Narrative Space and Mythic Meaning in Mark

NEW VOICES IN BIBLICAL STUDIES
edited by
Adela Yarbro Collins
and
John J. Collins

Other titles in the series:
SINAI AND ZION by Jon D. Levenson
BANDITS, PROPHETS, AND MESSIAHS by John S. Hanson and
    Richard A. Horsley

Narrative Space and Mythic Meaning in Mark

ELIZABETH STRUTHERS MALBON

1817

Harper & Row, Publishers, San Francisco

Cambridge, Hagerstown, New York, Philadelphia, Washington
London, Mexico City, São Paulo, Singapore, Sydney

FIRST EDITION

Library of Congress Cataloging-in-Publication Data

Malbon, Elizabeth Struthers.
Narrative space and mythic meaning in Mark.

Includes indexes.
1. Bible. N.T. Mark—Criticism, interpretation, etc.
2. Structuralism (Literary analysis) I. Title.
BS2585.2.M234   1986   226'.306   85-51550
ISBN 0-06-254540-X

86 87 88 89 90 HC 10 9 8 7 6 5 4 3 2 1

in memoriam
BETTY PHIFER
(Elizabeth Bowman Flory Phifer)
1930–1978

There were also women . . . who
. . . ministered . . .
—from Mark 15:40–41

Contents

Figures

Preface

This study has developed around three foci, three interrelated centers of interest: the meaning of the Gospel of Mark, the significance of space in a narrative, and the exegetical potential of structural analysis. Mark, narrative space, structural exegesis— this is the order of importance of these concerns.

This order is a signal of what is expected of the reader—primarily an acquaintance with and an interest in the Markan Gospel. In addition, he or she will need to be open, at least to some extent, to structural exegesis as a way of learning about Mark and about narrative space. But the reader need not have prior experience with the methodology of structural exegesis, which in this case is adapted from Claude Lévi-Strauss's studies of myth. Structural exegesis is the *method* of analysis; the *purpose* of analysis is a fuller understanding of the Gospel of Mark through an understanding of space in the narrative.

A study that has not one focus but three will encounter difficulties because of its breadth. Certainly it cannot try to take cognizance of the vast amount of scholarly work done in any *one* of the three broad areas: Markan studies,[1] investigations of space,[2] and structuralism.[3] Considerably fewer studies concentrate on the overlap or intersection of *two* of these three broad areas; such studies are investigations of Markan space,[4] Markan structural exegeses,[5] or structural exegeses of space in other New Testament texts.[6] Greater attention can be given to these studies that share two interests with the present work. The field of studies sharing all *three* interests (Mark/space/structuralism) is narrow indeed.[7] But in the structural exegesis of Markan space, the problem is less how extensive the scholarly literature is than how deep the analysis can go and still be helpful.

When the well-established tradition of detailed scholarly analysis of the Markan text comes into contact with the usually detailed (and sometimes intricate) steps of structural analysis as it reckons with the 288 spatial references in the Gospel of Mark, the results can be overwhelming. In order to be understandable as well as systematic, a structural exegesis must present all the relevant elements of the analysis without overburdening the reader with details. In the present study, every spatial reference of Mark is taken into account; however, because these details are not all equally important, stress is given to those aspects that have greater significance in the Gospel as a whole. Some readers may therefore find the present study too detailed and too methodologically rigid while others may find it too general and too methodologically soft. I am seeking to reach a middle—but not middling—audience of those who are willing to follow out a new methodology for the sake of increasing their understanding of an old—but ever current—text.

To potential readers who ask, "Why yet another study of the Gosepl of Mark?" I respond simply that the Gosepl of Mark has intrigued and challenged and rewarded yet another reader— me—and continues to challenge others to reconsider their own readings. To those who ask, "Why a structural exegesis?" I answer that it can aid us in listening carefully to a text we have heard so often that our ears have grown dull. Those who ask, "Why the focus on space?" require a somewhat fuller answer. Space is, as Mircea Eliade has shown, the necessary foundation for shaping a world. And certainly space shapes the narrative world of the Gospel of Mark in significant ways. But the spatial settings of a narrative, like the changing scenes of a stage play, are generally—and almost by definition—in the background. By moving this spatial framework to the foreground and thereby shifting our attention, we may perceive the whole in a new way; we may gain a new sense of its deeper meaning, its mythic meaning. There is, of course, much more to Mark than its narrative space, but the spatial framework is indeed a framework for the entire Gospel. By building on this frame, we may be better able to keep in mind the movements and meanings of the full story as we reread it with ever new questions.

To those who will be sharing in this process of rereading Mark, I offer the following specific suggestions for reading this book.

1. Since the Markan text is the foundation of this study, the

reader will need to have the Gospel of Mark not only in mind but also in hand while reading this book. (This book is not, however, a commentary on Mark; it makes no claim to completeness.)

2. The argument of the book can be followed without reference to the end notes. Because these notes may offer more than a nonspecialist would want and less than a specialist would expect, a word of explanation is in order. The purpose of the notes is not to offer a complete list of citations to the scholarly literature on all the topics touched upon (for example, emphasis is given to works available in English). Instead, the notes serve to credit sources that clarify the denotations (and connotations) of the Greek text of Mark and to suggest the fruitful interaction of structural exegesis and other approaches to Mark, especially redaction critical and literary critical approaches. Some readers may wish to ignore the notes entirely.

3. Chapter 1 is an exception to the book's dominant emphasis on exegesis of *Mark* rather than on *structural* exegesis. A new methodology almost always entails a new vocabulary, and structuralism has perhaps become infamous for its own. The first chapter explains my use of those—relatively few—specialized terms I find I cannot avoid. Some readers may find this methodological chapter the most difficult; however, it should not be skipped (with the possible exception of its notes). Chapter 1 is important in showing (a) how I discovered what I discovered about the meaning of Mark and (b) that my reading of Mark—which, like all readings, bears the individual stamp of the reader is not arbitrary. Let the reader who is eager to move on from abstraction to application note that the first chapter is the shortest.

4. Although Chapters 2, 3, and 4 are in some ways independent of each other, they should be read in sequence, for Chapter 2 shows in more detail how the method is applied.

5. Because the material is divided topically in Chapters 2, 3, and 4, these chapters are of unequal length. Chapter 3 is long. Take a breath perhaps a break—at its midpoint.

6. The figures (charts) summarize the textual evidence examined and the interpretive conclusions offered. The

figures are not magical; they need not be frightening. No special expertise is needed to read them, but they do not substitute for a text—mine or Mark's.

Structural exegesis, like all exegesis that seeks to avoid eisegesis, begins and ends with the text. Mark's text is open-ended, and an exegesis that seeks "to draw out the meaning of" Mark's text must describe that—and may well reflect it.[8] My study intends both to describe and to reflect the open-endedness of Mark. Further, as Marxsen observes of the open-ended ending of Mark, "in this very conclusive inconclusiveness lies the inner goal of the entire Gospel."[9] Here also my study of Mark, a study of the mythic meaning of its narrative space, intends to reflect the Gospel of Mark—to provoke thought but avoid closure, to manifest as its inner goal a conclusive inconclusiveness.

Acknowledgments

I am pleased to acknowledge the encouragement and constructive criticism I have received from readers of various recensions of this manuscript: in its earliest version, Robert A. Spivey and John F. Priest; and in its later stages, Robert L. Cohn, John R. Donahue, S.J., Adela Yarbro Collins, Frank Burch Brown, Hendrikus Boers, and Edward John McMahon II. My expression of appreciation to these readers implies not their agreement with all I have to say, but my gratitude for their friendly colleagueship and our collegial friendship. My appreciation also extends to Sue Mock for the initial typing of the manuscript, to Patty L. Carver for assistance in preparing the indexes, to Diane Journell for help in proofreading, and especially to Suzie Vankrey Karlin for much-valued assistance at each of these stages.

Small portions of Chapters 1, 2, and 5 first appeared—with additional materials—in the *Catholic Biblical Quarterly* (44/2 [1982]: 242-55). Parts of Chapters 2 and 3, combined and expanded, appeared in the *Journal of Biblical Literature* (103/3 [1984]: 363-77). A segment of Chapter 4 was included in an article in *New Testament Studies* (31/2 [1985]: 282-92). Permission to reprint this material has been kindly granted by the editors and publishers involved.

Abbreviations

BTB	Biblical Theology Bulletin
CBQ	Catholic Biblical Quarterly
HTR	Harvard Theological Review
HUCA	Hebrew Union College Annual
Int	Interpretation
JAAR	Journal of the American Academy of Religion
JBL	Journal of Biblical Literature
JES	Journal of Ecumenical Studies
JR	Journal of Religion
JTS	Journal of Theological Studies
NTS	New Testament Studies

1. Investigating Markan Space

In those days Jesus came from Nazareth of Galilee and was baptized by
John in the Jordan. . . . The Spirit immediately drove him out into the
wilderness. . . . Now after John was arrested, Jesus came into Galilee,
preaching the gospel of God, . . . And passing along by the Sea of Galilee,
he saw Simon and Andrew . . . and . . . said to them, "Follow me . . ."

—from MARK 1:9–17[1]

Space, it has often been noted, is of special importance in the
Gospel of Mark. Yet commentators have just as often described
the Markan geography and topography as confused or confusing. Perhaps it is this very conjunction of significance and confusion that has attracted biblical interpreters to an investigation
of narrative space in Mark.

Approaches to biblical space in general and to Markan space
in particular have been various. Some scholars have investigated
spatial locations in biblical narratives solely in terms of historical
geography.[2] Others have examined both the geographical and
the theological significance of such locations, one location at a
time.[3] Many Markan commentators, while not focusing on spatial
location in Mark, have first commented on its general "confusion," then traced scattered examples of that "confusion" to either the history or the theology of the Gospel's composition.[4] A
few exegetes have investigated the significance of one focal spatial location in the Markan Gospel, for example, the wilderness.[5]
And several interpreters have examined the significance of the
Markan spatial designations "Galilee" and "Jerusalem" by considering them in opposition.[6] In general, *historical* concerns about
the composition of Mark's Gospel seem to motivate this latter
group of scholars. Yet those who investigate the significance of
how Markan spatial locations interrrelate (and the discussions of
Galilee and Jerusalem mark a beginning[7]) have taken a step beyond the other approaches in sensing that space in the Gospel
of Mark must be surveyed not in isolated units but in its total—
and *literary* —context.[8] Now another step is called for.

The present study is marked by concern for the Markan Gospel as a literary and theological whole and for its narrative space as a system of relationships. The focus will be more on the function of the narrative than on the intention of the narrator, more on how the story is read than on why it was written. The approach is more literary than historical.[9] The specific task of this study is to consider all Markan spatial locations in their system of relationships and to consider the significance of this manifest narrative system in terms of an underlying, nonmanifest, "mythological" system. The methodology is an *adaptation* of the methodology of the French structural anthropologist Claude Lévi-Strauss for analyzing myth.[10]

Lévi-Strauss's method of analysis has grown out of the study of traditional mythic texts. Although the Gospel of Mark is not, strictly speaking, a myth, a mythic structure may also be operative in a text, like Mark, that does not represent the pure type. "We can easily understand," Daniel Patte suggests, that a mythic structure "might be at work in non-mythological religious texts— e.g., in Jesus' parables—yet it is also at work in subtle ways in any human communication."[11] Mythic structure, as Lévi-Strauss has formulated it, has been studied in the narratives of Genesis,[12] the book of Job,[13] selected parables of Jesus,[14] the passion narrative,[15] and portions of the letters of Paul.[16] New insights for biblical exegesis have resulted from such studies. Prospects for investigating mythic structure in the gospels are especially intriguing, for the gospels are perhaps best understood as Norman Perrin has depicted them: myth interpreting history and history functioning as myth.[17] This study is based on the conviction that analysis of the mythic structure or structures underlying the Gospel of Mark as a literary and theological whole can be a valid and enlightening approach to its meaning. The foundational question is not whether the Gospel of Mark is a myth, but whether attention to a mythic dimension contributes to an understanding of the Gospel of Mark.[18]

LÉVI-STRAUSSIAN ANALYSIS

Lévi-Strauss, in investigating the myths of a number of cultures, has theorized that myth operates to mediate irreconcilable opposites by successively replacing them by opposites that do permit mediation. In other words, myth is a way of thinking that involves the progressive mediation of a fundamental opposition. But how does myth work? And how must a hearer or reader work to understand myth?

Myth is like a musical composition, Lévi-Strauss posits. Just as a piece of music "composed of several voices is held within bounds by constraints in two dimensions, first by its own melodic line which is horizontal, and second, by the contrapuntal schemata (settings) which are vertical," so one may distinguish two aspects of the construction of a myth. The sequences of a myth, "the chronological order in which things happen," are analogous to the melodic line and "form the apparent content of the myth." "But," Lévi-Strauss continues, "these sequences are organized, on planes at different levels (of abstraction), in accordance with schemata which exist simultaneously, super-imposed one upon another."[19] Thus the schemata of a myth are analogous to the contrapuntal schemata of a piece of music, and they form the "latent content" of the myth. Alternatively Lévi-Strauss has suggested the related analogy of an orchestra score as illustrative of the structure of myth, for "in order to become meaningful," an orchestra score "has to be read diachronically along one axis—that is, page after page and from left to right—and also synchronically along the other axis, all the notes which are written vertically making up" one harmonic unit.[20] In other words, myths are two-dimensional. Sequences are diachronic, schemata are synchronic; sequences are syntagmatic, schemata are paradigmatic. Sequences tell the mythic story; schemata suggest the fundamental opposition the myth seeks to mediate.

But the discussion must move beyond the theoretical metaphor of a musical composition to the actual steps of the analysis, for the present study is Lévi-Straussian at the level of the method of analysis.[21] The analyses of Lévi-Strauss are frequently more powerfully suggestive than descriptively clear, more intriguing in their insights than consistent in their terminology. Thus they are not easy to summarize—or to apply. Nevertheless, this approach to mythic structure, adapted primarily from Lévi-Strauss's "The Structural Study of Myth" (1955) and "The Story of Asdiwal" (1967), may be outlined in terms of four steps.

First, the text must be reduced to its smallest essential and complete units, its "gross constituent units" as Lévi-Strauss terms them. Each of these units is not a thing but a relation, a relation comprised of a "function" and a "subject," or, as it were, a "doing" and a "doer." But "the true constituent units" of myth, Lévi-Strauss maintains, are not isolated relations but "bundles of relations." Thus relations of the same type must be gathered into bundles of relations, for "it is only as bundles that these relations can be put to use and combined so as to produce a meaning."[22] Grouping the relations of a myth into bundles of relations is possible because of the characteristic repetition of myth; each type of relation usually receives several manifestations scattered throughout the narrative, and together these relations form a bundle. Repetition, Lévi-Strauss concludes, has as its function "to make the structure of the myth apparent"; that is, myth exhibits a "structure which seeps to the surface, if one may say so, through the repetition process."[23] In alternate terminology, Lévi-Strauss refers to narrative "facts" (parallel to *relations*), which are presented in various "orders" (parallel to *bundles*).[24]

Second, the narrative as analyzed into relations (or facts) and orders (or bundles of relations) must be considered in terms of both the sequences and the schemata of the orders. The sequence of each order is simply the chronological order of its relations, the order in which events happen. The sequences of all the orders taken together form the "apparent content" of the narrative. The schema of each order is the formal, theoretical organization of its relations. Taken together, the schemata point to the fundamental opposition the myth seeks to mediate. Thus, to "tell" the narrative one would read all the relations in the order of their occurrence in the narrative; to "understand" the narrative one would attend to the internal organization of the bundles of relations.

A simple example may prove helpful at this point. A narrative might read:

The hero traveled south; then she traveled west;
then she traveled east.

Then the sequence of the relations of the geographical order would read:

south, west, east.

And the schema of the geographical order would be as follows:

north

west   east

south

North need not be manifest in the narrative sequence for this schema to be obvious. Accordingly, each order is read diachronically in terms of its chronological sequence and synchronically in terms of its theoretical schema. Note that these specialized terms form two sets:

chronological/diachronic/syntagmatic/sequence, and
mythological/synchronic/paradigmatic/schema.

Third, the various orders through which the narrative evolves must be compared and integrated. This "global integration," as Lévi-Strauss terms it, is possible because each order, "together with the symbolism proper to it,"[25] is understood as a transformation of an underlying logical structure common to all the orders. Thus two schemata may be integrated into a third schema, consisting of several binary oppositions, and this process may be repeated until the narrative is reduced to "two extreme propositions, the initial state of affairs and the final, which together summarize its operational function."[26] That is, the process of global integration of the various schemata gives us, as it were, the schema of the schemata, a statement of the fundamental opposition the mythic narrative seeks to mediate.

Fourth, and finally, one may apply to the schema of the schemata, and thus to the narrative as a whole, Lévi-Strauss's formula for describing the structure of a myth. According to Lévi-Strauss, a myth must be considered as the collection of all its variants, each of which represents a transformation of the fundamental structure—that is, the structure described by the formula.[27] And, since Lévi-Strauss also argues that each level (or order) within a narrative may be seen as "a transformation of an underlying structure common to all of them,"[28] it would appear that orders relate to the narrative as a whole as variants of a myth relate to the myth as a whole. Thus it would seem appropriate to apply Lévi-Strauss's formula for describing the structure of a complete myth to the structure of a narrative as a whole. In this case the formula would serve as the figuration of the schema of the schemata, that is, as a shorthand way of expressing the global integration of the schemata of the various orders. Since "mythological thought always works from the awareness of oppositions towards their progressive mediation,"[29] the pattern of this schema would be one of an initial opposition (A vs. B) replaced by another, but equivalent, opposition (C vs. D):

$$
\begin{array}{cc}
B & \\
 & D \\
 & C \\
A &
\end{array}
$$

This system of relationships may be expressed "A : B :: C : D" and read, "A is to B as C is to D." The formula expresses this relationship of equivalent opposition in a more complex form by considering two aspects of each element.[30]

THE PRESENT ANALYSIS

"A full structural analysis," as Dan Via has observed, "would be virtually endless."[31] The present analysis has an end. It does not attempt to analyze all orders of the Gospel of Mark, although it does examine one order—the spatial—thoroughly (suborder by suborder, then integrally) and throughout the entire Gospel. Because it is limited to one order of the text, the present study cannot complete all four steps of the Lévi-Straussian methodology as outlined above. There can be, of course, no global integration of the orders (step three)—although the three suborders examined are integrated in a way that parallels such a global integration. Nor can Lévi-Strauss's formula for the structure of myth be applied (step four), since the formula is intended to describe the global integration of all the orders of a text, or, as in Lévi-Strauss's use, all the variants of a myth. The present study, an analysis of the spatial order of the Gospel of Mark, carries out in detail step one, isolating relations, and step two, examining the sequence and the schema.

To shift Lévi-Strauss's analogy, a mythic narrative, like a symphony, is a complex artistic work. The work's orchestration involves several families of instruments—string, woodwind, brass, percussion; each of these families, in turn, comprises several kinds of instruments—for example, violin, cello, and bass. So too a myth evolves on various "levels" or in various "orders." The orders of the Gospel of Mark—spatial order, temporal order, and others—might be considered analogous to the various instrumental families heard in a symphonic work. Suborders of the Markan text, such as the geopolitical, topographical, and architectural suborders of the spatial order, might be considered analogous to the kinds of instruments within the families, such as clarinets, bassoons, oboes. The goal of the present study is to apply an adaptation of Lévi-Strauss's method of analysis to the spatial order of the Gospel of Mark—to listen, as it were, to the woodwinds of the symphony of Mark's Gospel.

As the spatial order of Mark's Gospel forms but one strand of an integrated literary and theological whole, the present analysis will remain incomplete, open-ended. An observation by Robert Polzin is apropos of such a study: "The brashness of a structuralist who hopes to arrive at intelligibility of a whole which may itself be a part of a larger whole rests upon this essential postulate of his approach: whatever may be the larger relationships of a whole with larger wholes, if it can be considered in any real sense a structure itself, it will reveal certain stable laws that cannot be lost but only integrated with the rules of its superstructure."[32] Thus the present proposal, modest perhaps in terms of Lévi-Strauss's overall goals, is not illegitimate in terms of structuralist research, nor is it insignificant for Markan exegesis. Markan narrative space,[33] although only one aspect of the Gospel, is a foundational or central aspect—to use two spatial metaphors.[34] In fact, Charles W. Hedrick argues that "the geographical references and spatial locations [of Mark], regardless of the occasional problems they pose, constitute the only immediately recognizable over-all narrative structure to an otherwise highly episodic narrative."[35]

A richly diverse set of narrative facts or relations makes up the spatial order of the Gospel of Mark. Each relation of the spatial order has to do, of course, with where some event of the narrative happens, its location in space. But this spatial location may be defined, and is defined in Mark, in a number of ways. Each of the following verses defines the spatial location of the narrative action in a different way; each contributes to the spatial order. " . . . Jesus came from Nazareth of Galilee . . ." (1:9). "And when Jesus had crossed again in the boat to the other side, a great crowd gathered about him; and he was beside the sea" (5:21). " . . . and immediately on the sabbath he entered the synagogue and taught" (1:21). In 1:9 a town and a political unit or region, Nazareth and Galilee, are specified. In 5:21 a topographical feature, the sea, is cited. In 1:21 an architectural enclosure, the synagogue, is mentioned. These three examples suggest the three types of relations that constitute the Markan spatial order: geopolitical (named regions, cities, towns), topographical (physical features of the earth, such as the sea, wilderness, mountains), and architectural (human-made structures, such as houses, synagogues, the temple).

Each of these three groups of spatial relations in the Markan narrative is quite complex in itself. Over seventy geopolitical relations in twenty-seven categories have been isolated, and the set of topographical relations is larger still. Because of the limits this complexity places on the comprehension of details, it will be necessary to consider each group as an integral suborder and examine both its diachronic sequence and its synchronic schema independently before reintegrating the three suborders for a consideration of the spatial order as a whole. It is important to remember that the process of explaining the composition of orders and suborders reverses the process of discovering their composition. The explanation begins with distinct orders and suborders; the analysis begins with a continuous text. The analyst tentatively isolates independent relations, then reads and rereads, arranges and rearranges, to determine and then to refine the various orders and suborders into which these relations may be grouped. Constant returning to the text serves as a check on this process of dissection and as a stimulus to the process of reintegration. An in-depth examination of each suborder of the Markan spatial order will follow three steps.

The first step is establishing the narrative facts—or isolating the *relations*—that comprise the suborder. Although the present analysis will stay closer to the actual words of the text than do the analyses of Lévi-Strauss, isolating the relations may not be reduced to word study. Three observations concerning relations make this clear.

1. Not every reference to a term literally pertaining to a certain order or suborder functions as a relation in that order or suborder in the Markan narrative. For example, the architectural term "house" (*oikos* or *oikia*) refers to an enclosed, private or familial space; but there is a significant difference between a reference to Jesus entering into the house of Simon and Andrew (1:29) and a reference to Jesus saying, " 'And if a house is divided against itself, that house will not be able to stand' " (3:25). The latter reference to the term *house*, a metaphorical usage, is indeed important in appreciating the connotative value of the term *house* throughout the text; however, this reference in 3:25 does not function to define the spatial location of any event of the Markan narrative and thus is not included among the relations of the architectural suborder.

2. Some references to terms not literally pertaining to a certain order or suborder function as relations in that order or suborder in the Markan narrative. For example, the term "boat" (*ploion*) is not a spatial designation. Yet the use of "boat," such as in 6:32, "And they went away in the boat to a lonely place by themselves," implies "boat on the sea," and "the sea" is a significant topographical designation in Mark. Thus "boat" in 6:32 is included in the topographical suborder in relation to the sea.

3. Some references to terms pertaining to a suborder are complex and function doubly—that is, in two suborders—in the Markan narrative. For example, the complex term "Mount of Olives" locates the narrative action both on a mountain (topographical) and just outside Jerusalem (geopolitical). The double reference doubles the relevant connotations that contribute to the total meaning effect of the complex term in its Markan context. Relations involving such terms will be recorded twice, once in each relevant suborder.

The relations of each suborder are presented in a chart that lists each relevant spatial term and cites its occurrence(s) in the text. When a relevant spatial term occurs more than once within a verse, small letters indicate each occurrence. Thus in Figure 1, for example, 10:46a and 10:46b indicate two occurrences of "Jericho" in 10:46, not—as is usual with this system of lettering—the first and second halves of verse 46. The process of isolating the relations making up each suborder must be completed carefully and systematically, lest the resultant sequence and schema be arbitrarily constructed.

The second step of the investigation of each suborder is examining the diachronic relationships of its relations—that is, its *sequence.* One observes, for example, that, whereas Galilee is the dominant geopolitical location throughout the opening portion of Mark, Jerusalem is the stage for the closing third, and yet the final geopolitical relation signals Galilee. This examination is made easier if each sequence is recorded in the form of a two-dimensional chart with horizontal rows and vertical columns. (Figures 2, 6, and 10 are such charts.) Each relation is signified on the chart by the citation (chapter: verse) of the text in which it occurs. For example, in Figure 2, "Geopolitical Sequence," 1:14 signifies, "Jesus came into Galilee." To trace the sequence, one reads the rows of the chart from left to right and from top to bottom, as one reads a page in a book. The sequence charts reflect not only the order of the verses involved but also the order of spatial relations *within* verses that include more than one spatial reference. By reading the rows of each sequence chart from left to right and from top to bottom one may "retell" the story of each suborder, its "apparent content." (I continue to use quotation marks around this last term of Lévi-Strauss's because I question his slighting the sequence—"apparent content"—in favor of the schema—"latent content."[36])

The third step involves focusing on the "latent content" of each suborder by analyzing the formal, theoretical organization of its relations, that is, its *schema.* The chart that represents the sequence of a suborder also suggests its schema, for each column signifies a bundle of relations. One may "understand" the suborder by disregarding the horizontal rows and attending to the vertical columns, each column being considered as a unit. These units, the narrative realities represented by the column headings, are the elements of the schema of the suborder.[37]

The present methodology refines that of Lévi-Strauss by distinguishing the "logic" of the hierarchical relationships of the various elements of the schema and the "mythologic" of the schema itself.[38] The logical hierarchy is supplied—implicitly in most cases—by the culture; both denotation and connotation are functions of the cultural code, which a mythic narrative must assume in order to be understood, but which it may also challenge. The mythological schema represents those distinctions among logical categories (supplied by the culture) that have been selected by the narrative as significant for the mythic process of opposition and mediation. Thus hierarchical relationships (showing subordination) are the key to the "logical" hierarchy, whereas oppositional relationships are the key to the "mythological" schema. For example, a portion of the logical hierarchy lying behind the spatial order of Mark might be sketched as:

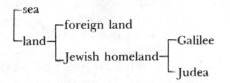

But the comparable portion of the mythological schema would be illustrated as:

```
(chaos)
              sea
                  foreign land
                                        Judea
                                        Galilee
                        Jewish homeland
         land
(order)
```

According to Lévi-Strauss, the schema suggests the latent, non-manifest opposition of the myth that underlies the manifest oppositions of the narrative as they move toward mediation. In the schematic diagrams, the terms in parentheses represent the non-

manifest (unconscious or preconscious), fundamental oppositions. The other terms represent the oppositions manifest in the
narrative. The arrangement of terms suggests the movement
from awareness of oppositions toward their progressive mediation, which Lévi-Strauss considers one of the main processes of
mythic thought. For example, the above (abbreviated) schema
may be read, "The fundamental, less than fully conscious, opposition CHAOS VS. ORDER is manifest in the Markan Gospel by
the opposition SEA VS. LAND, which is replaced by FOREIGN LAND
VS. JEWISH HOMELAND, which is in turn replaced by JUDEA VS.
GALILEE." The movement toward mediation is seen in the progressive weakening of the oppositions from the antithetical
CHAOS VS. ORDER to SEA VS. LAND (both ordered by God), to
FOREIGN LAND VS. JEWISH HOMELAND (both land), to JUDEA VS.
GALILEE (both part of the Jewish homeland).

After following these three steps—(1) isolating the *relations*, (2)
examining the *sequence*, (3) analyzing the *schema*—for each of the
three suborders (Chapters 2, 3, and 4), the relations of the spatial
order will be integrated for a look at its overall sequence and
schema (Chapter 5). The task is actually one of *re*integration because the separation of the suborders in the analysis shatters the
original integration of the text. To some extent the discussion
of the spatial order as a whole will recapitulate previous suggestions, just as earlier comments on the separate suborders will
have anticipated to some extent these conclusions. This spatial
integration will suggest the fundamental opposition that the spatial order of the Gospel of Mark seeks to mediate and the process
by which this mediation is brought about.

It is essential to remember that the terms of the spatial
schema—like those of the schemata of the three suborders—are
abstracted from the Markan text. On the one hand, they are
more *abstract* than the text and reflect the interaction of the analyst (a reader) and the text; on the other hand, they are abstracted *from the text* and reflect the constraints of the text on the
analyst. Verbal abstractions, of course, are neater—more easily
systematized—than their concrete textual embodiments; but
such abstractions from the text are not to be reified. The Markan text is the beginning—and the end; structural analysis is a
means. On this point I am in agreement with Dan Via: "If struc-

turalism were a monolithic, rule-bound methodology, I would still insist on bending or breaking the rules if the demands of the text under consideration required it. However, I do not see structuralism to be so monolithic and rule-ridden . . . ."[39]

While the present study is basically structuralist in its approach and literary in its overall orientation, it recognizes the relevance and interrelation of literary and historical questions for twentieth-century readers who seek to understand first-century texts. And while the present study is a structural exegesis, it does not unfold in isolation from other critical approaches to the New Testament, particularly studies of the language and the cultural and religious background of the New Testament and redaction critical studies of Mark.[40] In fact, throughout the investigation I have felt a certain empathy with William Wrede who, in an appendix to *The Messianic Secret*, wrote as follows of "predecessors of mine [who] did not become known to me until all the main ideas of my investigation and the basic lines of my plan were *already established*":

On individual points I was then able to learn much gratefully from them but equally have often coincided independently with them where it is a question of basic ideas held in common.

I am somewhat concerned to say this expressly, naturally for my own sake, but not just on that account. It has some value too for the subject-matter, that in certain ideas, . . . several people have found themselves on the same track.[41]

The unique contribution the present study seeks to make is twofold. to broaden understanding of Markan narrative space by considering *all spatial references* and to deepen understanding of Markan narrative space by considering the *system of interrelations* of these references. The task is a partial *structural exegesis* of the Gospel of Mark; the hope is that in the process of analyzing the *structure* of the spatial order of the Markan Gospel the *meaning* of the text will be *drawn out*. Thus, exegetical comments are not appended at the end of a structural outline, but the two are interwoven throughout, and, often, woven metaphorically. Metaphors are used not because Lévi-Strauss uses them, but for the cause for which Lévi-Strauss uses them: they point to that which the metaphors of myth and myths as metaphors point to, but which they cannot say because it cannot be said. It is for the reader to judge whether the endeavor avoids what has been called "one of the most serious difficulties any new approach may encounter: . . . the growing weariness with method that does not break through to meaning."[42]

2. Geopolitical Space

Jesus withdrew with his disciples to the sea, and a great multitude from Galilee followed; also from Judea and Jerusalem and Idumea and from beyond the Jordan and from about Tyre and Sidon a great multitude, hearing all that he did, came to him.

—MARK 3:7–8

Commentators are generally agreed upon two aspects of what is here isolated as the geopolitical suborder of the Gospel of Mark: (1) the geography of Mark is confused, and (2) the Markan distinction between Galilee and Jerusalem is important.[1] The apparent incompatability of these two assertions is generally resolved by assuming that the geopolitical terms and distinctions are not to be taken literally but figuratively and theologically. Once such interpretation begins, however, strict agreement among commentators ends. In relation to this discussion, the present goal is twofold: to broaden the base of deliberation and to deepen the level of understanding of interrelationships. Under examination will be not only Markan references to "Galilee" and "Jerusalem" but the system of all relations involving places signified by a proper place name in Mark's Gospel.[2] This set of narrative facts or relations may be labeled the geopolitical suborder because it concerns spatial areas of the earth (*geo-*), which are defined by human-made boundaries of civic or governmental units (*-political*). Of course, humanly designated boundaries and natural boundaries may overlap. The conjunction of geopolitical distinctions and *topographical* distinctions is especially plain with regard to the Jordan *River*, the *Sea* of Galilee, and the *Mount* of Olives. The double aspect of these references is discussed in Chapter 3 in the context of topographical space. Through a Lévi-Straussian approach to the mythic narrative, one is searching for a homology (a similarity in structure) between the geopolitical system and a cognitive (philosophical or theological) system. By understanding the system of relationships at the geopolitical level of the Gospel of Mark, one may be better

MARKAN POLITICAL GEOGRAPHY

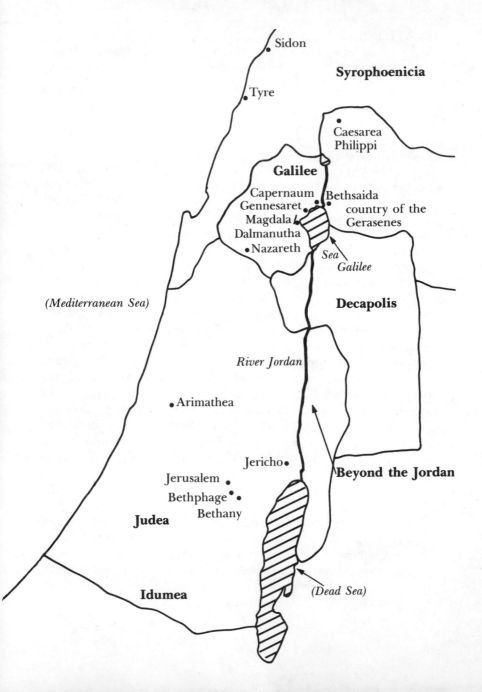

able to understand the significance of Mark's Gospel at the theological level.

RELATIONS

The seventy-two relations of the geopolitical suborder, in twenty-seven categories, are cited in Figure 1. The narrative facts making up the geopolitical suborder of the Markan spatial order are those relations designating events reported or projected in the Gospel of Mark in spatial relation to a specific, named village, city, country, region, area, mountain, sea, or river. The cities, towns, or villages of *Nazareth, Capernaum, Gennesaret, Dalmanutha,* and *Magdala* are in Galilee. *Jerusalem, Jericho, Bethphage, Bethany,* the *Mount of Olives, Gethsemane, Golgotha,* and *Arimathea* are in Judea. Outside the traditional Jewish homeland of Galilee and Judea are *Idumea,* an area *beyond the Jordan, Tyre, Sidon,* the *country of the Gerasenes,* the *Decapolis, Bethsaida, Syrophoenicia, Caesarea Philippi,* and *Cyrene.* The *Sea of Galilee* forms the eastern boundary of Galilee, and the *River Jordan* flows through the Sea of Galilee and southward to form the eastern boundary of Judea.

As a general rule, the relations of the geopolitical suborder are marked by proper nouns serving as place names, for example, Galilee, Jerusalem, Bethsaida. But there are exceptions. In two cases a proper adjective modifies a noun: the "Judean region" (*Ioudaia chōra,* 1:5), the "Jordanian river" (*Iordanē potamō,* 1:5). Elsewhere a proper noun is part of a phrase that serves as a place name: "beyond the Jordan" (*peran tou Iordanou,* 3:8; 10:1). At 5:1, an area is identified by reference to the name of its inhabitants, the Gerasenes, but the phrase the "country of the Gerasenes" (*chōran tōn Gerasēnōn*) makes clear the geopolitical designation of the space, not the people. My translations into English reflect the Greek grammatical forms.

In addition, six proper nouns or adjectives that are references to the inhabitant(s) of a town, city, or region—and not to the town, city, or region itself as a spatial location—serve as implicit place names: "Jerusalemites" or "inhabitants of Jerusalem" (1:5), "Nazarene" (1:24; 10:47; 14:67; 16:6), "Syrophoenician" (7:26), "Galilean" (14:70), "Cyrenian" (15:21), "Magdalene" (15:40; 15:47; 16:1).[3] Each of these terms functions as a geopolitical ref-

Figure 1 Geopolitical Relations

An action or event reported or projected in the Gospel of Mark occurs in spatial relation to:

Judea   1:5; 3:7; 10:1; 13:14
Jerusalem   3:8; 3:22; 7:1; 10:32; 10:33; 11:1; 11:11; 11:15; 11:27;
        15:41
        Jerusalemites   1:5
River Jordan   1:5
        the Jordan   1:9
Nazareth   1:9
        Nazarene   1:24; 10:47; 14:67; 16:6
Galilee   1:9; 1:14; 1:28; 1:39; 3:7; 6:21; 9:30; 14:28; 15:41; 16:7
        Galilean   14:70
Sea of Galilee   1:16; 7:31
Capernaum   1:21; 2:1; 9:33
Idumea   3:8
beyond the Jordan   3:8; 10:1
Tyre   3:8; 7:24; 7:31
Sidon   3:8; 7:31
country of the Gerasenes   5:1
Decapolis   5:20; 7:31
Bethsaida   6:45; 8:22
Gennesaret   6:53
Syrophoenicia
        Syrophoenician   7:26
Dalmanutha   8:10
Caesarea Philippi   8:27
Jericho   10:46a; 10:46b
Bethphage   11:1
Bethany   11:1; 11:11; 11:12; 14:3
Mount of Olives   11:1; 13:3; 14:26
Gethsemane   14:32
Cyrene
        Cyrenian   15:21
Golgotha   15:22
Magdala
        Magdalene   15:40; 15:47; 16:1
Arimathea   15:43

erence in the Markan narrative because each could be translated "of" the place or "from" the place,[4] paralleling Jesus "from Nazareth" at 1:9 and Joseph "of Arimathea" at 15:43 and indicating location in geopolitical space. None of these terms is employed as a self-designation; all are applied either by the narrator or by another character. Furthermore, these references to inhabitant(s), in addition to the two references to towns linked to personal names at 1:9 and 15:43, may generally be considered as flashbacks at the geopolitical level. When referred to as *Nazarēnos*, "the Nazarene," in the Markan text, Jesus is never in Nazareth; the appellation reminds us of a past time when Jesus was in Nazareth, when he grew up in Nazareth.[5] Peter the Galilean and Mary Magdalene, both from Galilee, and Simon the Cyrenian, from North Africa, are in Judea when so called. The Jerusalemites appear outside the city in the wilderness by the River Jordan, and Joseph of Arimathea, a Judean city northwest of Jerusalem,[6] emerges at Golgotha. With the exception of the Syrophoenician woman who appears in the region of Tyre and Sidon, each designation suggests some past movement of the person from his or her native place to his or her present location.[7] Thus each passage is included in the geopolitical suborder. On the other hand, "Greek" (7:26), "Israel" (12:29; 15:32), and "Jews" (7:3; 15:2, 9, 12, 18, 26) serve not as geopolitical references denoting physical space, but as sociological references denoting groups of people, each with a distinctive culture.

The inclusion of proper names of inhabitant(s) of a city or area in the geopolitical suborder is an exception to the general rule that geopolitical relations are marked by proper nouns designating places. One might ask whether a second exception may be made to this rule in order to include general spatial references that imply specific, previously named locations, for example, "the village" for Bethsaida at 8:23 and 8:26, or "the sea" for the Sea of Galilee in many verses. The emphases of the Markan text, however, are more faithfully followed by including in the geopolitical suborder only those references marked by a proper name (e.g., "Jerusalem" or "Nazarene") and considering general spatial references (e.g., "the city" or "the sea") in the context of the topographical suborder.

Finally, one notes several complex spatial references within the geopolitical suborder. The two terms of a complex reference are joined grammatically, as in "Nazareth of Galilee" (*Nazaret tēs Galilaias*) at 1:9. The conjunction of two geopolitical terms forming "Nazareth of Galilee" serves to intensify the reference to Jesus' home. The other complex spatial references represent geopolitical/topographical conjunctions and are listed here for discussion later in relation to the topographical suborder: "country of Judea," "river Jordan," "Sea of Galilee," "country of the Gerasenes," "Mount of Olives." With the set of relevant geopolitical relations now established, attention turns to the diachronic sequence of their narrative manifestation and to the significance of this sequence for the meaning of the Gospel of Mark.

SEQUENCE

The sequence of an order or suborder is simply the chronological order of its narrative facts or relations, representing the "apparent content" of the narrative. The sequence of the geopolitical suborder, a complex system of seventy-two relations in twenty-seven categories, is summarized graphically in Figure 2. A brief overview of the sequence of the suborder, that is a "retelling" of the narrative at the geopolitical level, will precede a consideration of various patterns manifested in the sequence and their significance in the overall meaning of Mark's Gospel.

OVERVIEW

The geopolitical sequence of the Markan narrative opens at the River Jordan with "all" the country of Judea and "all" the inhabitants of Jerusalem coming out to John (1:5). Jesus too comes to John, from Nazareth of Galilee (1:9). Afterwards Jesus returns to Galilee and begins his ministry with preaching (1:14) and calling disciples (1:16). The Galilean ministry continues with teaching and preaching in synagogues (1:21, 39) and casting out demons (1:24, 39). Jesus' fame spreads "everywhere throughout all the surrounding region of Galilee" (1:28),[8] and large crowds gather to him at his "home" in Capernaum (2:1). Though Jesus withdraws with his disciples to the Sea of Galilee, an even greater multitude comes to him there, not only from Galilee but also from Judea, Jerusalem, Idumea, beyond the Jordan, and Tyre and Sidon (3:7–8)—that is, from all directions, from west and south and east and north.[9] These people, "hearing all that he did" (3:8), come to Jesus seeking healing. Others, apparently also hearing all that he did—and all the excitement it created among

Figure 2 Geopolitical Sequence

An action or event reported or projected in the Gospel of Mark occurs in spatial relation to:

Judea	1:5
Jerusalem	1:5 · 3:8 · 3:22 · 7:1 · 10:32 · 10:33 · 11:1 · 11:11 · 11:15 · 11:27 · 15:41
River Jordan	1:5 · 1:9
Nazareth	1:9 · 1:24 · 10:47
Galilee	1:9 · 1:14 · 1:28 · 1:39 · 3:7 · 6:21 · 7:31 · 9:30 · 14:28 · 14:70 · 15:41 · 16:7
Sea of Galilee	1:16 · 1:21 · 2:1 · 7:31 · 9:33
Capernaum	2:1 · 9:33
Idumea	3:8
beyond the Jordan	3:8 · 10:1
Tyre	3:8 · 7:24 · 7:31
Sidon	3:8 · 7:31 · 7:31
country of Gerasenes	5:1
Decapolis	5:20 · 7:31
Bethsaida	6:45 · 6:53 · 8:22
Gennesaret	6:53
Syro-phoenicia	7:26
Dalmanutha	8:10
Caesarea Philippi	8:27
Jericho	10:46a · 10:46b
Bethphage	11:1
Bethany	11:1 · 11:11 · 11:12 · 14:3
Mount of Olives	11:1 · 13:3 · 14:26
Gethsemane	14:32
Cyrene	15:21
Golgotha	15:22
Magdala	15:40 · 15:47 · 16:1
Arimathea	15:43

the people—come to Jesus: scribes from Jerusalem (3:22; 7:1), seeking not healing but confrontation.

From this Galilean base of ministry Jesus and his disciples set out on wider travels: across the Sea of Galilee to the country of the Gerasenes (5:1) and to Bethsaida (6:45; 8:22); overland, north to Tyre and Sidon (7:24,[10] 31) and then east and south through the Decapolis (7:31); later north again, east of the lake, to Caesarea Philippi (8:27). All of these journeys are made in the broader context of a Galilean ministry; amid the foreign travels Jesus periodically returns to Gennesaret (6:53) or Dalmanutha (8:10)[11] or Capernaum (9:33), all in Galilee. Passing "through Galilee" (9:30) is a basic spatial mode of Jesus' ministry. As broadly as Jesus travels, his name and fame travel farther, borne on the lips of those who come to him from as far away as Syrophoenicia (7:26) in the north and Idumea (3:8) in the south and who go away from him not only throughout Galilee to the west but also throughout the Decapolis (5:20) to the east. The itineraries of the Markan journeys are not always clear (e.g., 7:31), and significant detours are sometimes reported (e.g., 6:45, 53), but the narrative impact is that the actions of this Galilean, this Nazarene (1:24; 10:47; 14:67; 16:6), have more than a local significance.

From Capernaum (9:33) Jesus departs with his disciples on one final journey. He travels south to the region of Judea and east to the region beyond the Jordan (10:1).[12] As in Galilee, here crowds gather to him again, and, as his custom has been, again he teaches them (10:1). Finally he is "on the road, going up to Jerusalem" (10:32, 33). On the way Jesus and his disciples come through Jericho where Bartimaeus joins them (10:46). They stop outside Jerusalem, at the Mount of Olives, near Bethphage and Bethany (11:1), to prepare for the entrance into Jerusalem (11:11). And, though Jerusalem has been the goal of their journey, Jesus and the disciples actually stay in Bethany, returning there (11:11, 12; 14:3) after daily trips into Jerusalem (11:11, 15, 27). The Mount of Olives (13:3; 14:26) and Gethsemane (14:32) also serve as places of retreat from the city of Jerusalem, the city of Jesus' arrest, trial, and condemnation to death. Jesus is crucified at Golgotha (15:22), outside the walls of Jerusalem, and laid in a rock tomb.

Thus the narrative action seems to end in Judea. The close of the geopolitical sequence, however, turns the reader's attention away from Judea and back to Galilee. From the Mount of Olives, Jesus informs his disciples that after he is raised up he will go before them to Galilee (14:28). At the cross, the reader is given a flashback to Galilee in the description of the women "who, when he was in Galilee, followed him, and ministered to him" (15:41). At the empty tomb, the women and the reader are given a flash-forward to Galilee where Jesus is going and where " 'you will see him, as he told you' "(16:7).

Thus the sequence of the geopolitical suborder is not static, but dynamic. It is not an ordered list of place names (which is, admittedly, about all that can be captured on a chart such as Figure 2), but a complex pattern of lively journeys by a number of characters throughout the cities, villages, and countryside of Galilee, Judea, and various regions beyond.

JESUS AND JOHN

The sequence of the geopolitical suborder opens not with the location in space of Jesus, the central character of the Markan narrative, but with the spatial location of John. John is at the River Jordan,[13] and "all" the country of Judea and "all" the inhabitants of Jerusalem are coming out to him (1.5)[14] to hear and respond to his "preaching a baptism of repentance for the forgiveness of sins" (1:4).[15] Jesus also comes to John at the Jordan (1:9). Two other Markan geopolitical relations involve John: at 1:14 John's arrest before Jesus comes into Galilee is reported; at 6:21 Herod summons "the leading men of Galilee" to a banquet that ends with the decapitation of John. Thus the geopolitical suborder draws attention to these milestones of John's career: he preaches in Judea and people from Judea come out to him (1:5); he is arrested or handed over (1:14, *paradothēnai*); he is killed at a gathering of persons from Galilee (6:21).

Beyond the superscription (1:1), the first two references to Jesus in Mark, the first two narrative actions of Jesus, are linked dramatically to John. Jesus comes from Nazareth of Galilee to John in Judea and is baptized by him in the Jordan, outside Jerusalem (1:9). (The narrative fact that both John and Jesus spend time "in the wilderness" will be examined when considering topographical space.) Jesus returns to Galilee, "preaching" and saying " 'repent' " (1:14–15), but only after John's arrest. The story of John and the story of Jesus overlap; the geopolitical suborder manifests this link by specifying a common spatial location for John and Jesus at the Jordan, in Judea, near Jerusalem. Yet the geopolitical suborder also signals the distinction between John and Jesus: both are associated with bodies of water; but John is associated with the River Jordan, which flows through the Sea of Galilee, while Jesus is associated with the Sea of Galilee itself. (See Figure 3, showing the geopolitical hierarchy, and Figure 7, showing the topographical hierarchy.) Both the River Jordan and the Sea of Galilee mark theological boundaries as well as geopolitical ones: the boundary between sin and forgiveness is crossed by John's "baptism of repentance" (1:4); that between Jewish exclusiveness and Gentile inclusiveness is crossed by Jesus' mastery over the Sea of Galilee. (This generalization will be discussed in relation to topographical space.)

In addition, the geopolitical suborder draws attention to the common overall pattern of the careers of the two boundary-crossers. Jesus preaches in Galilee (1:14)—and other places—and people from Galilee—and other places (3:7–8)—come to him; he is arrested or handed over (15:1, *paredōkan;* also many other references[16]); he is killed in Judea. This pattern parallels that of John's career. But the geopolitical suborder also suggests that their parallel careers do not make Jesus and John equal in status. John's ministry is centered in Judea, his death is among Galileans; Jesus' ministry is centered in Galilee, his death is in Judea. The reversal in spatial orientation and the wider scope of Jesus' ministry signal geopolitically the difference between John and Jesus; the difference is explicated theologically by John's speech in 1:7–8: " 'After me comes he who is mightier than I . . . .' "

In addition to establishing a link with John, Jesus' initial journey from Nazareth of Galilee to Judea, near Jerusalem, serves another function: it foreshadows Jesus' final journey to Judea, to Jerusalem. In the beginning Jesus journeys to Judea to be baptized by John into a ministry that leads, in the end, to a journey to Jerusalem to be crucified. The Markan Jesus would appear to interpret the first journey as a metaphor for the second in asking James and John, " 'Are you able . . . to be baptized with the baptism with which I am baptized?' " (10:38). But Jesus' initial return to Galilee from Judea also foreshadows Jesus' final return to Galilee from the tomb in Judea (16:7). The crucial importance of 1:14 as the inauguration of Jesus' ministry is generally recognized, but it must be noted that his ministry opens with a *return* to Galilee from Judea. In the opening of Mark, Jesus' return to Galilee is reported; in the closing of Mark, Jesus' return to Galilee is anticipated. At the initial return to Galilee, Jesus comes "preaching the gospel of God" (1:14). At the final return to Galilee, it would appear, Mark comes preaching "the gospel of Jesus Christ, the Son of God" (1:1).[17] The preaching of Mark follows the preaching of Jesus, which follows the preaching of John.

JESUS OF NAZARETH

At his entrance onto the narrative scene, Jesus is described as coming from Nazareth (1:9). And at the tomb, where the women expect to see Jesus for the final time, Jesus is identified as "of Nazareth" (16:6). Of course, *Nazarēnos* may serve to identify this Jesus among many persons of the same name;[18] after 1:1, however, it is unlikely that any doubt remains concerning which Jesus is intended. Nevertheless the term *Nazarene* appears in Mark four times after the reference to Nazareth in 1:9, each time designating Jesus. This appellation serves as a reminder of Jesus' rootedness in his home town, of his ties to his family, and thus of his humanity. *Nazarenos* is appended to Jesus' name when such a reminder may well be necessary, when Jesus' actions seem more than human. In his manifestations of healing power—when recognized as " 'the Holy One of God' " by soon-to-be-exorcised unclean spirits (1:24), when cried out to as " 'Son of David' " by the soon-to-be-healed blind Bartimaeus (10:47)—Jesus is called " 'Jesus of Nazareth.' " (But also in the midst of his most human passion, when denied by Peter [14:67], Jesus is identified as " 'the Nazarene.' ") Most emphatically, at the empty tomb, when death is recognized as real but not final, " 'Jesus of Nazareth, who was crucified,' " is proclaimed as he who " 'has risen' "

(16:6).[19] At the very moment when it appears that Jesus has broken through the human boundaries of death, the title *Nazarēnos* reaffirms his humanity.

The final geopolitical comment about Jesus "of Nazareth" is that he is going " 'before you to Galilee' " (16:7). One way of understanding the significance of the promised return to Galilee is by noting the types of activities carried out in Galilee initially. These activities include calling disciples (1:16), teaching in synagogues (1:21, 39) and beside the sea, casting out demons (1:39) and healing the sick, and in general "preaching the gospel of God" (1:14). These activities are not easily separated, for their accounts are intricately interwoven in the Markan narrative. The initial preaching is followed immediately by the calling of disciples. The initial exorcism in the Capernaum synagogue is embedded in an account of Jesus' teaching: " 'a new teaching with authority' " (1:27, my translation). Is this Galilean composite of proclamation and discipleship and power and authority a sign of what will be seen in Galilee where " 'he is going before you' "? The final reference to Galilee, a promise given in the spatial order, serves to move the story beyond its literal ending in Jerusalem while at the same time recalling not only the narrative's beginning but its dominant geopolitical mode. In some sense the Markan experience of Jesus' Galilean ministry seems to be proleptic of the post-resurrection experience of the followers of Jesus. " 'The time is fulfilled, and the kingdom of God is at hand' " (1:15), the Markan Jesus preaches upon his initial return to Galilee; the proclamation is not inappropriate for the promised final return to Galilee of the Markan ending.

JESUS' JOURNEYS AROUND GALILEE

The geopolitical suborder of the Gospel of Mark is dynamic, involving *coming* from Nazareth, *going* to Galilee, *crossing* the Sea of Galilee to Bethsaida, *journeying* to Tyre and Sidon. Through chap. 9, the journeys of the Markan Jesus may be defined in relation to their home base, Galilee. Jesus travels from Galilee to Judea and back (1:9; 1:14); Jesus travels "throughout all Galilee" (1:39); Jesus travels from Galilee to the country of the Gerasenes and back (5:1; 5:21); and so on. The major journeys made by the Markan Jesus appear to be anticipated by journeys of other characters in one of two ways: (1) Jesus' fame, or word of his deeds, is spread by a person or persons, either unsolicited or commanded, in an area Jesus will later traverse; (2) persons come to Jesus from regions Jesus will later enter.

On two occasions, word about Jesus is specified as traveling before Jesus, moving out from him, throughout an area. Jesus' fame precedes him (1:39) throughout Galilee, for it spreads "everywhere throughout all the surrounding region of Galilee" (1:28) even before the Markan Jesus has traveled beyond Capernaum for the first time. What Jesus has done is preached in the Decapolis by the healed Gerasene demoniac (5:20) before Jesus himself preaches there (7:31). In each case, a later journey of Jesus is positively anticipated. By contrast, at 6:45 Jesus sends the disciples before him to Bethsaida, but, according to the Markan text, they do not go as sent. Rather, they land, after a dramatic mid-sea encounter with Jesus, at Gennesaret (6:53). Since Jesus, accompanied by the disciples, does eventually land at Bethsaida (8:22), it may be said that the projected but detoured journey negatively anticipates Jesus' later journey.

Because elsewhere in the Markan narrative anticipatory journeys by others do prepare the way for later journeys by Jesus, this exception—this preparatory journey commanded at 6:45 but interrupted at 6:53—is especially interesting. To be sure, the voyages section of the Markan narrative is not particularly clear. Commentator after commentator has noted that the Markan geography can scarcely be taken literally because of its perplexities. Theories of how and why the departure and arrival points of the Markan voyages are as confused or confusing as they are have been argued on the basis of the rearrangement of traditional materials.[20] In attempting to make sense of the Markan text as it stands, however, one must consider all the geopolitical references in the sequence in which they occur in the text. Thus, in order to interpret the interrupted anticipatory voyage to Bethsaida, one must, first, sketch its place in the overall system of voyages and, second, consider what activities took place during the delay.[21]

Briefly, one may trace the Markan voyages as follows. At 4:35 a crossing from west to east is proposed; at 5:1 the successful completion of the crossing is marked by the arrival at "the country of the Gerasenes." Mark 5:21 signals a return voyage from east to west. That Jesus is on the west at this point is confirmed by the reference to his home town (*patris*) in 6:1. At 6:32 Jesus and the disciples take a side trip along the west coast "in the boat to a lonely place." At 6:45 Jesus commands (*ēnagkasen*) his disciples to cross the lake, from west to east, to Bethsaida. *Anagkazō*, used only here in Mark, means "force," "compel"; the "word implies unwillingness on the part of the disciples."[22] And, in fact, command is not completion (4:35 and 5:1 also illustrate this separation), for, after the dramatic episode of Jesus' walking on the sea and the disciples' misunderstanding, the boat "came to land at Gennesaret" (6:53), still on the west. The land journeys of 7:24 and 7:31 (admittedly a confusing verse) appear to take the group from the west side to the east side of the lake via a northerly, overland route. Thus the voyage "in the boat" to the district of Dalmanutha would be from east to west.[23] At 8:13 they again depart to the other side; that is, they set out from the west, and after the mid-lake conversation about loaves they come "to Bethsaida" on the east at 8:22.[24]

The east side of the lake is, of course, outside the Galilean homeland of Jesus and his disciples. Jesus, in asking his disciples to go before him to Bethsaida (6:45), is asking them to move out to others, to move beyond their own people, their own religious tradition—not that this is something Jesus has not already done himself. (Earlier, Jesus, accompanied by the disciples, performed an exorcism in the country of the Gerasenes [5:1] on the east coast, where the presence of the swine confirmed the eastern side of the lake as Gentile.) As commanded, the disciples set out in the boat, but they are "distressed in rowing" because of the wind (6:48, my translation), fearful at Jesus' appearance because they do not recognize him, and (as the Markan narrator adds) without understanding "about the loaves" for "their hearts were hardened" (6:52). Are the disciples, according to Mark, also distressed, fearful, and without understanding about going to Bethsaida?

Between the projected anticipatory voyage of the disciples to Gentile Bethsaida (6:45) and the confirmed arrival there of Jesus and the disciples (8:22), Jesus, accompanied by the disciples, performs the following actions: (1) argues against the laws of ritual purity, which serve to separate Jews and Gentiles, and against the hypocrisy of the Pharisees; (2) travels to the most distant foreign (Gentile) cities of Mark, Tyre and Sidon, where he confirms the faith of the Gentile woman that even dogs (Gentiles) deserve the children's (Jews') crumbs; (3) heals in the Decapolis, east of the lake and the river, beyond the Galilean, Jewish homeland; and (4) miraculously feeds a multitude on the east (Gentile) side as he had earlier done on the west (Jewish) side. Finally Jesus and the disciples return to Galilee (8:10, Dalmanutha), and only then do they set out by boat once more (8:13) and successfully reach Bethsaida (8:22). At Bethsaida, Jesus enables a blind man to see by working a two-stage healing. Narratively, it would appear that Jesus works in at least two stages to enable the disciples to "see," to perceive the scope of his ministry, to understand that there is bread for the people on the east as well as on the west of the sea, for Gentiles as well as for Jews.[25] In the detour from the journey commanded by Jesus, the disciples display their blurred vision.

In contrast, the Gerasene, when sent "home" to tell "how much the Lord has done" for him (5:19), goes beyond the command of Jesus; he proclaims "in the Decapolis how much Jesus had done for him" (5:20), anticipating positively Jesus' own journey through the Decapolis. Jesus' disciples, when sent to Bethsaida before him, do not go as far as Jesus commands; they land at (Jewish) Gennesaret, anticipating negatively Jesus' eventual successful arrival at (Gentile) Bethsaida where the blind may see.[26]

On other occasions Jesus' journeys are anticipated by persons coming to Jesus from regions to which he will later go. Before Jesus is reported to have traveled beyond Galilee teaching and healing, a multitude comes to him from Judea, Jerusalem, Idumea, beyond the Jordan, and Tyre and Sidon (3:7-8).[27] (Since the Markan Jesus has already been "throughout all Galilee" [1:39], here the multitude from Galilee is said to have "followed" [ēkolouthēsen] him while the multitude from other regions "came" [ēlthon] to him). Later, Jesus himself goes to each of these places (with the exception of Idumea) that have first come to him in a metaphorical way through their inhabitants: Tyre and Sidon (7:24, 31), Judea (10:1), beyond the Jordan (10:1), and Jerusalem (10:32). Thus Jesus retraces, in reverse, the steps of those who come to him from Judea and from foreign regions. Jesus' reception by persons wherever he goes is anticipated by his reception of persons from wherever they come.

Jesus' journey to Jerusalem is anticipated in an analogous way. Scribes come down (*katabantes*, 3:22) from Jerusalem to confront Jesus (3:22; 7:1), and Jesus and his followers go up (*anabainontes*, 10:32; *anabainomen*, 10:33; *sunanabasai*, 15:41) to Jerusalem and to confrontation with the religious establishment. "Going up" is regularly used of "going" to a city and is especially appropriate in relation to Jerusalem because Jerusalem was higher than the surrounding region.[28] But the contrasting movements to and from Jerusalem serve as more than descriptive geography in the Markan narrative.[29] The scribes, with their concerns for order in the religious group in the face of a disruptive exorcist (3:22) and for ritual purity (7:1), represent the religious establishment of Jerusalem. Thus the accusations delivered to Jesus by the scribes who come down from Jerusalem anticipate the accusations against Jesus when he is delivered to the chief priests and the scribes upon going up to Jerusalem. This decisive "going up" to Jerusalem of Jesus contrasts with the coming down (3:22) from Jerusalem of the scribes. Jesus and the scribes move in opposite directions, not only spatially but also theologically. As further analysis will illustrate, Jesus seeks to break down and break open the exclusive categories of the sacred and the profane, which the scribes—and the entire religious establishment— seek to maintain. Jesus' rejection in Jerusalem is anticipated in his rejection by the scribes from Jerusalem.

JESUS' JOURNEY TO JERUSALEM

From chap. 10 forward, the movement of the Markan Jesus may be defined by his destination, Jerusalem. Jesus' going up to Jerusalem is not described in geographical detail, but several key geopolitical signposts of the journey are given. Although going to Judea is mentioned at 10:1 and setting out on a journey is specified at 10:17, Jerusalem is first named as the goal of the journey south at 10:32. In addition, this pivotal passage introduces the third and final passion prediction and reverberates with the resurrection account in the motifs of the way, going ahead, disciples, amazement, and fear. A second signpost on the way to Jerusalem is the explicit and repeated mention of Jericho in 10:46. Here Jesus and the disciples are drawing nearer to the climax of Jesus' ministry. But immediately before coming to Jericho the disciples are no closer to understanding the significance of this climax, as witnessed in the request of James and John for honor. Just outside Jericho, however, Bartimaeus, who was blind physically but sighted to the significance of Jesus, is healed and follows Jesus "on the way" (10:52). As coming through Jericho marks the approach to Jerusalem geographically, so the encounter with Bartimaeus marks the approach to Jerusalem—and all that it means—theologically.

A third, and complex, geopolitical signpost on the way to Jerusalem is given at 11:1: "... they drew near to Jerusalem, to Bethphage and Bethany, at the Mount of Olives ...." The order in which the names of the outlying villages are mentioned is somewhat peculiar since Bethphage is closer to Jerusalem than is Bethany.[30] Here, however, the three places seem to function together as a place *near* Jerusalem but *not* Jerusalem. The three places *outside* Jerusalem together serve as the staging ground for the entry procession *into* Jerusalem.

Although Bethphage is not listed again, Bethany and the Mount of Olives continue to serve as spatial locations over against Jerusalem. Jesus has made his way to Jerusalem, but he makes his stay in Bethany, entering Jerusalem in the morning, returning to Bethany in the evening. Jerusalem is the power base of the opposition to Jesus, the home of the temple and of the scribes, Jesus enters Jerusalem to look around (11:11), to drive out those who buy and sell in the temple (11:15), to teach (11:27); but he returns to Bethany or to the Mount of Olives. Jesus' power has another base—both spatially and theologically.

Jesus' round trips from Bethany to Jerusalem serve as the spatial frame for the significant incident of the cursing of the fig tree (11:12–27).[31] The withering of the cursed fig tree is generally recognized as a metaphor for the fall of Jerusalem, of the temple, of the Jewish religious establishment.[32] The Markan Jesus stands over against the religious establishment, over against the temple, and thus over against Jerusalem. The antithesis between Bethany where Jesus stays and Jerusalem where Jesus visits underlines this confrontation. But Bethany is not a place for escaping the realities of Jerusalem. In Bethany (14:3) Jesus welcomes the anointing of his body with oil, the anointing " 'beforehand for burying'" (14:8). In directly approaching his death, Jesus personally takes on the fate of Jerusalem; he comes from Bethany to Jerusalem one last time.

The contrast is even more explicit between the Jerusalem temple and the Mount of Olives; "he sat on the Mount of Olives opposite the temple" (13:3). From this position, Jesus responded to his disciples' questions concerning the time and the sign of the coming destruction of the temple and of Jerusalem. In addition to the special connotation of a mountain as a place for divine revelation (discussed below in relation to the topographical term *oros*), metaphorical significance is suggested here in Jesus' seated posture and in the traditional associations of the Mount of Olives. Sitting, "the usual position of Jewish rabbis while teaching,"[33] is indeed the posture of authoritative teaching for the Markan Jesus. Two extended teaching sessions are presented in Mark: the parable discourse in chap. 4 and the eschatological discourse in chap. 13. Each is prefaced by reference to Jesus' seated posture. Jesus sat in a boat on the sea (or, in the Greek, literally "sat on the sea": *kathēsthai en tē thalassē*) and taught the crowd "many things in parables" (4:1–2). Jesus "sat on the Mount of Olives opposite the temple" (13:3) and taught four of his disciples about the end of the age. Although more segmented by changes in audience, Jesus' discourse in the temple in 11:27–12:44 may perhaps be considered a third extended teaching session. Interestingly enough, the preface to this discourse specifies that Jesus was "*walking* in the temple" (11:27); only at the close of his teaching in the temple did Jesus sit: "he sat down opposite the treasury" (12:41). But soon thereafter "he came out of the temple" (13:1), and "he sat on the Mount of Olives opposite the temple" (13:3). The seat of the Markan Jesus' authority is not the temple, but the mountain (13:3) and the sea (4:1)—the Sea of Galilee and the Mount of Olives.

The Mount of Olives was, from ancient times, a place of prayer (2 Samuel 15:30, 32) and the scene of Ezekiel's vision of the glory of the Lord (Ezekiel 11:23). Later the Mount of Olives was associated by the rabbis with the resurrection of the righteous dead and the coming of the Messiah.[34] Most dramatically, the Mount of Olives was the destined place of the initiation of the end of the age, the eschatological judgment, the day of the Lord: "On that day his [the Lord's] feet shall stand on the Mount of Olives which lies before Jerusalem on the east; and the Mount of Olives shall be split in two from east to west by a very wide valley; so that one half of the Mount of Olives shall withdraw northward, and the other half southward" (Zechariah 14:4). J. B. Curtis argues that "Zechariah's cleft in the mountain was meant to represent an exit from the netherworld for the resurrection of the dead."[35] If so, the imagery of Zechariah, built upon by Mark, may reflect elements of the mythology of Negral, "the Destroyer," the Assyro-Babylonian god of death and the netherworld. Negral, in his West-Semitic manifestations as Molech, the god of the Ammonites, and Chemosh, the god of Moab, was worshiped on one spur of the Mount of Olives, called the Mount of the Destroyer,[36] in Israel's monarchical period (2 Kings 23.13; cf. 1 Kings 11:7). In the Yahwistic tradition, however, the god Negral was demoted to the rank of demon and became, in the words of Curtis, "the Destroyer, perhaps the one who went about on the night of Passover to slay the first-born of the Egyptians (Exod. 12:23)." Curtis concludes that it is thus "appropriate that Jesus on the night of his arrest—Passover evening, according to Mark—should retire to the Mount of Olives, the mountain sacred to the god of death, to become reconciled to death (Mark 14:26–42)."[37]

The Mount of Olives, therefore, functions in Mark not only as an eschatological space, but also as a critical space in the career of Jesus. Returning to the Mount of Olives with his disciples after the Last Supper, the Markan Jesus speaks of the striking of the shepherd and the scattering of the sheep. This allusion to, or near quotation of, Zechariah 13:7, although eschatological in a general sense in its original context, is here applied specifically to Jesus' death, after which he will be "raised up" to go before his disciples to Galilee (14:28). From the Mount of Olives Jesus gives his disciples the eschatological warning: " 'Take heed, watch; for you do not know when the time will come' " (13:33). And to the Mount of Olives Jesus returns, giving Peter the personal warning of the three times Peter will deny him. From the Mount of Olives Jesus anticipates both the eschatological end and its destruction and his personal end, his death, thus bringing the two into conjunction.

Gethsemane (14:32) and Golgotha (15:22) are stations along the inevitable way to this death, marking the initial arrest and the final crucifixion. The only New Testament references to Gethsemane are here and in the parallel passage, Matthew 26:36. *Gethsemane* is generally taken to mean "an oil press,"[38] that is, a press for olives, and is thus linked with the Mount of Olives.[39] As he prays at Gethsemane, Jesus again asks the disciples to "watch"; this time the command is more directly personal as a preparation for Jesus' end than eschatological as a preparation for the world's end. The Markan text leaves no doubt concerning the significance of Golgotha; it is the "place of a skull" (15:22), the place of death. *Golgothan* is the Greek equivalent of the Aramaic *golgolta'*, "skull";[40] the connotation of death is clear whether the location received its name from a hill shaped like the top of a skull[41] or from its use for executions.[42] Like Bethphage, Bethany, and the Mount of Olives, Gethsemane and Golgotha—central to the culmination of Jesus' ministry—are outside the gates, over against Jerusalem, beyond the realm of the center of the Jewish religion.

Jerusalem is the real and symbolic center of traditional Judaism in Mark's Gospel—and the scene of Jesus' condemnation to death. Each action of Jesus in Jerusalem intensifies the conflict between the two religious perspectives manifest respectively in Jesus of Nazareth and the chief priests, scribes, and elders of Jerusalem. When the chief priests and the scribes hear of Jesus' overturning of the tables of the temple money-changers, they seek "a way to destroy him" (11:18). When the chief priests and the scribes and the elders perceive that Jesus has told the parable of the wicked tenants against them, they try to arrest him (12:12). The outcome of the conflict in Jerusalem becomes increasingly clear. But Jerusalem is not the final geopolitical reference of Mark. According to Mark's Gospel, Jerusalem cannot confine Jesus of Nazareth of Galilee—not spatially, not theologically.

PAST AND FUTURE

Golgotha, naturally enough, is the final Markan geopolitical reference in the present time of the narrative. It is not, however—and significantly, the final geopolitical reference in Mark, being followed by seven geopolitical references that are flashbacks and one that is a flash-forward. In fact, in the final portion of the Markan Gospel (from 13:14 on) geopolitical flashbacks together with flash-forwards dominate present geopolitical references more than three to one. These past and future narrative facts or relations both integrate and extend the Markan story.

Of the ten flashbacks from 13:14 through 16:6, all but two involve the linking of a character with his or her native town or region. The closing of Mark manifests an amazing accumulation of this type of reference. Jesus is called Jesus "of Nazareth" not only in the midst of his all-too-human passion (14:67) but also in the midst of his resurrection, his breakthrough beyond the human boundaries of death (16:6). The designation *Nazarēnos* integrates these disparate aspects of the story of Jesus. Identification of Peter as " 'a Galilean' " (14:70) serves to link him with Jesus, " 'the Nazarene' " (14:67), as even the Markan bystanders observe, saying to Peter: " 'Truly you are one of them; for you also are a Galilean' " (14:70, my translation[43]). Similarly, Mary Magdalene, Mary of Magdala in Galilee, is implicitly joined with Jesus of Nazareth in Galilee (1:9) by her compound name; such a link is made explicit in the double geopolitical flashback of 15:41. The presence of these Galileans, Peter and Mary, with Jesus in Judea bridges, at the geopolitical level, the story of Jesus' ministry in Galilee and death in Judea. Both Mary and Peter, Mark specifies (16:1, 7), may extend the story of Jesus. When Mary and Peter go home to Galilee they will see that Jesus has gone before them.

When Jesus was in Galilee his ministry carried him not only throughout Galilee but to Judea and to foreign regions as well, and persons from each of these three major areas came to him. When Jesus was in Judea, his crucifixion and burial again brought to him persons from each of these three major areas: from North Africa, Simon the Cyrenian who carried his cross (15:21); from Galilee, Mary Magdalene and the other women who observed his crucifixion (15:40–41) and made preparations for his burial (15:47; 16:1); from Judea, Joseph of Arimathea

(15:43) who laid him in a tomb. Again Jesus is the focal point of Galilee, Judea, and foreign regions; again the closing geopolitical relations function to integrate the Markan Gospel.

The functions of integration and extension of the Markan story of Jesus are served most obviously in the double geopolitical flashback at 15:41. Here Mary Magdalene and the other Mary and Salome are described as those "who, when he was in Galilee, followed him, and ministered to him." As a flashback this description recalls, at the time of the Judean crucifixion, the Galilean ministry. Joining the three named women at the cross are "many other women who came up with him to Jerusalem" (15:41). "Followed" (ēkolouthoun) and "ministered" (diēkonoun) are discipleship words in Mark, almost technical terms for roles of service.[44] Going up to Jerusalem—and all that it signifies in terms of facing suffering, in terms of denying oneself, taking up one's cross, and following him (8:34)—is also a demand of discipleship. Mark 15:40–41 links named and unnamed women with the disciples of Jesus in this spatial and theological move. The continued presence of these women with Jesus, in Galilee for ministry and service, in Judea for suffering and death, integrates these various aspects of Jesus' career—and of the career of all disciples. In following Jesus (15:41), these women, these disciples, join and may extend the story of the one who goes before them (16:7).[45]

The two references to Jesus going before others to Galilee (14:28; 16:7), together with a single reference to persons in Judea fleeing to the mountains (13:14), constitute the three flashforwards of the final portion of Mark. All three are given as Jesus' words; at 16:7 Jesus' words are reported by a messenger and should be rendered as direct discourse, rather than as indirect discourse.[46] At the geopolitical level the Markan Jesus anticipates the future not simply for himself but for his followers as well. The reference to Judea in 13:14 does not specify the spatial location of characters within the present time of the narrative but propels the reader into the future, of which Jesus warns: " 'But when you see the desolating sacrilege set up where it ought not to be (let the reader understand), then let those who are in Judea flee to the mountains . . . .' " The verse, included in

Jesus' eschatological discourse, has long intrigued and confused interpreters. The destination of those who are to flee, "the mountains," will be discussed in Chapter 3 as an element of the topographical suborder, but here one may at least note that the phrase "the mountains" suggests uninhabited areas as opposed to populous areas, such as the city of Jerusalem.[47] The designation of those who are to flee, "those who are in Judea," is open-ended and is expanded even more by the parenthetical aside that pulls the reader into the text. Judea is to be the scene of some strange and estranging catastrophe. Attention is shifted beyond Jerusalem and beyond the present to the future.

The same orientation is given in 14:28. While in Judea, Jesus tells his disciples, " 'I will go before you to Galilee.' " The words of the young man at the empty tomb in Judea, " 'he is going before you to Galilee' " (16:7), echo Jesus' words: *proaxō humas eis tēn Galilaiun; proagei humas eis tēn Galilaian.* The women at the tomb, and through them the disciples and especially Peter, are not *told* to go to Galilee—a fact usually overlooked, if not contradicted,[48] by most commentators, but apparently observed by one commentator, R. H. Lightfoot, concerning the parallel statement at 14:28.[49] Rather, the return of these Galileans to their homeland is assumed. Lightfoot also recognizes that the proper question to ask in determining the significance of "Galilee" at 16:7 is "In what light is Galilee regarded in the entirety of Mark's gospel?"[50] In Galilee Jesus' followers had experienced the authority of teaching and the power of healing in Jesus. From Galilee they had ventured out to foreign regions, witnessing through Jesus' actions the breakdown of barriers--geopolitical, sociological, theological. In Galilee they had often been blind to Jesus to his walking on the sea, to his multiplying the loaves, to his steadfastness in taking the way from Galilee to Jerusalem, from life to death. To this Galilee they must now return. Jesus has been killed, but their lives go on. They have left everything to follow Jesus; they have only Galilee to which to return. The surprising and yet familiar thing, the promising thing, is that Jesus "who was crucified" is going before them, "going to Galilee," going where they must go—home, to begin life anew. "'There,'" the Markan young man tells them, "'you will see . . . .'"

SCHEMA

In order to see the mythic pattern of opposition and mediation of the geopolitical suborder, one must turn from a look at its diachronic structure, its sequence, to a view of its synchronic structure, its schema. The schema of an order or suborder is the formal theoretical organization of its narrative facts or relations, representing the "latent content" of the narrative, in contrast to the "apparent content" represented by the sequence. Each column of Figure 2, showing the geopolitical sequence, represents a bundle of relations; each column heading reflects a kind or type of relation. These *types* of relations are the elements of the schema of the geopolitical suborder, wherein they are arranged abstractly, theoretically. Lying behind the mythological schema presupposed by the Markan geopolitical suborder is a logical hierarchy of all the specific, named locations referred to in the Markan narrative as representative of the political geography of Palestine and its surrounding areas in the first century A.D. This logical hierarchy is supplied—implicitly in most cases—by the culture of which Mark's Gospel is a part; in our analysis, the hierarchy is presented as the "branching tree diagram" given in Figure 3, which may be read, "The political geography presupposed by the Gospel of Mark involves two major categories— *Jewish homeland* and *foreign lands*—and a third category in between—*boundaries. Jewish homeland* is further subdivided into *Galilee* and *Judea; Galilee* is further specified in terms of five villages or towns, etc."

Not every distinction of the logical hierarchy is represented as an opposition within the mythological schema. As part of the mythic process of opposition and mediation, certain distinctions among locations have been blurred in the Markan narrative and other distinctions accented. At the level of the sequence, the logical distinction between Capernaum and Gennesaret is relevant; at the level of the "latent content," represented by the mythological schema, all the villages or towns of Galilee together point to the travels of Jesus and the spread of his fame throughout all Galilee as opposed to Judea or foreign regions. The logical hierarchy (Figure 3) and the sequence distinguish Idumea to the south, the area beyond the Jordan to the east, and Tyre and Sidon to the north; the mythological schema reflects the unity

Figure 3 Geopolitical Hierarchy

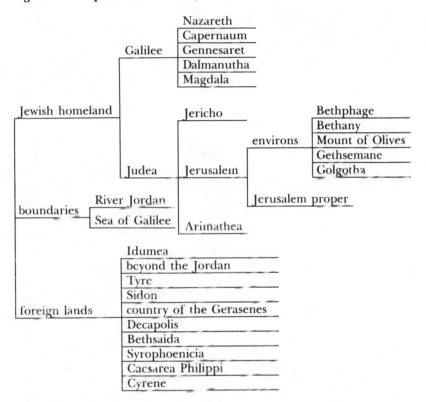

of these locations as foreign lands from which multitudes come to Jesus (3:8) and to which Jesus later travels (7:24, 31; 10:1). The mythological schema, presented as a series of oppositions moving toward mediation, is given in Figure 4 and may be read, "The opposition JEWISH HOMELAND vs. FOREIGN LANDS is replaced by the opposition GALILEE vs. JUDEA, which gives way to the opposition ENVIRONS OF JERUSALEM vs. JERUSALEM PROPER." The terms in parentheses in Figure 4 represent the nonmanifest, fundamental opposition underlying the oppositions manifest in the narrative and will be clarified in the process of considering the narrative connotations of the succeeding oppositions.

The schema of the geopolitical suborder of the Gospel of Mark

Figure 4   Geopolitical Schema

(familiar)

    Jewish homeland

        Galilee

            environs of Jerusalem

            Jerusalem proper

        Judea

    foreign lands

(strange)

will be analyzed opposition by opposition. Of each pair of opposed terms one may ask three questions: (1) How is this opposition manifest in the narrative? (2) On what basis are these terms opposed? (3) Is any movement toward mediation of this opposition suggested in the narrative?

JEWISH HOMELAND VS. FOREIGN LANDS

JEWISH HOMELAND is given narrative expression in Mark by reference to the regions of Galilee and Judea and various cities, towns, and villages within those regions. Jesus, a Jewish native of Galilee, travels freely throughout Galilee and Judea, and persons come from throughout both areas to him. The Jewish character of Galilee and Judea is suggested by Mark in two ways: (1) the presence there of Jewish centers of worship and (2) the presence there of Jewish religious leaders. Jesus teaches and heals in synagogues in Capernaum (1:21; 3:1) and throughout Galilee (1:39; 6:2). In Jerusalem, Jesus visits and teaches in the temple (11:11, 15, 27; 12:35; 13:1; 14:49). Beyond the Jewish homeland of Galilee and Judea, neither synagogue nor temple is mentioned.

Jesus is confronted by Jewish religious leaders of several types throughout the Jewish homeland. In Galilee, Jesus debates with scribes (2:6, 16), some of whom have come down from Jerusalem

(3:22; 7:1), and with Pharisees (2:24; 7:1; 8:11)[51] who very early plot against him (3:6). (On one Markan occasion, 9:14, scribes do appear outside the Jewish homeland, in Caesarea Philippi, arguing not with Jesus but with the disciples.) In Judea, and especially in Jerusalem, this dialogue with scribes (11:27; 12:28) and Pharisees (10:2;[52] 12:13) continues and also includes Sadducees (12:18) and chief priests and elders (11:27) as well. In Jerusalem, the chief priests and scribes join in plotting against Jesus (11:18; 14:1); the two groups are then joined by a third, the elders, in carrying out Jesus' arrest (14:43) and trial (14:53; 15:1), although in all these activities leadership seems to belong to the chief priests (14:10, 47, 55; 15:3, 11). Finally the chief priests and the scribes mock Jesus at his crucifixion (15:31). Yet not all the relations between Jesus and Jewish religious leaders in the Jewish homeland are adversary relations. In Galilee, Jesus heals the daughter of the ruler of the synagogue; in Judea, one conversation with a scribe closes with Jesus saying, " 'You are not far from the kingdom of God' " (12:34). Taken together these references to Jewish institutions and their leaders confirm for the reader of Mark that Judea and Galilee form the Jewish homeland.

The narrative manifestations of FOREIGN LANDS in the Markan gospel include Idumea, beyond the Jordan, Tyre, Sidon, the country of the Gerasenes, the Decapolis, Bethsaida, (by implication) Syrophoenicia, Caesarea Philippi, and (by implication) Cyrene. Mark's geographical assumptions concerning these foreign areas and Jesus' journeys through them sometimes prove confusing when plotted on a map reflecting physical reality. For example, at 7.31 it is reported that Jesus "returned [to Galilee?] from the region of Tyre [north of Galilee], and went through Sidon [north of Tyre!] to the Sea of Galilee [south and east of Tyre and Sidon], through the region of the Decapolis [east and south of the Sea of Galilee!]."[53] The "foreignness," as it were, of these cities and areas is more crucial in Mark's Gospel than their precise location or Jesus' exact itinerary in reaching them.[54] Narrative signs such as the great herd of swine in the country of the Gerasenes (5:11–13) or the conversation with the Syrophoenician woman about the children's crumbs for the dogs (7:26–29) signal the foreign, Gentile character of these places.

Bethsaida is clearly marked in the text as being on "the other side" of the sea (6:45; 8:13, 22) from Galilee, that is, beyond the borders of Galilee. No geographical description is given with the reference to Caesarea Philippi (8:27),[55] nor is the itinerary clear in regard to the reference to the land beyond the Jordan (10:1). These place names seem to serve as labels for foreign regions in general. Nowhere is this more clear than at the accumulation of place names at 3:7–8. After referring to a multitude following Jesus from Galilee, the narrator refers to a multitude coming from Judea and Jerusalem (west), and from Idumea (south), beyond the Jordan (east), and Tyre and Sidon (north). Galilee and Judea constitute the Jewish homeland, and the other regions and cities establish the boundaries of the foreign regions surrounding the Jewish homeland. The Markan point seems to be that people come to Jesus from everywhere, from throughout the Jewish homeland and from the foreign lands beyond.

These geopolitical labels often appear carefully placed in the Markan Gospel in order to locate incidents on either foreign or Jewish soil. For example, the complex, and not quite clear, pattern of land and sea voyages functions, in effect, to place healings and a miraculous feeding on each side of the Jewish/foreign (Gentile) border. Jesus' return across the Sea of Galilee from the east to the west (5:21) serves as the introduction to his encounter with Jairus, the ruler of the synagogue, in Galilee (5:22). The landing at Gennesaret (6:53), in Galilee, immediately precedes Jesus' dialogue with the Pharisees (7:1). The journey to and from Tyre and Sidon (7:24, 31) forms a frame for the conversation with the Syrophoenician woman (7:25–30).[56] Jesus and the disciples return to the west side of the lake, to Dalmanutha (8:10), only to depart again almost immediately (8:13), but in between Jesus confronts the Pharisees in Galilee. Thus the geographical boundaries between the Jewish homeland, especially Galilee, and foreign regions parallel the distinctions between Jewish scribes and Gentile swine-herders, between a synagogue ruler and a Syrophoenician woman. Jesus, of course, crosses the boundaries and engages both.

In the Markan Gospel, the Jewish homeland is clearly home— home to Jesus and home to the disciples. Together Galilee and Judea not only connote but also denote the familiar. Thus one might say that JEWISH HOMELAND, as one pole of an opposition given narrative expression in the Gospel of Mark, manifests the basic concept and reality of the FAMILIAR, which is one pole of the fundamental, nonmanifest opposition underlying the geopolitical suborder of Mark. The other pole of the manifest opposition is FOREIGN LANDS; the corresponding pole of the nonmanifest opposition is, quite clearly, the STRANGE. Figure 4 presents in parentheses the poles of the fundamental opposition FAMILIAR vs. STRANGE. As will become clear later, the strange is not merely benign or indifferent, but threatening.

Following this consideration of (1) how the opposition JEWISH HOMELAND vs. FOREIGN LANDS is manifest in the Markan narrative and (2) on what basis (FAMILIAR vs. STRANGE) these terms are opposed, the discussion moves to the third question: Is any movement toward mediation of this opposition suggested in the narrative? An affirmative answer is anticipated by the earlier observation that Jesus is sought out by multitudes from both sides of the home/foreign, Jewish/Gentile boundary; that the Markan Jesus, Jesus of Nazareth in Galilee, repeatedly crosses this boundary and ministers openly to residents on both sides. Perhaps the Sea of Galilee—and Jesus' relation to it—best represents this mediation narratively. The sea forms a natural boundary on the east of Galilee, but it does not keep Jesus in bounds. Jesus calms the sea (4:37–41), walks on the sea (6:47–52), and, while crossing the sea, reminds his disciples that there was plenty of "bread" for those on the eastern, Gentile side of the sea as well as for those on the western, Jewish side (8:14–21). The Sea of Galilee, the supposed boundary between the Jewish homeland and foreign lands, becomes instead the bridge between them.[57]

Furthermore, because Galilee is, within Mark's Gospel, the gathering place for the various multitudes (3:7–8) as well as the home base for Jesus' foreign travels, Galilee itself, in a sense, mediates between JEWISH HOMELAND and FOREIGN LANDS. Galilee seems to have played a similar mediating role in first-century history and culture. The name *Galilee* means "ring, circle" and was likely given to the district "in recognition of the circle of Gentile nations which had infiltrated the region."[58] But some commentators seem to overreact to this connotative aspect of

Galilee, equating "Galilee" in Markan usage with "Gentile" or the "Gentile mission" of the early church.[59] Although for the Gospel of Matthew, Galilee may be the "Galilee of the Gentiles" of Isaiah 9:1 (see Matthew 4:15), for Mark the situation is more complex; and Galilee is perhaps, in an admittedly less poetic phrase, "Galilee of the mediator(s) between the Jews and the Gentiles."

Mediation is the basic process of myth, according to Lévi-Strauss, for "mythical thought always works from the awareness of oppositions towards their progressive mediation."[60] Lévi-Strauss details the process of progressive mediation as follows: " . . . two opposite terms with no intermediary always tend to be replaced by two equivalent terms which allow a third one as a mediator; then one of the polar terms and the mediator becomes replaced by a new triad and so on."[61] In the present case of the schema of the geopolitical suborder, the two opposite terms with no intermediary are FAMILIAR and STRANGE. They are replaced by two equivalent terms, JEWISH HOMELAND (equivalent to FAMILIAR) and FOREIGN LANDS (equivalent to STRANGE), which allow a third one, SEA OF GALILEE, as a mediator. Then, according to Lévi-Strauss's description, one of the polar terms and the mediator become replaced by a new triad and so on. In the geopolitical schema of Mark, the polar term FOREIGN LANDS is replaced by JUDEA and the mediator SEA OF GALILEE is replaced by GALILEE to form the second manifest opposition, GALILEE vs. JUDEA.

GALILEE VS. JUDEA

As redaction critics have noted, Galilee receives particular stress in Mark's Gospel. Galilee is the homeland of Jesus and the home base of all his travels. Nearly the first two-thirds of the narrative is set in Galilee. And, by a series of flashbacks and flashforwards, attention is focused on Galilee at the end. The present action of the Markan Gospel, however, both begins and ends in Judea, and Judea is the setting of the final third of the story. Galilee and Judea are manifest in the Markan narrative not only by reference to the two regional names but also by reference to various cities, towns, or areas within each region.

Together Galilee and Judea make up the Jewish homeland; within the Gospel of Mark, however, Galilee is the homeland within the homeland because Jesus is "from Nazareth of Galilee" (1:9) and from Galilee he calls his disciples. Thus, in relation to Galilee, Judea is foreign to the central characters of Mark. This Markan orientation is perhaps somewhat surprising, since Judea, region of Jerusalem, center of Jewish worship and Jewish religious institutions and leadership, might have been anticipated as the homeland within the Jewish homeland in comparison to Galilee, surrounded by foreign lands and their influence. But the Gospel of Mark challenges such expectations, presenting Judea not only as a strange place but as a threatening one, and characterizing Galilee not only as the familiar home from which Jesus and the disciples have come but as the final home to which they will return.[62] Thus GALILEE must be understood as a representation of the FAMILIAR pole of the fundamental opposition underlying the geopolitical suborder, replacing JEWISH HOMELAND as the opposites move toward mediation. Accordingly, JUDEA is to be perceived as a narrative representation of the STRANGE pole, replacing FOREIGN LANDS.

An observation about Mark 1:5 by R. H. Lightfoot is especially interesting in light of the assertion that Mark has challenged the positive expectations that would normally be associated with Jerusalem. Lightfoot states that "the very strong expressions in Mk. 1:5, that all the country of Judea and all the dwellers in Jerusalem went out to him, are probably not to be regarded as picturesque exaggeration, but emphasize that which was only to be expected at the appearance of the herald of the end."[63] Thus at the very beginning of Mark's Gospel, Jerusalem, all Jerusalem, is glimpsed in a positive, hopeful light. Jerusalemites witness and are responsive to the preparatory events of the kingdom of God. Thus the opening of the Markan narrative illustrates an awareness of the positive view of Jerusalem that is challenged and denied in the remainder of the text. The critique is stronger because the potential is acknowledged.[64]

Movement toward the mediation of the opposition GALILEE vs. JUDEA is suggested narratively by the journeys of Jesus (and his followers) between the two regions. Initially Jesus travels from Galilee to Judea and returns to Galilee preaching " 'the kingdom of God is at hand' " (1:15). Finally Jesus journeys from Galilee to Judea, and his return to Galilee is promised. Nothing is narrated of the events along the way of Jesus' initial journey to and from Judea, but Jesus' final journey to Judea is punctuated by three important encounters: with the rich man who seeks to inherit eternal life, with James and John who seek places of honor in Jesus' glory, with Bartimaeus who seeks his sight and follows Jesus "on the way" (10:52). The encounter with Bartimaeus is geopolitically marked; Bartimaeus joins the Galilean followers of Jesus in Judea, outside Jericho, on the road to Jerusalem. The road to Jerusalem, from the security of home in Galilee to the threat of estrangement in Judea's capital, functions as the mediator of the second manifest opposition of the Markan geopolitical suborder, GALILEE VS. JUDEA.

ENVIRONS OF JERUSALEM VS. JERUSALEM PROPER

In accordance with the mythic process of progressive mediation, the opposition GALILEE VS. JUDEA is replaced by an equivalent opposition formed by replacements of one of the polar terms, JUDEA, and the mediator, ROAD TO JERUSALEM. JUDEA is replaced by its chief city, JERUSALEM, and ROAD TO JERUSALEM is replaced by ENVIRONS OF JERUSALEM (including Bethphage, Bethany, Mount of Olives, Gethsemane, and Golgotha), giving the opposition ENVIRONS OF JERUSALEM VS. JERUSALEM PROPER. The places included among the environs of Jerusalem are all locations surrounding Jerusalem but distinguished from Jerusalem proper, outside the gates.[65] Jerusalem is the power base of the religous establishment that opposes Jesus. The environs of Jerusalem provide a base for Jesus' encounters in the city. Bethphage, Bethany, and the Mount of Olives seem to serve together as the staging ground for Jesus' entry into Jerusalem (11:1). Jesus resides in Bethany, entering Jerusalem in the morning, returning to Bethany in the evening. The Mount of Olives (13:3; 14:26) and Gethsemane (14:32) provide a place for Jesus to be with his disciples, over against Jerusalem. Even Jesus' death, brought on by the religious authorities in Jerusalem, occurs outside the city, at Golgotha (15:22). As the Markan chief priests, scribes, and elders oppose Jesus, so Jerusalem proper opposes the environs of Jerusalem.

Refuge from the opposition of religious leaders in Jerusalem is provided Jesus and his disciples in Bethany. There Jesus stays in a private home, presumably the home of a friend, Simon the Leper (14:3), where he is treated kindly—anointed by a woman. While Jesus is in Judea, near Jerusalem, Bethany offers him the familiarity of "home." Of course, in post-biblical Judaism, all pilgrims, from Galilee or from the Diaspora, could expect a "home" *in Jerusalem* during the great feasts. "The citizens [of Jerusalem] had to entertain foreign pilgrims for nothing, for Jerusalem is the possession of all Israel. One of the 10 miracles of God in the sanctuary, i.e., while the temple still stood, was that no one in Jerusalem ever said to another that there was no room to put him up for the night."[66] Because, at Passover, pilgrims often outnumbered inhabitants, the city limits of Jerusalem were extended to include Bethphage (less than a mile from the city) to accommodate them all "in Jerusalem."[67] But the Markan Jesus stays *about two miles outside the city, in Bethany.*

Jerusalem, on the other hand, offers a strange and threatening series of events: arguments with religious leaders and temple officials, arrest, interrogation, beatings, condemnation to death. The Mount of Olives, which is "opposite the temple" (13:3), and Gethsemane, whose name means "an oil press" and apparently indicates a location on the Mount of Olives, also serve as a home base for Jesus and his disciples as these events unfold. The enduring teaching and true prayer that should be, but are not, the concerns of the Jerusalem temple (see especially 11:15–19) are localized instead on the Mount of Olives (see especially 13:31) and at Gethsemane (14:32–42). Golgotha, the place of a skull (15:22), not Jerusalem, the city of Israel's kings, is the scene of the—admittedly ironic—crowning of the "King of the Jews," the "King of Israel" (15:21–32). Surprisingly, Mark's Gospel finds the traditional and familiar motifs of messiahship, teaching, prayer, and kingship estranged from Jerusalem itself but at home in Bethany and at the Mount of Olives, Gethsemane, and Golgotha. The Jewish prophetic tradition, including a recurring emphasis on Jerusalem as the "city of sin and judgment,"[68] surely forms part of the background of the Markan portrayal of Jerusalem. The Jewish tradition, however, also affirms Jerusalem as the city of God, the "city of the eschatological age and salvation";[69] and this the Markan Gospel rejects. Thus the terms ENVIRONS OF JERUSALEM and JERUSALEM PROPER are opposed on the same basis that GALILEE and JUDEA or JEWISH HOMELAND and FOREIGN LANDS are opposed: the fundamental opposition of FAMILIAR and STRANGE.

To a certain extent the opposition ENVIRONS OF JERUSALEM vs. JERUSALEM PROPER is an unstable one; the composite terms of the first element tend toward mediation of the fundamental opposition. On the Mount of Olives Jesus attempts to familiarize his disciples with the strange events to come, especially the strange events in Jerusalem. At Gethsemane Jesus prays to God in the familiar tones of a son to his father, while his prayer at Golgotha reflects, in addition, a feeling of estrangement from God. If familiarity implies security and strangeness threat, then one may perceive that these oppositions draw closer to mediation in Bethany and at Gethsemane. The threat of Jerusalem is the threat of death. But Jesus, in accepting the anointing at Bethany as the anointing " 'beforehand for burying' " (14:8), has begun to neutralize that threat, to incorporate it into his anticipated future, to familiarize himself and his followers with its strangeness. At Gethsemane Jesus prays that the threat of death coming from Jerusalem might be removed, but that above all the will of the "Father" be done. Thus Jesus appropriates the strange threat of death by understanding it within a larger pattern than that of his struggles with the Jerusalem religious authorities, that is, within his familiar—and familial—pattern of relating to God as a son to a father.

On the basis of these observations, it might seem possible to extend the geopolitical schema beyond the opposition ENVIRONS OF JERUSALEM vs. JERUSALEM PROPER; however, this is not advisable. Repetition is the device by which the oppositions of a mythic narrative are clarified. Bethphage, Gethsemane, and Golgotha are named but once each and the Mount of Olives and Bethany only three and four times respectively; in comparison with the frequencies of other elements of the geopolitical schema, these frequencies do not demand separate treatment for Bethphage, Gethsemane, Golgotha, the Mount of Olives, and Bethany.

Although movement toward mediation is sensed with each pair of opposed geopolitical terms, no final mediator is presented within the geopolitical schema. The significance of this lack must be evaluated within the context of the Markan spatial order as a whole. But, at this point, the following observations at least may be made: (1) It is not here assumed that the Gospel of Mark is a myth but, rather, that it has a mythic dimension; and the lack—at one level, or, rather, sublevel, of the narrative—of the mediator predicted by Lévi-Strauss's methodology does not invalidate this presupposition. (2) The Gospel of Mark seems, in fact, to manifest a parabolic dimension as well as a mythic dimension, and the reversal of the expected connotations of Galilee and Jerusalem would appear to be a significant manifestation of this parabolic dimension,[70] whereas the mediation expected of the mythic dimension receives clearer expression elsewhere (for example, in the topographical suborder). (3) The Markan Gospel (whether mythic or parabolic or both) is embedded in a historical/cultural context; and, within that situation, geopolitical mediation (e.g., between GALILEE and JERUSALEM) may not have been either desirable or possible for the Markan author or the Markan community.

Whatever the reason—or, more likely, reasons—for the absence of a geopolitical mediator, the effect is a residual tension at the geopolitical level of the Markan narrative.[71] At the close of the Gospel of Mark, Jesus' spatial location is neither Jerusalem nor its environs, neither Judea nor Galilee, but somewhere in between; Jesus is in movement (16:7). For the followers of Jesus—after the strange and surprising event of the resurrection outside Jerusalem—nothing, not even the familiarity of home in Galilee, is likely ever to be the same.

3. Topographical Space

And after he had taken leave of them, he went up to the mountain to pray. And when evening came, the boat was out on the sea, and he was alone on the land.

—MARK 6:46–47

While the geopolitical suborder is made up of those relationships that would be obvious from a political map, the topographical suborder is composed of relationships that would be observed from an aerial photograph or a relief map. From the air, one would see no dotted lines marking political boundaries, no pink "nations" and green "nations." But one would see rivers, lakes, seas, wilderness areas, mountains, cities and villages (although not their names), and roads, that is, the physical features of the earth, both natural (for example, mountains) and human-made (for example, cities).[1] Certain of these topographical features, as elements of the Gospel of Mark, have called forth critical attention. The significance of the mountain setting of the transfiguration (9:2) is generally noted by commentators,[2] as is that of Jesus' miracles on the sea (4:35–41; 6:45–52).[3] Attention has also been given to Markan references to the wilderness.[4] The present goal, however, is to examine the complexity of *all* the topographical designations of the Markan Gospel within the pattern of their narrative presentation. The mountain, the sea, the wilderness—the topographical locations of Mark—are more than mere stage settings for the dramatic action, for each space has its own character that is incorporated into the action. Together their relational and connotative values contribute to the narrative significance. In seeking to locate within a topographic system the action reported and projected in the Gospel of Mark, one may be better able to locate within a theological system the meaning manifested in Mark's Gospel.

RELATIONS

The 151 relations of the topographical suborder, in twelve categories, are cited in Figure 5. The narrative facts constituting the topographical suborder of the Markan spatial order are those relations designating events reported or projected in the Gospel of Mark in spatial relation to *way* (or *road*), *wilderness, region, river, heaven, sea, city, village, earth, mountain, the country,* or *marketplace.* Although the term for "wilderness," *erēmos,* literally means "desert," it refers not necessarily to a hot and dry area of sand, but to an unpopulated, isolated (i.e., deserted) area.[5] Inhabited areas, on the other hand, are suggested not only by *city, village, marketplace,* and *region,* but by *the country* as well. "The country" *(agroi)* is not a wild or unpopulated area but a rural, as opposed to an urban, region where people live and work (see 5:14 and 6:36).

If *topographical* is defined strictly as "of, or relating to, the physical features of the earth," the inclusion of *heaven* within this category demands a word of explanation. Because, in the Hebrew cosmography presupposed by the Gospel of Mark, heaven was conceived as a layer or zone above the earth—that is, defined spatially in relation to the earth—the topographical suborder seems the appropriate place to consider references to heaven. Also, if the discriminations that can be made from an aerial photograph are key to defining topographical features, the inclusion of *region* within the topographical suborder demands a word of explanation. The boundaries of a region may be natural or political or both. There are clear political aspects to Mark's use of four Greek words for "region"; of eleven occurrences, eight are grammatically linked to a proper place name, and the remaining three (5:10, 17; 6:55) are at least associated with a proper place name. Yet, in an effort to reflect accurately Mark's double spatial emphasis at these points, references to "region" are included within the topographical suborder. When occurring in phrases such as "the region [*RSV* "country"] of Judea" (1:5), "region" is perhaps little more than a classifier. When "the region of" is applied to a city, however, as in "the region of Tyre" (7:24, 31) or "the region [*RSV* "district"] of Dalmanutha" (8:10), "region" broadens the spatial designation beyond that of the geopolitical labeling of the city. Like "the country" *(agroi),* "region" (or "territory" or "district") does indicate in general a broad area of the earth.

The topographical suborder is an especially complex one. In

isolating its relations we must consider four special cases: (1) synonymous or nearly synonymous topographical terms, (2) nontopographical terms that function topographically, (3) topographical terms that function metaphorically rather than topographically, and (4) terms that function in two spatial categories.

As Figure 5 shows, the Greek text of Mark's Gospel employs sets of synonymous or nearly synonymous terms to designate each of several topographical spaces. For the sake of clarity, one basic English translation for the dominant meaning of each set of Greek terms has been chosen and will be used throughout the analysis. The single Markan reference to *tribos* ("path," 1:3) and the one to *amphodon* ("street," 11:4) are considered along with the multiple references to *hodos* ("way" or "road"). *Erēmos* ("uninhabited region" or "desert"), *erēmia* ("desert," "grassland," or "wilderness"), and *erēmos topos* ("wilderness place") are classified as designations of *wilderness*. Four Greek words contribute to the topographical category *region*: *chōra* ("region"), *perichōros* ("surrounding region"), *horia* ("region" or "territory"), and *meros* ("region" or "district"). *Kōmopolis*, literally "village-city," which occurs but once in Mark (at 1:38), is counted both with references to "village" (*kōmē*) and with references to "city" (*polis*).

Patris is a more problematic topographical term. At 6:1 *patris* (literally "of one's fathers"[6]) is translated as "own country" in the *Revised Standard Version* but as "home town" in *Today's English Version*.[7] Many commentators understand *patris* at 6:1 as an implicit reference to Jesus' native town or village, Nazareth.[8] The reference to Jesus' family in 6:3 would seem to support this view. Thus *patris* at 6:1 is included in the topographical suborder along with references to *village* (*kōmē*).

Several non-topographical terms, or terms that may only be considered topographical in a general or implied sense, function to locate Markan events in topographical space. The Markan use of the term *nephelē* ("cloud") signifies the space "heaven" (9:7 [cf. 1:11]; 13:26; 14:62 [*nephelōn tou ouranou*]).[9] The word *thalassa* ("sea") occurs frequently in Mark's Gospel, but the sea as a spatial location is also signaled by other terms, often appearing in conjunction with *thalassa* or with each other: *ploion* ("boat"), *ploiarion* ("small boat"), *peran* ("the other side"), *embainein* ("to embark"), *diaperan* ("to cross over"), *elaunein* ("to row"), *prosormizesthai* ("to

Figure 5   Topographical Relations

An action or event reported or projected in the Gospel of Mark occurs in spatial relation to:

hodos (way)   1:2; 1:3a; 2:23; 6:8; 8:3; 8:27; 9:33; 9:34; 10:17; 10:32a; 10:46; 10:52; 11:8

    tribos (path)   1:3b

    proagein (to go before)   6:45; 10:32b; 11:9; 14:28; 16:7

    amphodon (street)   11:4

erēmos (wilderness)   1:3; 1:4; 1:12; 1:13

    erēmos topos (wilderness place)   1:35; 1:45; 6:31; 6:32; 6:35

    erēmia (wilderness)   8:4

chōra (region)   1:5; 5:1; 5:10; 6:55

    perichōros (surrounding region)   1:28

    horia (region; territory)   5:17; 7:24; 7:31a; 7:31b; 10:1

    meros (region; district)   8:10

potamōs (river)   1:5

ouranos (heaven)   1:10; 1:11; 6:41; 7:34; 13:25a; 13:25b; 13:27; 13:31; 14:62b

    nephelē (cloud)   9:7a; 9:7b; 13:26; 14:62a

thalassa (sea)   1:16a; 1:16b; 2:13; 3:7; 4:1a; 4:1d; 4:1e; 4:39; 4:41; 5:1b; 5:13a; 5:13b; 5:21d; 6:47b; 6:48b; 6:49; 7:31

    ploion (boat)   1:19; 1:20; 4:1b; 4:36a; 4:36b; 4:37a; 4:37b; 5:2; 5:18b; 5:21b; 6:32; 6:45b; 6:47a; 6:51; 6:54; 8:10b; 8:14

    ploiarion (small boat)   3:9

    embainein (to embark)   4:1c; 5:18a; 6:45a; 8:10a; 8:13a

    peran (the other side)   4:35; 5:1a; 5:21c; 6:45c; 8:19b

    diaperan (to cross over)   5:21a; 6:53a

    elaunein (to row)   6:48a

    prosormizesthai (to moor)   6:53b

polis (city)   1:33; 1:45; 5:14; 6:33; 6:56; 11:19; 14:13; 14:16

    kōmopolis (village-city)   1:38

kōmē (village)   6:6; 6:36; 6:56; 8:23; 8:26; 8:27; 11:2

    kōmopolis (village-city)   1:38

    patris (native village)   6:1

gē (earth)   2:10; 4:1; 6:47; 6:53; 8:6; 9:20; 13:27; 13:31; 14:35; 15:33

oros (mountain)   3:13; 5:5; 5:11; 6:46; 9:2; 9:9; 11:1; 13:3; 13:14; 14:26

agros (the country)   5:14; 6:36; 6:56; 11:8; 13:16; 15:21

agora (marketplace)   6:56; 7:4; 12:38

moor a boat"). Were all the markers except *thalassa* ignored, the analyst's overall view of the Markan topographical suborder might be little changed; however, following the Markan emphases at this point does illustrate clearly the density of Markan references to events on the sea. The reader is reminded insistently of this spatial location when it occurs in the narrative.

A final example of a seemingly non-topographical term that serves to locate Markan characters topographically is the verb *proagein*, "to go before." "To go before" entails movement and directionality. Movement and directionality are also implied in being "on the way" (*en tē hodō*). In fact, *proagein* (6:45) may be translated "lead the way" and *proagei* in 16:7 (paralleling 14:28), "he is *on his way* before (you)."[10] Additional weight is given the consideration of *proagein* as a signal for *hodos* ("way" or "road") by two Markan passages that link both terms. Mark 10:32 opens, "And they were on the road [*en tē hodō*], going up to Jerusalem, and Jesus was walking ahead [*ēn proagōn*] of them . . . ." Mark 11:8–9 reads, "And many spread their garments on the road [*eis tēn hodon*], and others spread leafy branches which they had cut from the fields. And those who went before [*hoi proagontes*] and those who followed cried out, 'Hosanna! Blessed is he who comes in the name of the Lord!' " It is clear in each case that the one or ones who go before are on the way, or road. The literal road in both cases is the road from Galilee to Jerusalem. Two additional, and parallel, uses of *proagein* suggest implicitly, rather than explicitly, this same road. The movement promised at 14:28 and 16:7, however, is in the opposite direction—from Jerusalem to Galilee. The future tense at 14:28 and the present tense at 16:7 emphasize the process of going before on the way as opposed to the resultant arrival.

The fifth and final Markan use of *proagein* to be discussed is the term's first occurrence in the text, 6:45, "Immediately he made his disciples get into the boat and go before [*proagein*] him to the other side, to Bethsaida, while he dismissed the crowd." Initially this usage of *proagein* seems not comparable with those at 10:32, 11:9, 14:28, and 16:7. The latter imply a road on the land, but the former involves crossing the lake. Yet both are concerned with making a way, traveling, journeying, and this is the central meaning of *hodos* within the topographical suborder of Mark. Nevertheless, the contrast between making a way on the land and making a way across the sea is a real one and underlies a further narrative contrast between the successful carrying out of a journey and a detoured journey. Those traveling on their way to Jerusalem at 10:32 and 11:8–9 do arrive at their given destination, and the journey of Jesus on his way to Galilee (14:28; 16:7) is still in progress within the narrative time of Mark's Gospel. But the projected journey of the disciples, their going before Jesus to Bethsaida, is aborted. After struggling with the wind and with the terrifying sight of Jesus walking on the water, the disciples land at Gennesaret (6:53).[11] The significance of this contrast is made clear within the narrative by the employment of *proagein* at 6:45 as well as at 10:32, 11:9, 14:28, and 16:7. Everywhere *proagein* signals a spatial location *en tē hodō*.

But one might ask whether the verb *proagein* is unique in its implication of the topographical location generally signified by *hodos*. Verbs such as *erchesthai* ("to come" or "to go,") are clearly too general and too varied in their meanings to be read as specific spatial markers. But the verb *akolouthein* ("to follow") might appear to suggest being "on the way." Such is not so clearly the case, however, as with *proagein*. Like *proagein*, *akolouthein* suggests movement; but unlike *to go before*, *to follow* in and of itself does not consistently suggest one spatial location. The term *way* is not an integral part of a translation of *akolouthein*, as it may be of *proagein*. Of course, *on the way* may be quite naturally linked with *to follow* as well as with *to go before*. Such a linkage occurs three times in Mark, twice in the very verses where *to go before* is linked with *the way* (10:32, RSV "the road," "walking ahead," "followed"; 11:8–9, RSV "the road," "went before," "followed") and once in between (10:52, RSV "followed," "on the way"). But *to follow* occurs fifteen other times in Mark, embedded in a wide variety of contexts. Jesus is followed to a house (2:15; 5:24; 14:54; at 14:13 two disciples are instructed to follow " 'a man carrying a jar of water' " to a house) or to the shore of the sea (3:7) or to his native place (6:1). Of greater import in deciding whether *akolouthein* is a topographical marker suggesting *hodos* are the numerous metaphorical uses of *to follow* signifying discipleship (1:18; 2:14 bis; 8:34 bis; 9:38; 10:21; 10:28; 15:41). Jesus being the only "destination" indicated, such metaphorical usages are more sociological and theological than spatial in their connotations. Furthermore, the physical and metaphorical meanings overlap. Mark 15:41 exemplifies the varied meanings of following: the women at Jesus' crucifixion were those "who, when he was in Galilee, followed him." Did they follow him as disciples, or follow him in a physical sense, or both? Probably both. Did their following place them only on the road, or also in the village, in the country, by the sea, and elsewhere? Probably the latter. Thus, *akolouthein*, with its manifold meanings in its varied contexts, is not taken to be a topographical marker signifying *en tē hodō*.

In summary, *cloud, in the boat, to the other side, to embark, to cross over, to row, to moor,* and *to go before* are, strictly speaking, nontopographical terms that, nevertheless, function to locate Markan action in topographical space. Thus references to them are to be included in the topographical suborder.

In contrast, some uses of topographical terms in Mark do not function to locate events in narrative space and are, accordingly, to be excluded from the topographical suborder. These uses are by no means unimportant; their significance lies in part in their clarification and enrichment of the connotations of the ordinarily topographical terms they embed in other contexts. At the topographical level, all these instances are metaphorical applications—metaphorical being defined in its broad sense to include metaphors per se, parables as extended metaphors, similes, and figures of speech. Examples occur with *heaven, earth, sea, mountain,* and *way.*

Of the seventeen Markan occurrences of the word *ouranos,* "heaven,"[12] eight occur in narrative contexts functioning other than as spatial locators. The Greek *ouranos* has two centers of meaning: *heaven* as "sky" (or "air" or "atmosphere") and *heaven* as "dwelling place of God."[13] The first meaning is called for in 4:32, "the birds of the heaven" (*RSV* "air"), a poetic figure of speech from a parable of Jesus, echoing such biblical passages as Daniel 4:12 and Psalm 104:12 (LXX 103:12). The second meaning of *ouranos,* "God's dwelling place,"[14] is more frequently drawn upon in Mark, Jesus teaches his disciples to forgive others " 'so that your Father also who is in heaven [i.e., God] may forgive you' " (11:25). Because heaven is God's dwelling place, it is the dwelling place of the angels, God's messengers, as well (12:25; 13:32). Although the conventional figures of speech, "'Father . . . in heaven'" and "'angels in heaven,'" on the lips of the Markan Jesus disclose the presupposed Jewish cosmology, they do not orient narrative actions in space. Because heaven is the abode of God, *heaven* can, by metonymy and because of circumlocution, be employed in place of the divine name.[15] Both Jesus and the Jewish religious leaders employ *ouranos* in this sense in discussing the baptism performed by John (11:30, 31; cf. 11:25);[16] and when Jesus encourages the man of great possessions to "'give to the poor'" and thus "'have treasure in heaven'" (10:21), the apparent goal is "treasure with God."[17] There is no question, at 10:21 or 11:30–31, of spatial location of Markan events. Such is also the case at 8:11 where the Pharisees are reported "seeking from him a sign from heaven," that is, a sign given by God.[18] As will become obvious when considering the Markan contexts in which *ouranos* does function to locate events in topographical space, 8:11 provides an instructive contrast to 6:41 and 7:34. Action does not take place *in* heaven at 6:41 and 7:34, but Jesus, by his action, orients himself *to* heaven; thus his spatial location is determined in relation to heaven.[19]

As we try to determine the boundary between metaphorical and topographical functioning of *ouranos*, Mark 13:31 presents a unique dilemma. On the one hand, the spatial term *heaven* is joined to the spatial term *earth*, together signifying "the totality of creation,"[20] to form a basically temporal metaphor.[21] The metaphor is expressed negatively, the duration of Jesus' words is not (just) the duration of heaven and earth. Rephrased as a simile, the statement of the Markan Jesus would be, "my words will not pass away *as* heaven and earth will pass away." On the other hand, 13:31 is *not* worded as a clear simile, and its metaphorical aspect is somewhat different from the above-mentioned metaphors and figures of speech employing *ouranos*. The statement "'Heaven and earth will pass away'" is a flash-forward of narrative action concerning the basic poles of all spatial location. Something is projected to happen not so much *in* heaven or earth as *to* heaven and earth. (In a comparable case, something happens *to* the sea at 4:39.) Heaven and earth as spatial locations will cease to exist; spatial location will be invalidated at its very foundation. Thus, even though heaven and earth do function as a combined metaphor of the non-eternal at 13:31 (cf. Isaiah 40:8; 51:6; Psalm 102:25–27), the clear spatial dimension of this saying, a narrative flash-forward of action in relation to topographical space, leads to the inclusion of this reference in the topographical suborder.

Like *ouranos*, the Greek *gē*, "earth," has more than one meaning; its reference ranges from "soil" (e.g., 4:5, 8), to "ground" (e.g., 9:20; 14:35), to "land" (e.g., 4:1; 6:47), to "the world" (e.g., 4:31b; 9:3).[22] About half of the Markan references to *gē* are metaphorical uses rather than instances of topographical location of narrative action. The majority of such uses occur in the similes and metaphors of the seed parables of Mark 4: the sower (4:5a, 5b, 8) and interpretation (4:20), the seed growing secretly (4:26, 28), the mustard seed (4:31a, 31b). *Gē* also occurs within the simile describing the whiteness of the garments of the transfigured Jesus: "glistening, intensely white, as no fuller on earth could bleach them" (9:3). Later it will be instructive to consider the placement of these metaphorical usages of *gē* in relation to the references to *gē* within the topographical sequence; however, these usages are not themselves a part of the topographical sequence.

Central to the topographical sequence of the first eight chapters of the Gospel of Mark is the Sea of Galilee. Although specifically named only twice in the narrative (1:16a; 7:31), references to "the sea" are numerous and are supplemented by phrases implying the sea. Of these many narrative facts or relations involving the sea, only two have no bearing on the spatial location of narrative action of the Markan text, 9:42 and 11:23.[23] These two are the only references to "sea" in the second half of Mark's Gospel, and both are embedded in hypothetical statements. The hyperbolic metaphor operative at 9:42 might be phrased, "An appropriately dire consequence for the serious offense of causing 'little ones' to stumble is being cast in the sea to drown."[24] Similarly, the metaphor functioning behind 11:23, employing the topographic term *mountain* as well as *sea*, might be stated, "The power of belief is the power of causing a mountain to be cast in the sea."[25] Both of these hypothetical and hyperbolic statements of the Markan Jesus disclose an assumption that the sea is a powerful agent of destruction, whether in a positive sense—destroying a mountain as a witness to the power of belief (11:23), or in a negative sense—destroying a person as a sign of the danger of hindering other believers (9:42). Thus the sea is a threatening entity. This assumption is to be kept in mind when the place of the sea in the topographical sequence and schema is examined. Non–topographical applications enrich the reader's understanding of the connotative value of topographical terms.

Such enrichment is also obvious in relation to the topographical term *hodos*, "way." *Hodos*, like *ouranos* and *gē*, reflects several dimensions of meaning. Like the English translation, "way," *hodos* may signify a path or road (e.g., 4:4, 15; 10:46), a journey (6.8; 10:17), or a system of doctrine or a way of life (12:14).[26] These shadings of meaning may overlap (e.g., at 10:52, where *hodos* suggests both the road to Jerusalem and the way of discipleship), making an absolute distinction between literal and figurative meanings impossible as well as unnecessary.[27] Nevertheless, three Markan occurrences of *hodos* are separable from the topographical sequence as metaphorical applications and not locations of Markan events. *Hodos*, like *gē*, occurs in the metaphors of Jesus' parable of the sower (4:4) and its interpretation (4:15), where *hodos* means on one level "the path" in the grainfield, and on another "where the word is sown" but produces no fruit. Also *hodos* is employed metaphorically, as a figure of speech, by the Markan Pharisees and Herodians who say to Jesus, " '[you] truly teach the way of God' " (12:14).[28] Although sarcastic in tone and devious in spirit, Jesus' questioners are right in word. The "way" that Jesus travels in the Gospel of Mark leads literally to the city of Jerusalem but points to the "way of God." So the nonspatial applications of *hodos* support and extend the spatial designations.

Although " 'the way of the Lord' " in 1:3 may appear to have a metaphorical meaning comparable to "the way of God" in 12:14, the earlier reference is included in the topographical suborder because the physical aspect of *way*—that is, as a road—is developed by carry-overs of the imagery of Isaiah 40:3, including the use of the synonym *path* (*tribos*) and the injunction to make the Lord's way "straight." The entire clause beginning with "as it is written" modifies "John the baptizer appeared," and thus the scriptural quotations (involving "way" and "wilderness") are given as a description of the Markan character. Thus 1:2, 1:3a, and 1:3b are included within the topographical suborder as relations indicative of the spatial orientation of the event of John's appearing before Jesus, although a metaphorical meaning lies not far below this surface.[29] *En tē hodō* is especially amenable to metaphorical interpretation in the Gospel of Mark and occupies a focal position in the spatial sequence and schema.[30]

Additional metaphorical—and thus non-topographical—usages occur with the topographical terms *agros* (10:29–30) and *patris* (6:4). *Agros* is a surprisingly complex word in Mark. In the singular, *agros* generally means "field"—that is, a cultivated plot of ground, as at Mark 13:16—but it may signify "the country," as at 15:21. In the plural (six of eight cases in Mark), the significance of *agros* is "estate(s)" or "lands" (10:29, 30), "the country" or "hamlets" (5:14; 6:36, 56; 11:8).[31] Especially when the meaning "estates" is possible, the spatial/metaphorical distinction between uses of *agros* may be ambiguous. Jesus' saying at 10:29–30 is a case in point. Framed by references to a journey (10:17, 32)—a spatial relocation—and paralleling in part Peter's immediately prior reference to the disciples' spatial relocation (10:28; note *aphēkamen*, "we have left"), Jesus' words about *agrous* at 10:29–30 may also suggest a spatial relocation. Following Jesus' teaching concerning riches (10:17–31), *agrous* at 10:29–30 appears to serve metaphorically for riches.[32] But the hyperbole at 10:30 best demonstrates the figurative character of the saying; the phrase "and mothers," as an early twentieth-century commentator pointed out, "suffices to shew that the relations enumerated in v. 30 are not to be understood literally."[33] In addition, the form of the saying reminds the reader of the form of the metaphorical sayings at 9:42 and 11:23—an opening " 'Amen [*RSV* "Truly"], I say to you' " (9:41; 11:23; 10:29), followed by a hypothetical subject (9:41, 42; 11:23; 10:29).

Patris at 6:4 is embedded in a generalized saying of Jesus: " 'A prophet is not without honor except in his own country . . . .' " This "common proverb" has "numerous parallels"[34] and functions almost as a figure of speech concerning prophetic unpopularity. Thus this use of *patris* does not serve to locate in space any event of the Markan narrative, although it has surely influenced the choice of the term *patris* in 6:1. Therefore, *patris* at 6:4, along with *agros* at 10:29 and 30, is excluded from the topographical suborder because it functions metaphorically rather than topographically.

Finally, a number of narrative facts or relations in the Gospel of Mark function doubly as spatial references—that is, they locate the narrative action on two spatial axes simultaneously. These complex spatial references are not to be confused with Markan passages in which a number of spatial references are simply clustered together, such as at 6:56, "And wherever he came, in villages, cities, or country, they laid the sick in the market places . . . ." The two terms of a complex spatial reference are joined grammatically in the Greek; within the spatial order of Mark this occurs in one of three ways.

1. A compound word may be formed of two spatial terms; thus *kōmopolis*, village-city,[35] whose only New Testament occurrence is at Mark 1:38, is formed by joining *kōmē* to *polis* and is to be considered within the sequence of both spatial designations. Both elements of this complex spatial reference are topographical; in the remaining examples one element is topographical, the other geopolitical.

2. A spatial adjective may modify a spatial noun. At 1:5 the geopolitical adjective *Ioudaia* ("Judean") modifies the topographical noun *chōra* ("region"), and the geopolitical adjective *Iordanē* ("Jordanian") modifies the topographical noun *potamō* ("river").

3. A spatial noun may be specified by another spatial noun in the genitive case; this is the most frequent form of complex spatial reference in Mark. Included in this category are the "Sea of Galilee" (1:16a; 7:31), the "Mount of Olives" (11:1; 13:3; 14:26), and the "villages of Caesarea Philippi" (8:27). In addition, six complex references, employing three different nouns signifying, in general, "region," follow this third pattern: with *chōra*, the "region [*RSV* "country"] of the Gerasenes" (5:1); with *horia*, the "region of Tyre" (7:24, 31a), the "region of the Decapolis" (7:31b), and the "region of Judea" (10:1); with *meros*, the "region [*RSV* "district"] of Dalmanutha" (8:10).

Each of these complex spatial references is marked at two points in the spatial sequence, once within the geopolitical suborder and once within the topographical suborder—with the exception of *kōmopolis*, which is marked at two points within the topographical suborder. Most such references are simply the natural, perhaps the technical, ways of designating specific, named places; the geopolitical sense (e.g., "of Judea") overpowers the topographical sense ("region"). "Sea of Galilee" and "Mount of Olives," however, are important on the level of both suborders; the connotations of the sea presupposed by Mark are manifest in the Sea of Galilee; the Mount of Olives is important in Mark both as a specific location outside Jerusalem and as a mountain. To a consideration of the significance of *sea* and *mountain*, as well as *heaven, earth, river, wilderness, way, city, village, the country, region,* and *marketplace,* within the diachronic structure of the Gospel of Mark, the discussion now turns.

SEQUENCE

The diachronic structure of an order or suborder is given in the sequence. The sequence of the topographical suborder, a complex system of 151 relations in twelve categories, is summarized in Figure 6.

OVERVIEW

The topographical sequence of the Markan narrative opens with linked references to "the way" (1:2, 3a, 3b) and "the wilderness" (1:3): "the voice of one crying in the wilderness: Prepare the way . . . ." The voice becomes concretized in John the Baptist in the wilderness (1:4). When Jesus appears, contact is made between the topographical extremes of heaven and earth at the baptism (1:10, 11); then Jesus, like John, is located in the wilderness (1:12, 13), where he is tested. Following these initial events in topographic space, action shifts to the sea, which becomes the focal point for the first half of the narrative.

By the sea Jesus calls disciples (1:16a, 16b, 19, 20) and teaches and heals the crowds (2:13; 3:7, 9; 4:1a–e). Jesus crosses the sea freely (4:35; 5:1a, 1b, 2, 18a, 18b, 21a–d; 6:53a, 53b, 54; 8:10a, 10b, 13a, 13b) and at one point commands his disciples to cross the sea before him (6:45a–c). Three voyages involving Jesus and the disciples are dramatically marked by events or conversations of consequence (stilling the storm: 4:36a, 36b, 37a, 37b, 39, 41; walking on water: 6:47a, 47b, 48a, 48b, 49, 51; conversation about bread: 8:13a, 13b, 14). The threatening power of the sea is manifest, but the power of Jesus' word is portrayed as stronger; Jesus stills the storm and walks on the water, overcoming the threat of the sea; Jesus causes the swine possessed by unclean spirits to rush to their deaths in the sea (5:13a, 13b), turning the threat of the sea to his own purpose. (The threatening, destructive power of the sea is similarly to be turned to the purposes of believers according to Jesus' metaphorical uses of "the sea" at 9:42 and 11:23.) The sea is the center of movement in topographic space for Jesus (7:31), as is the river for John (1:5).

Two topographic locations in particular serve as a counterpoint to the *cantus firmus* of the Markan Jesus' orientation to the sea: the wilderness and the mountain(s). The wilderness had defined Jesus (following John) in the opening of Mark's Gospel, and throughout the first half of the story Jesus withdraws, by foot or by boat (6:32), to wilderness areas (1:35, 45; 6:31, 32, 35; 8:4). Initially Jesus is driven by the Spirit into the wilderness, where he experiences the testing of Satan and the ministry of angels (1:12, 13). Later Jesus takes the initiative in withdrawing to wilderness areas for prayer (1:35) or for hoped-for rest (1:45; 6:31, 32, 35). Like the wilderness, the mountain is generally an isolated area in the Markan context. Withdrawals by Jesus to a mountain, sometimes alone (6:46), sometimes with all his disciples (3:13; 11:1; 14:26), sometimes with a select few (9:2, 9; 13:3), punctuate the full length of the topographical sequence. But the crowd sometimes seeks out Jesus even on the mountain (5:5, 11) or in the wilderness (1:45; 6.31, 32, 35; 8:4); thus, not even topographically isolated areas can totally isolate the Markan Jesus. Furthermore, events on a mountain, a traditional setting of solemn, divine acts, intensify Jesus' involvement with others— especially his disciples (3:13; 9:2, 9; 13:3; 14:26).

Throughout the Markan narrative, the inhabitants of cities (1:33; 6:33), villages, the country, and entire regions (6:55–56) gather to Jesus as they first gathered to John (1:5). Jesus travels

Figure 6 Topographical Sequence

An action or event reported or projected in the Gospel of Mark occurs in spatial relation to:

	way	wilder-ness	region	river	heaven	sea	city	village	earth	moun-tain	the country	market-place
1	—1:2	1:3										
2	1:3a											
	1:3b	1:4	1:5	1:5	1:10							
					1:11							
		1:12										
		1:13				1:16a						
						1:16b						
						1:19						
						1:20						
			1:28				1:33					
		1:35					1:38	1:38				
							1:45					
		1:45								2:10		
						2:13						
3		2:23 *(grainfields)*				3:7			3:13			
						3:9						
						4:1a						
						4:1b						
						4:1c						
						4:1d						
						4:1e				4:1		
						4:35						
						4:36a						
						4:36b						
						4:37a						
						4:37b						
						4:39						
						4:41						
						5:1a						
						5:1b						
			5:1			5:2				5:5		
			5:10							5:11		
						5:13a						
						5:13b	5:14					5:14
			5:17			5:18a						
						5:18b						
						5:21a						
						5:21b						
						5:21c						
						5:21d		6:1				
								6:6				
4	6:8	6:31				6:32						
		6:32					6:33					
		6:35									6:36	
									6:36			
				6:41		6:45a						
	6:45 *(go ahead)*					6:45b						
						6:45c				6:46		
						6:47a			6:47			
						6:47b						
						6:48a						
						6:48b						
						6:49						
						6:51						

Figure 6   Topographical Sequence *cont.*

way	wilder-ness	region	river	heaven	sea	city	village	earth	moun-tain	the country	market-place
					6:53a				6:53		
					6:53b						
					6:54						
		6:55					6:56				
						6:56				6:56	6:56
											7:4
		7:24									
		7:31a			7:31						
		7:31b	7:34								
8:3	8:4								8:6		
					8:10a						
					8:10b						
		8:10			8:13a						
					8:13b						
					8:14	8:23					
						8:26					
						8:27					
8:27									9.2		
			9.7a								
			9:7b						9:9		
								9:20			
9:33											
9:34		10:1									
10:17											
10:32a											
10:32b											
10:46											
10:52									11:1		
							11:2				
11:4											
11:8										11:8	
11:9						11:19					12:38
									13:3		
									13:14	13:16	
					13:25a						
					13:25b						
					13:26			13:27			
					13:27						
					13:31			13:31			
						14:13					
						14:16					
14:28								14:26			
								14:35			
					14:62a						
					14:62b					15:21	
								15:33			
16:7											

throughout these inhabited areas preaching and healing (city: 1:38; 6:56; village: 1:38; 6:1, 6, 56; 8:27; the country: 6:56; region: 5:1; 7:24, 31a, 31b; 8:10; 10:1), and his fame travels even farther and faster (city: 1:45; 5:14; the country: 5:14; region: 1:28). But once Jesus is asked by the inhabitants to leave a region

(5:17), and once Jesus heals a blind man outside a village and asks him not to enter it (8:23, 26). At 6:36, the disciples suggest that Jesus send the people from the wilderness to the country and villages to buy food for themselves, but Jesus does not consent. On certain occasions, however, people do move into one or another of the inhabited areas to make special preparations: to "the village opposite" to procure a colt at 11:2, to the country to cut branches for Jesus' welcome at 11:8, to the city to prepare for the Passover meal at 14:13, 16. Perhaps the cluster of references at 6:55–56 best epitomizes references to inhabited areas within the topographical sequence: the people "ran about the whole neighborhood [chōran, "region"] and began to bring sick people on their pallets to any place where they heard he was. And wherever he came, in villages, cities, or country, they laid the sick in the market places and besought him . . . . "

The journeys of Jesus and others throughout the inhabited areas (city, village, the country, region, marketplace) and to the isolated areas (wilderness, mountain) of the Markan topography are all, of course, on the earth. Although Jesus does travel between some areas by boat, on the sea, the areas themselves are on the land. But some events scattered throughout the Markan narrative are specifically linked to the earth (or land or ground). Jesus commands the crowd to sit down on the ground to be fed (8:6), but both the "epileptic" boy and Jesus at prayer in Gethsemane fall (pesōn; epipten) to the ground (9:20; 14:35). At the crucifixion the whole earth becomes dark (15:33). In some cases the contrast between earth (or land) and sea is made emphatically clear in the Markan text: at 4:1 Jesus is on the sea and the crowd is on the land, while at 6:47 Jesus is on the land and the disciples are on the sea. (See also 6:53.) In other cases, land (or earth) is contrasted with heaven: " 'the Son of man has authority on earth to forgive sins' " (2:10) now, and later " 'you will see the Son of man sitting at the right hand of Power, and coming with the clouds of heaven' " (14:62). Elsewhere heaven and earth are linked to signify the whole created universe (13:27, 31).

None of the events narrated in the present time of Mark occur in heaven as a topographical location, but heaven is important in terms of the spatial orientation of several crucial episodes.

Twice (in the present time of the narrative) heaven is opened to the earth, centering on Jesus: at the baptism (1:10, 11) and at the transfiguration (9:7a, 7b). Twice (also in present narrative time) Jesus on earth looks up to heaven: in blessing the loaves and fishes (6:41) and in healing a deaf person (7:34). The final episode spatially related to heaven is the prophesied end time when the order of the heaven will be shaken (13:25a, 25b, 31) and the Son of man will appear (13:26, 27; 14:62a, 62b). These references to the activities in heaven at the end time, together with the warning to " 'flee to the mountains' " (13:14) and not to turn back in the country (or "field," 13:16), are included in the eschatological discourse of the Markan Jesus and are flash-forwards at the topographical level.

In the second half of the Gospel, Jesus sits on a mountain (13:3) and speaks of heaven (eschatological discourse); in the first half of the Gospel, Jesus sits on the sea (4:1) and speaks of the earth (seed parables). In the opening half of Mark's Gospel, travel on the sea is dominant; in the closing half of Mark's Gospel, travel on the way, or the road, is dominant. "The way" opens the Gospel of Mark topographically and scattered references to "the way," including "going before," occur from that point on (2:23; 6:8; 6:45; 8:3). Beginning with 8:27, however, this topographic modality intensifies. Jesus and the disciples are frequently located there. On the way to Caesarea Philippi, Jesus asks, " 'Who do men say that I am?' " (8:27). On the way to Capernaum, the disciples, having failed to understand the significance of who Jesus is, discuss who is the greatest among them (9:33, 34). As Jesus sets out on the way, a rich man asks, " 'Good Teacher, what must I do to inherit eternal life?' " (10:17). This final way is the road to Jerusalem, a way of suffering, of fear, of amazement (10:32a, 32b). Along the way, outside Jericho, blind Bartimaeus sees and follows Jesus "on the way" (10:46, 52). Joyous people line the way with garments and branches for Jesus' entry into the city (11:8, 9). Yet the city of Jerusalem, which has been the destination, the goal of the way, throughout much of the Gospel, is not, according to the topographical sequence, the end point after all. Following their final meal together, Jesus declares to his disciples that after he is raised up he is going on the way before them to Galilee (14:28). This is the promise the young man repeats to the women at the empty tomb (16:7) and the final topographical reference of the Markan Gospel. Mark opens with John preparing the way and closes with Jesus on the way.

Thus the sequence of the topographical suborder is not a static relief map but a dynamic pattern of movement across narrative space. On the surface, the Markan topography is neither startling nor unimaginable, but as a narrative representation of the world it bears significance for the overall meaning of Mark. The patterns of movement of Jesus and others within topographic space suggest Jesus' response to the world and the world's response to Jesus.

ON THE WAY

The initial and final references of the topographical sequence of the Gospel of Mark are, more or less explicitly, to "the way," forming a spatial frame for the narrative. The first narrative fact or relation presents a prophecy from the past (1:2–3), the final one a promise for the future (16:7), and both past and future impinge upon the narrative present. Between these poles, further references to the way occur throughout the sequence, and a significant cluster is presented between 8:27 and 11:9. Thus the way provides a unifying framework for the topographical suborder.[36]

The sequence of the topographical suborder, like that of the geopolitical suborder, opens not with the location in space of Jesus, but with a prophecy presented in topographic terms and fulfilled topographically in John. The *hodos* of the near quotations of Malachi 3:1 in Mark 1:2 and of Isaiah 40:3 in Mark 1:3 together serve as markers of the coming of "the Lord." In the Septuagint passage paraphrased in Mark 1:3, "the Lord" refers to Yahweh, God. By a substitution in the text of Isaiah 40:3, however, the Markan Gospel suggests that "the Lord" is Jesus Christ. Instead of Second Isaiah's phrase, " 'make straight . . . a highway *for our God*,' " Mark gives " 'make *his* [i.e., the Lord's] paths straight,' " thus maintaining an ambiguity in regard to the designation "Lord" that allows application of the prophecy to Jesus in a messianic sense.[37] To "prepare" the way, to make the "paths [*tribos*—Mark 1:3; Isaiah 40:3, LXX] straight" is not simply to build or prepare a road, but to do everything necessary to smooth the journey and make ready the welcome of the heralded one (cf. Isaiah 40:4 and Luke 3:5).[38] When John "appear[s] in the wilderness" (1:4) heralding a "mightier" one (1:7), the prophesied preparation of the way is concretized within the narrative space of Mark's Gospel.

As biblical texts provide the background for John's preparation of the way, twice biblical allusions enrich the reader's understanding of Jesus' actions and words in relation to the way. Early in Mark's story, Jesus and his disciples make their way (*hodos*)[39] through a grainfield on the sabbath and the disciples pluck ears of grain (2:23) in violation of the sabbath rules for rest (Exodus 34:21). In defending this action before the accusing Pharisees, Jesus suggests a parallel between his actions and those of David (1 Samuel 21:1–6) and concludes that " 'the Son of man is Lord even of the sabbath' " (2:25–28). A second episode, again conjoining the way and the provision of food, is narrated at 8:1 and following. Jesus does not wish to send the crowd away hungry, for they will " 'faint on the way' " (8:3); so Jesus multiplies the seven loaves available, just as God, through Elijah, had multiplied the meal in the jar of the widow (1 Kings 17:8–16), or through Elisha, the twenty loaves of barley (2 Kings 4:42–44).[40] Jesus provides bread for all "in the desert" (8:4), just as God, through Moses, had provided manna in the desert (Exodus 16). It is interesting to note, however, that, whereas the account in Exodus develops in detail the point that no manna is left over (except that on the day before the sabbath a two-days' supply is gathered), the Markan account, like that in 2 Kings, develops the opposite point that a surplus remains after all have eaten. These actions and words in relation to the way should suggest to the disciples who Jesus is.

As John prepares the way for Jesus, Jesus points the way for the disciples. That way is not easy; its demands are strict: no bread, no bag, no money (6:8). Within the Markan story, the disciples experience both the success of a land journey (*hodos*) of preaching and healing such as Jesus has made (6:7[41]) and the failure of a sea journey (*proagein*) in anticipation of Jesus' journey (6:45). That "on the way" is an enacted spatial metaphor of discipleship is made even more clear by the questions and discussions raised as characters are in movement on the road. These questions are part of the cluster of relations concerning the way beginning at 8:27. " 'Who do men say that I am?' " (8:27), Jesus asks the disciples on the way to Caesarea Philippi. The disciples answer: people say that you are John the Baptist, or Elijah, or one of the prophets (8:28). Then, still on the way, Jesus poses a second question: " 'But who do you say that I am?' " (8:29). Peter confesses, " 'You are the Christ' " (8:30), but demonstrates the limits of his understanding of this answer by rebuking Jesus for predicting the suffering of the Son of man (8:31–33).

Later the other disciples join their spokesman Peter in misunderstanding Jesus, for on the way to Capernaum, and after Jesus' teaching, " 'If any man would come after me, let him deny himself and take up his cross and follow me' " (8:34), the disciples discuss who among them is the greatest (9:33, 34). A final question is asked, this time *of* Jesus as he is setting out "on the way" (my translation of *eis hodon,* 10:17); a rich man asks: " 'Good Teacher, what must I do to inherit eternal life?' " Jesus' final reply echoes his teaching to the disciples: " ' . . . go, sell what you have, and give to the poor, . . . and come, follow me' " (10:21); that is, deny yourself and follow on the way. Thus, in the Markan pattern of questions and discussions posed on the way, two concerns are interwoven: "Who is the leader?" and "What does following entail?"

These concerns are made concrete "on the road, going up to Jerusalem" (10:32a). Jesus leads the way (*proagein,* 10:32b) and following is shown to entail amazement and fear, for the way leads to suffering and death for the Son of man.[42] The first two passion predictions appear to be given as Jesus and the disciples are traveling (8:31–33; 9:30–32); the third and fullest passion prediction is specifically located "on the road" (10:32–34). Further along the way to Jerusalem, by the road outside Jericho (10:46), the leader is recognized by blind Bartimaeus not only as Jesus of Nazareth but also as the Son of David, as one whose mercy may give sight. Receiving physical sight to match his spiritual insight, Bartimaeus follows Jesus "on the way" (10:52).

While many commentators have noted the more-than-spatial significance of one or another Markan reference to "on the way,"[43] few, if any, have considered the pattern of *all* such references as a unifying framework. But the importance of "the way" in the mid-section (8:22–10:52) of the Markan Gospel, the "discipleship section," has increasingly been recognized.[44] For some interpreters, however, the story here is chiefly of the disciples losing the way: "Theirs is the road to ruin."[45] Certainly the Markan disciples of Jesus illustrate colorfully the difficulties of following on the way. But perhaps light is shed on the difficulties Markan characters experience in understanding and following the way of Jesus by Wilhelm Michaelis's comment on the references to the ways of God in the Septuagint: "There are not wanting passages which assume that men can really follow these ways of God. In most cases, however, these are self-protestations . . . [e.g., Job 23:11; Psalms 17:4; 18:21; 37:34; 39:1; 119:15]. But there is an impressive number of passages painting a different picture. Men (including Israel, to which most of the passages refer) do not observe the ways of God (Mal. 2:9) and will not know them (Jer. 5:4f.; Wis. 5:7)."[46] The way is never easy. And, in Mark's Gospel, the way is not to be understood until the journey to Jerusalem is more than complete.

One final episode of the journey to Jerusalem is signaled by the topographic marker "on the road": Jesus' entry into the city. At Jesus' instruction, two disciples bring a colt from a street (*amphodon*, 11:4) in a nearby village. At their own initiative, many people spread on the road (*hodos*, 11:8) their garments and leafy branches, while those who go before (*proagein*, 11:9) Jesus on the road and those who follow cry, " 'Hosanna! Blessed is he who comes in the name of the Lord' " (11:9). It is an event appropriate to the final consummation of an important journey. Yet, according to Mark's Gospel, the way of Jesus does not end in the city of Jerusalem.

After celebrating the Passover meal in Jerusalem, Jesus and the disciples go out to the Mount of Olives. It is there Jesus announces that after the resurrection he will go before them to Galilee (14:28).[47] At the empty tomb the young man repeats Jesus' earlier promise for the future as an actuality that is now beginning:[48] " '. . . he *is going* before you to Galilee' " (16:7); he is on the way. Thus the topographical sequence of the Gospel of Mark ends with its least static element, "on the way." *Hodos* and *proagein* signal not so much one place among others as a way between places, a dynamic process of movement.[49] This topographical pattern is a microcosm of the entire Markan Gospel: John prepares the way, Jesus leads the way, disciples are called to follow on the way.[50]

IN THE WILDERNESS

An echo of this pattern, John/Jesus/disciples, is heard in the wilderness. First John appears "in the wilderness" (1:4); then Jesus is driven "out into the wilderness" (1:12–13); later Jesus goes out to the wilderness and Simon (Peter) comes to him (1:35); finally Jesus and the disciples withdraw to the wilderness and a multitude comes to them (1:45; 6:31, 32, 35; 8:4). Within the topographical suborder of Mark, one is concerned not with locating "the wilderness" specifically in terms of the physical geography of first-century Palestine, but with understanding the significance of *the wilderness* in terms of the system of Markan spatial relations in which it is embedded and in terms of the larger, traditional system of associations of the wilderness presupposed by Mark.

The Jewish Scriptures, *the* Holy Scriptures for Mark, offer two major foci for interpreting *the wilderness:* (1) the wilderness as the place of both divine testing and divine providence during the exodus from Egypt and (2) the prophesied transformation of the wilderness in the end time or the messianic age.[51] Both aspects are incorporated into Mark's Gospel. Ulrich Mauser, in his study *Christ in the Wilderness: The Wilderness Theme in the Second Gospel and its Basis in the Biblical Tradition,* clearly illustrates the double aspect of the exodus tradition of the wilderness. "The desert stories of Exodus and Numbers," Mauser summarizes, "almost always combine two elements: danger and divine help. The wilderness is the place that threatens the very existence of Yahweh's chosen people, but it is also the stage which brightly illumines God's power and readiness to dispel the threat."[52] For example, the Hebrew people appear to be trapped between Pharaoh's army and the Red Sea (danger, testing), but Yahweh makes a way for their escape through the sea (help, providence). Or again, the Hebrew people are murmuring because of their lack of food in the desert (danger, testing), but Yahweh provides manna for them (help, providence). On the other hand, we read in Isaiah of a second exodus through the wilderness. A voice announces the transformation of the wilderness (40:3–4). As Mauser notes, "Everything in the nature of the desert which is troublesome for the journey of the redeemed will be transformed into a condition insuring an easy passage";[53] the way will be made straight (Isaiah 40:3). Then the wild beasts of the wilderness (see Isaiah 34:9–15) will be tame and harmless (Isaiah 11:6–9; 43:20) or absent altogether (Isaiah 35:7, 9). In the renewed wilderness, the people will receive the gift of the Spirit of God (Isaiah 63:10–14; 32:15; 44:3).[54]

The Markan prologue draws significantly upon this rich wilderness tradition, combining the themes of repentance and renewal.[55] Immediately following the superscription, Mark writes: "As it is written in Isaiah the prophet, . . . 'the voice of one crying in the wilderness: Prepare the way of the Lord . . . ' " (1:2–3). But Mark's full "quotation" from "Isaiah" is actually a composite paraphrase of Malachi 3:1 (cf. Exodus 23:20) and Isaiah 40:3. The Hebrew of Isaiah 40:3 connects "in the wilderness" with "prepare" rather than with the "voice." Mark's usage in this matter, however, conforms to the Septuagint.[56] Mark's purpose of illustrating the fulfillment of the prophecy in John requires a voice (later John) in the wilderness (1:4) rather than a voice (in no specified place) crying "prepare the way in the wilderness." For Mark, the wilderness is not so much the scene of the preparation of the way as the identifying location of the one preparing it. John's spatial location serves to confirm the prophecy's fulfillment in him.[57] Even the syntax makes the connection obvious, for verse 4 "stands as the conclusion" of verse 2: "As it is written . . . John the Baptizer appeared . . .," the quotations from the Hebrew Scriptures in verses 2–3 being parenthetical.[58] A second confirmation of prophetic fulfillment is given in the parallel between John's clothing in 1:6 and that of Elijah in 2 Kings 1:8, since Elijah, it was believed on the basis of Malachi 4:5–6, would return as the forerunner of the end time and/or the Messiah.[59] A third confirmation is given in John's speech concerning the "mightier" one to follow, that is, a speech enacting the role of the forerunner of the Messiah.

With John, the renewal of the wilderness is proclaimed; with Jesus the transformation is made manifest. The Spirit, that is the Spirit of God that has just descended from heaven like a dove, drives (*ekballei*) Jesus into the wilderness (1:12–13). The verb *ekballei* is a strong and forceful one, used mainly to describe the expulsion of unclean spirits (1:34, 39; 3:15, 22, 23; 6:13; 7:26; 9:18, 28, 38). When Jesus casts out (*ekballei*) an unclean spirit he exhibits power over it. When the Holy Spirit casts Jesus out into the wilderness (a double reversal: unclean spirit/Holy Spirit; Jesus casts out/Jesus is cast out), the power of the Spirit over Jesus is manifest.[60] Thus the temptation story concurs with the baptism story: Jesus is under the power of the Spirit. God, through the Spirit, initiates these actions. Similarly, the initiative was God's in leading the Hebrew people into the wilderness. And, of course, both the initiation of the end time and the renewal of the wilderness rest with God.

Like the wilderness of the exodus, the wilderness of the Markan prologue entails both testing, here by Satan,[61] and providence, here through angels (cf. 1 Kings 19:5, 7; note also the *angelos*, "messenger," mentioned in Mark 1:2 [cf. Exodus 23:20]).[62] Like the renewed wilderness of the messianic age, this wilderness is inhabited by wild beasts no longer wild; Jesus is "with" them as one is "with" one's family and friends. This passage should also be understood "against the background of the common Jewish idea that the beasts are subject to the righteous man and do him no harm . . . ."[63] Examples of this idea include the story of Adam, Job 5:22, Psalm 91:11–13, the *Testament of Benjamin* 5:2, and especially the *Testament of Naphtali* 8:4: "If you do good, my children, both men and angels shall bless you, and the Devil shall flee from you and the wild beasts shall fear you and the Lord shall love you."[64] Perhaps the forty days of Jesus' stay in the wilderness allude to both foci of the wilderness tradition—testing and renewal—recalling both the forty years in the wilderness of the exodus tradition and, more exactly, the forty days of strength that Elijah, the prophesied forerunner of the messianic age, received from the food given by the angel in the wilderness (1 Kings 19:4–8). A third possible allusion is to the forty-day fast of Moses on Mount Sinai (Exodus 34:28; Deuteronomy 9:9, 18). These allusions need not be exclusive.[65]

The four references to the wilderness in the Markan prologue, 1:3, 4, 12, 13, are the only Markan occurrences of *erēmos* as a noun; this form is presumably derived from the Septuagint text of Isaiah 40:3 as quoted in Mark 1:3. Although the theological connotations of wilderness are primary, the wilderness of the prologue would be located geographically in Judea.[66] The next five Markan references to the wilderness (1:35, 45; 6:31, 32, 35) employ the phrase *erēmos topos*, "wilderness place" or "deserted place,"[67] and would be located geographically in Galilee. It is the theological significance, however, that is again of first importance.

The exodus tradition of danger and help in the wilderness supports the Markan narrative development. After an initial outpouring of healing power, Jesus withdraws to a wilderness place (1:35)[68] to pray. (Because of some danger or testing in regard to the kind of response elicited in the ministry so far? For divine help?[69]) When Simon (Peter) finds Jesus there, or rather "pursues" or "tracks down" Jesus in the wilderness (*katediōxen*, "tracks down," is a *hapax legomenon* in the New Testament and nearly always used in a hostile sense, e.g., Genesis 31:36[70]), Jesus returns to preach throughout Galilee (1:36–39). But the news of Jesus' healing of a leper spreads, "so that Jesus was no longer able to enter into a city but was outside in a wilderness place" (1:45, my translation). But no place is long deserted after the arrival of the Markan Jesus, and people come out to Jesus from everywhere (1:45). Later Jesus, with the disciples, again withdraws from the crowds to a wilderness place to "rest a while," for "they had no leisure even to eat" (6:31). But the wilderness provides neither rest nor leisure; Jesus and the disciples arrive by boat (6:32) only to be met by a crowd of more than five thousand people who have arrived before them on foot (6:33). What is provided in the wilderness (6:35) is divine sustenance, bread broken and multiplied. The first Markan reference to Moses (1:44) is framed by *erēmos topos* at 1:35 and 1:45; at 6:31, 32, 35, *erēmos topos* recalls Yahweh's provision of manna to those led by Moses in the wilderness. This image of divine sustenance is repeated at 8:4 in the feeding of the four thousand. At 8:4 *erēmia* is employed (a *hapax legomenon* in Mark), and the geographical location would be the east side of the Sea of Galilee.

In summary, all Markan narrative facts or relations involving the wilderness occur in the first half of the Gospel. To be miraculously fed in the wilderness is to stand in line with those called out of Egypt in the past. To prepare a way in the wilderness, to be at peace with the wild animals in the wilderness, is to be in line with the prophecies of those who have looked for the coming of the Messiah in the future.

ON THE SEA

Like the narrative facts or relations involving the wilderness, those involving the sea occur in the first half of Mark's Gospel. The opening of the topographical sequence is fugue-like in its introduction of the narrative pattern way/wilderness/sea. The "way" melody begins the composition (1:2, 3a, 3b) and is followed immediately by strains of the "wilderness" theme (1:3, 4, 12, 13); both themes continue and a third, the "sea," is introduced (1:16a, 16b, 19, 20) after a few bars of the second. This third theme is played *forte*.

Before examining in detail the pattern of the Markan presentation of references to the sea, two preliminary observations are in order concerning the Markan naming of the sea—the first concerning *tēs Galilaias*, "of Galilee," the second concerning *thalassa*, "sea." The first and final Markan usages of *thalassa* for spatial location, 1:16a and 7:31, are complex, each combining a geopolitical with a topographical marker: *thalassa tēs Galilaias*. These specific citations frame the ministry of Jesus, which encircles the sea. Jesus is "of Galilee" (1:9), and the sea that is central to his travels is, according to Mark, also "of Galilee" (1:16a; 7:31). Since "the name as applied to the lake does not appear until the gospels use it,"[71] and since Mark was likely the first Gospel written, Mark's naming is not without importance; it strengthens the tie between Jesus and the sea. But in actuality the so-called "Sea of Galilee" is a lake—a large, but inland and freshwater, lake. The Markan use of *thalassa*, "sea," instead of the more precise *limnē*, "lake," has been characterized as thoroughly Semitic.[72] Whatever the motivation for the choice of *thalassa*, the term serves in Mark with richer scriptural connotations and as a more significant contrast to *land* or *earth* than would *lake*, as will be observed later in connection with the schema and now in regard to the topographical sequence.[73]

Cited in a single column of Figure 6 are all those relations that locate Markan events in relation to the sea; the set might be subdivided into "by the sea" and "on the sea." By the sea Jesus calls his first disciples, and immediately they leave the sea and follow him (1:16a, 16b, 19, 20). By the sea Jesus teaches the multitudes (2:13; 4:1a–e) and heals those who come to him from every direction (3:7, 9). Jesus also teaches and heals in synagogues (e.g., 1:21–27, 39), the traditional setting for teaching;

but the seaside provides an additional setting for the teaching of Jesus, a teaching that moves beyond traditional limits.

In crossing the sea, Jesus may also be said to cross traditional limits. Jesus travels on the sea freely and frequently; such action is so typical that sometimes only a phrase marks it at the topographical level (5:21a–d; 6:32; 8:10a, 10b). Three voyages on the sea, however, are narratively elaborated and dramatize both teaching and healing. While on the sea the disciples are given opportunity to learn who Jesus is, to understand the nature and source of the power that comes through him.[74] Having crossed the sea with Jesus, the disciples are witnesses to the healing nature of that power in the lives Jesus touches.

The first crossing, from west to east, follows Jesus' private instruction of the disciples (4:34). The crossing itself is marked with numerous topographical designations (4:35, 36a, 36b, 37a, 37b, 39, 41; 5:1a, 1b, 2), serving to intensify the drama by this step-by-step accounting.[75] As frequently depicted in the imagery of the Psalms, the sea, the wind, the storm are under the power of God. To still the storm and save those in danger is also the power of the Lord (Psalm 107:23–32). But this is what Jesus does on the first crossing, rebuking the stormy sea as he earlier rebuked an unclean spirit (4:39, paralleling 1:25, *phimousthai*, "to be silent"; cf. Psalms 104:7; 106:9; 107:29),[76] so that the disciples are "filled with awe" and ask themselves, "'Who then is this, that even wind and sea obey him?'" (4:41). Immediately upon his arrival on the other side of the sea, in the country of the Gerasenes (5:1), Jesus is met by a demoniac, presumably a Gentile, whom he heals by casting out the unclean spirits that had possessed him. After the episode, Jesus crosses "again in the boat to the other side" (5:21) where he is met by Jairus, a Jew, whose daughter he "heals" by raising her from the dead—that is, by restoring her spirit that had departed from her. The manifestations of Jesus' power by the sea are to be interpreted in light of the manifestations of Jesus on the sea, and vice versa.

A second voyage on the sea is likewise emphasized by multiple topographical signals (6:45a–c, 47a, 47b, 48a, 48b, 49, 51, 53a, 53b, 54), but it begins quite differently: the boat with the disciples is "in the middle of the sea" and Jesus is "on the land" (6:47, my translation). The disciples have been sent by Jesus ahead to Bethsaida (6:45); yet they have made little progress, being "distressed in rowing for the wind was against them" (6:48a, my translation).[77] When Jesus, who has been praying on a mountain (6:46), comes to them "walking on the sea" they are "terrified" (6:49–50). Jesus reassures them in the solemn words of the revelation formula spoken by Yahweh to Moses from the burning bush, *egō eimi*, " 'I am' " (6:50; cf. Exodus 3:14, LXX). As before, the wind ceases; as before, the disciples are astounded and do not really understand the significance of this event on the sea (6:51–52). And finally, as before, when they reach land (not at Bethsaida, but at Gennesaret) persons immediately come to Jesus, and he heals them (6:53–56).

By the third narratively elaborated voyage on the sea, a west-to-east crossing (8:13–22), the pattern is clear: Jesus and the disciples start out across the sea (8:13a, 13b); a significant event, this time a conversation, occurs midway (8:14–20); the disciples fail to understand its significance (8:21); when they come to land again Jesus heals someone (8:22–26). For Mark's purposes, Jesus' mid-sea teaching about the multiplication of the loaves is as dramatic as his stilling the storm or walking on water. Both the importance and the difficulty of understanding about the loaves were foreshadowed in a previous sea voyage (6:52). Twice the disciples have witnessed the power of Jesus over the sea and over the bread, power like that of Yahweh over the Red (or Reed) Sea and over the manna. But the disciples remain blind to the implications (8:21). Upon landing at Bethsaida (8:22), Jesus twice tries to heal a blind man, and finally the man does see and see clearly. Whether events occur "on the sea" or "by the sea," the sea is central to the spatial orientation of Jesus' ministry of healing and teaching, his ministry of power.

In addition to the manifestations of Jesus' power over the sea by calming it or walking on it, Mark portrays Jesus as utilizing the generally destructive power of the sea for his own purposes. Jesus grants the request of the legion of unclean spirits to enter the swine rather than be sent out of the country of the Gerasenes, but the possessed swine then rush down the bank into the sea (5:13a) and are drowned in the sea (5:13b). Elsewhere Jesus suggests, in hyperbole, that the destructive power of the sea may be used by those who have faith (11:23) and against those who hinder faith (9:42). This destructive, chaotic power of the sea is the very power Jesus confronts and overcomes in ordering the sea by stilling the storm and walking on the water. The power Jesus manifests on the sea is akin to the power he manifests by the sea, the power of teaching and healing.

At certain points in the Markan narrative, care seems to have been taken to distinguish the sea from the land as a spatial location. Mark 4:1 and 6:47 present the opposition most strongly. At 4:1 the crowd is on the land, beside the sea, and Jesus is on the sea, sitting in a boat, near the land. The Greek text juxtaposes "sitting" with "on the sea" rather than with "in the boat," thus accenting the more fundamental sea/land (*thalassa/gē*) distinction. The scene is the setting for Jesus' teaching the crowd in parables, especially parables of seeds planted in the earth (*gē*). At 6:47 Jesus is alone on the land and the disciples are in the boat out "in the middle of the sea" (my translation).[78] The scene is the setting for Jesus' walk on the sea. The opposition between sea and land is outlined here as it is presented diachronically in the topographical sequence. Later the opposition will be considered as it is operative synchronically in the topographical schema.

BETWEEN EARTH AND HEAVEN

All Markan topographical relations, except the sea and heaven, implicitly entail the land or the earth (*gē*). Certain narrative facts or relations, however, bring out this spatial orientation in an explicit way and, apparently, for a variety of reasons. At 8:6 Jesus commands the crowd *anapesein epi tēs gēs*, that is, literally, "to recline (as at table) on the earth." Understandably, the *Revised Standard Version* has translated the command "to sit down on the ground," but the significant disjunction is thus lost. Along with many of the details of the miraculous feeding, the use of *anapesein*, appropriate to a formal meal or banquet, rather than *kathēsthai* ("sit"), appropriate to an outdoor meal or picnic, points to the church's celebration of the Eucharist and to the imagery of the Messianic Banquet (cf. Mark 6:39–40 and 14:22–25).[79] By the juxtaposition of *anapesein* and *epi tēs gēs*, the Markan account of the miraculous feeding is overlaid with ritual and eschatological significance.

Elsewhere in Mark, two separate episodes are perhaps linked at the connotative level by two similar uses of *epi tēs gēs*. At 9:20 it is reported that an apparently epileptic boy was brought to

Jesus and "fell on the ground" (*pesōn epi tēs gēs*). At 14:35 it is reported that Jesus, in praying at Gethsemane, "fell on the ground" (*epipten epi tēs gēs*). In addition to the clear lexical parallel, less obvious but significant narrative parallels exist between the two episodes. First, both the epileptic boy and Jesus at prayer fell on the earth in the felt presence of a greater power: the boy when the dumb spirit afflicting him saw Jesus; Jesus as he began to pray, " '*Abba*, Father, all things are possible to thee; remove this cup from me; yet not what I will, but what thou wilt' " (14:36). It is clear at 14:35 that falling on the earth presents an attitude of supplication and prayer.[80] Secondly, both episodes portray the power of prayer in disturbing circumstances. To the disciples who had been unable to drive out the dumb spirit, Jesus responded, " 'This kind cannot be driven out by anything but prayer' " (9:29); it is a response unique in Mark's Gospel and unique to Mark's Gospel. After praying at Gethsemane, Jesus, although initially "greatly distressed and troubled" (14:33), said *apechei*, " 'It is enough' " (14:41), in the sense of having in full what is due or what is sought.[81] Third, both encounters involved a sense of death. When the dumb spirit came out of the boy, the boy was *hosei nekros*, "as if dead" (9:26, my translation); as Jesus began to pray, his soul was "sorrowful, even to death [*eōs thanatou*]" (14:34). In fact, the Greek word for "dead body" or "corpse," *ptōma* (6:29; 15:45), literally means "that which has fallen," deriving from the same root as "to fall," *piptō*.[82]

Finally, both pericopes incorporating the phrase "fell on the earth" (*RSV* "ground") occur in contexts shaped by predictions of Jesus' death and resurrection. The account of the healing of the epileptic boy follows Jesus' comment on the Son of man's resurrection from the dead (9:9–13) and is followed by the second passion and resurrection prediction (9:30–32). Even within the account of the healing, resurrection language is employed: the boy, who was as dead, "arose," *anestē* (9:27).[83] The narration of Jesus' prayer at Gethsemane follows that of Jesus' statements at the Mount of Olives in anticipation of his death and resurrection (14:26–31) and is in turn followed by the report of his arrest, which moves the narrative toward death and resurrection (14:43–50). Thus, within the echo of the repeated phrase "fell on the earth," there resound as well the tones of death and resurrection. The topographical marker *epi tēs gēs* is a spatial signal of a more-than-spatial narrative sense.

The narrative facts or relations involving the earth (*gē*) at 2:10, 13:27, and 13:31 are associated in another sense; each suggests the scope of some aspect of the authority of the Son of man or Jesus. " 'The Son of man has authority on earth to forgive sins' " (2:10), Jesus proclaims, having just manifested such authority. At the end time, the Son of man will have power and authority to " 'send out the angels, and gather his elect from the four winds, from the ends of the earth to the ends of heaven' " (13:27); that is, the Son of man will have authority not just on earth but throughout the universe. Finally, Jesus will have authority beyond the universe: " 'Heaven and earth will pass away,' " Jesus says, " 'but my words will not pass away' " (13:31). By the repetition of the topographic term *gē* in each of these three contexts, the Gospel marks the sequence of the expanding authority of Jesus as the Son of man—now, in the future, forever.

At 13:27 and 31, earth is both contrasted with and linked with heaven.[84] The ends of earth are not the ends of heaven but together they define the universe (13:27); the universe, both earth and heaven, will pass away (13:31). At 15:33 an event that occurs on earth appears to presuppose an occurrence in heaven; darkness covering the whole earth from noon to three o'clock suggests a darkening of the sun in heaven, such as that predicted at 13:24 (cf. Amos 8:9–10). Mark 13:24 is one in a series of descriptions of eschatological catastrophes foretold to overcome heaven and earth, narrative flash-forwards at the topographical level: 13:25a, "and the stars will be falling from heaven"; 13:25b, "and the powers in the heavens will be shaken";[85] 13:26, "and then they will see the Son of man coming in clouds [of heaven] with great power and glory" (cf. 14:62; cf. Daniel 7:13); 13:27, and the Son of man "will send out the angels to gather his elect . . . from the ends of the earth to the ends of heaven."[86] All this will happen at the end time, totally transforming heaven and earth, the basis of all spatial location. But beyond even the Markan Jesus' descriptions of the transformations of the end time is his proclamation in 13:31 that " 'heaven and earth will pass away,' " that is, cease to exist.[87] Then, since in the ancient oriental, Hebrew, and New Testament world views heaven and earth together constitute the cosmos (Genesis 1:1; Psalm 115:15–16[88]), all spatial location will be disestablished at its very foundation. Orientation in space will be replaced by orientation to Jesus' " 'words' " (13:31). The significance of this startling narrative fact will be examined when we consider the schema of the topographical suborder.

Within the sequence of the topographical suborder, one may ask, "Who is this Jesus whose words will have authority beyond heaven and earth?" Some clues have been given in relations involving the topographic designation *earth* (e.g., 2:10); others are offered in narrative facts relating Jesus and heaven.[89] In Jewish thought around the turn of the eras, heaven and earth were considered separate realms. Communication across their unseen and distant boundary was not normally expected.[90] Long ago the voice of God (from heaven) had spoken directly to the prophets (on earth), but now "even the holiest rabbis were allowed to hear only the echo of it, the 'daughter of the voice' (*bath qol*) as it was called."[91] Long ago God had sometimes "bowed the heavens" (e.g., Psalms 18:9; 144:5; 2 Samuel 22:10) and come down to earth to assist human beings. But now the way between heaven and earth seemed blocked. Yet hope remained that God would "rend the heavens and come down" (Isaiah 64:1; see John 1:51; Acts 7:56; Revelation 11:19; 19:11).[92] Mark's Gospel affirms the realization of that hope.

Two episodes in the Markan Gospel, each including two relations involving heaven, manifest the openness of heaven to Jesus, and two episodes manifest the openness of Jesus to heaven. In the former category are the baptism and the transfiguration of Jesus. The heavens are literally opened to Jesus at 1:10, splitting[93] as Jesus emerges from the river, allowing the descent of the Spirit like a dove. Communication between heaven and earth, between the divine and the human, is then established— by the initiative of the divine but on a human model: a voice from heaven speaks, " 'Thou art my beloved Son' " (1:11).[94] What was once a wide gulf between two realms has now been bridged; the heavenly and the earthly are as close as parent and child. This motif is repeated in the transfiguration account: "And a cloud [a topographical marker signaling heaven] overshadowed them . . ." (9:7). In the Jewish Scriptures, particularly in the exodus account, clouds are important in theophanies, as accompanying signs of God's presence (Exodus 16:10; 19:9, 16; 24:15–18; 33:9; 34:5; 40:35; Leviticus 16:2; Numbers 11:25),[95] but the biblical cloud both conceals and reveals the divine presence.[96] And this motif also finds expression in Mark: " . . . and a voice came out of the cloud, 'This is my beloved Son; listen to him [akouete autou]' " (9:7; cf. Deuteronomy 18:15, LXX, autou akousesthe[97]). In listening to Jesus, Mark seems to suggest, one will hear words of God because in Jesus communication between heaven and earth has been reestablished.

In between the divine/human encounters of the baptism and the transfiguration, in which heaven is oriented toward Jesus, the Markan Jesus twice orients himself toward heaven. In "taking the five loaves and the two fish," Jesus "looked up to heaven" (6:41); that is, he turned spatially to heaven and sprititually to God in prayer. And when he "blessed, and broke the loaves" and "divided the two fish among them all" there was more than enough food to feed over five thousand people. The miraculous results of communication from earth to heaven rival those of communication from heaven to earth. In healing a deaf man Jesus also looked up to heaven (7:34), from where the Spirit had come down (1:10). And when Jesus said, " 'Be opened,' " the man's "ears were opened . . . and he spoke plainly" (7:34–35), just as the voice from heaven would later speak plainly to the three disciples, " 'listen to him' " (9:7), let your ears be opened (cf. 4:9; 4:23; 8:18). Jesus' action in turning toward heaven contrasts with the failure of the Pharisees to orient themselves toward heaven or to recognize that heaven had been opened to the earth through Jesus. The Pharisees did come to Jesus, but they "began to argue with him, seeking from him a sign from heaven [that is, from God], to test him" (8:11). Jesus sighed (8:12). Twice in the Markan Gospel Jesus is said to have sighed. At 7:34 the sighing is linked with "looking up to heaven," that is, preparing for divine/human communication. Perhaps the connotation is the same at 8:12.[98] The Pharisees' "seeking" did not involve placing themselves in a spatial location in relation to heaven as Jesus did; their orientation did not change; they participated in no divine/human communication.

FROM THE MOUNTAIN

In a cosmographic system in which God dwells in the heaven above and human beings dwell on the earth below, the mountain forms a natural location for divine/human encounters. The mountain represents the earth reaching heavenward; the distance from heaven to a mountaintop is not so great. (See Figure 7, showing the topographical hierarchy.) This theological significance of the mountain underlies many narratives of the Jewish Scriptures, which in turn underlie Mark's Gospel. The biblical image of the mountain, and Mark's appropriation of it, is composite.

Early in his ministry Jesus goes up "on the mountain" (3:13) and there appoints twelve "to be with him, and to be sent out to preach and have authority to cast out demons" (3:14–15), that is, to be disciples. According to William Wrede: "This mountain is not to be sought on the map . . . . It is an ideal mountain."[99] In appointing twelve disciples on the mountain, the Markan Jesus would appear to establish the New Israel.[100] The old Israel, with its twelve tribes, had been established by appointment by God, through Moses, from Mount Sinai (Exodus 19). It is to be noted, however, that when the narratives of Exodus and Mark are examined as parallels, Jesus plays not so much the role of Moses as the role of God. Jesus does the calling in Mark as God does the calling in Exodus. God calls only Moses to come up on the mountain (19:20), and through Moses the people are called to the foot of the mountain; all those whom Jesus calls come up on the mountain.

With these twelve disciples Jesus travels in Galilee, and then they cross over the Sea of Galilee to the country of the Gerasenes. There a demoniac, who wandered among the tombs and "on the mountains" (5:5) injuring himself, comes to Jesus and is healed, rescued from the legion of demons who had possessed him. The demons are sent into a herd of swine feeding "near the mountain" (5:11, my translation of *pros tō orei*), and the swine, in place of the man, now suffer the torment of possession—and death. The story of a person's rescue from the threat of death and the substitutionary death of an animal that "happens" to be nearby, all taking place on a mountain, is also an aspect of the biblical account of Abraham and Isaac (Genesis 22). The Markan Jesus, like the God of Genesis, provides the rescue; but, like Abraham, Jesus "sacrifices" the provided animal(s). Because of its nearness to heaven, the mountain serves as an archetypical location for divine rescue or healing and for the divine establishment of the community, old or new.

Because of its nearness to heaven, the mountain serves also as the focal point for divine/human communication. That the Markan Jesus goes up "on the mountain" (6:46) to pray—that is, to converse with God—is not so surprising in the light of the traditional encounters of Abraham, Moses, and Elijah with God on the mountain.[101] At 6:46 it would appear that Jesus initiates the conversation. This Markan reference to prayer on the mountain is followed immediately by the account of Jesus walking on the sea and saying to the disciples at 6:50, *egō eimi*, " 'I am' " (*RSV* " 'it is I' "). The simple yet solemn proclamation recalls that of Yahweh to Moses from the burning bush on Mount Horeb: *egō eimi*, " 'I am' " (Exodus 3:14, LXX). In addition, the disciples to whom Jesus speaks, just as the Pharoah to whom Moses spoke the words God gave, did not understand for "their hearts were hardened" (Mark 6:52; cf. Exodus 10:1 and passim). Thus Mount Horeb witnesses a hierophany in the fire, and the mountain on which Jesus prays preludes a hierophany on the water. In addition, divine revelation on the mountain occurred in the country of the Gerasenes, where Jesus was recognized as " 'Son of the Most High God' " (5:7).

God's initiation of the divine/human communication involved in the transfiguration (9:2–8) is clear, and the brightness of Jesus' garments, the cloud and the voice, and especially the "six days" (cf. Exodus 24:16) recall the encounter of Moses with God on Mount Sinai,[102] but also perhaps Elijah's encounter with God in the "voice" on Mount Horeb (1 Kings 19). These connotative possibilities are strengthened by the appearance of Moses and Elijah with the transfigured Jesus on the "high mountain" (only at 9:2). The biblical tradition of the mountain as the place of divine revelation and meeting, manifested in the Law (Moses) and the Prophets (Elijah), is woven into the fabric of Mark's Gospel. The divine message given at the transfiguration (9:7) parallels that given at the baptism (1:11), but the mountain setting of the transfiguration and the more public address of the voice from the cloud (of heaven) on that occasion heighten the significance of the divine/human communication within the narrative.

The final mountain on which Jesus is located within the Markan topography is the Mount of Olives (11:1; 13:3; 14:26). Here at least three aspects of biblical imagery of the mountain are engaged: (1) the mountain as a place of divinely authoritative teaching; (2) the Mount of Olives as the place of the initiation of the catastrophes of the day of the Lord, the end time; (3) the mountain as a place of encounter between God and the prophets. First, the Ten Commandments, the very kernel of divinely authoritative teaching in the Jewish tradition, were received from God by Moses on Mount Sinai. Jesus' discourse while sitting (the traditional position of a rabbi while teaching) on the Mount of Olives is the longest section of uninterrupted teaching material in Mark, and the mountain setting helps establish its authority. The content is eschatological rather than religio-ethical, however, and Jesus' role seems more analogous to that of God on Mount Sinai than to that of Moses. Second, according to Zechariah 14:4, the Lord's feet shall stand on the Mount of Olives on the day of the Lord; from that point the earth-shaking events of the end time will radiate outward. From the Mount of Olives, Jesus gives his eschatological discourse, warning of the heaven- and earth-shaking events to come at the end time. The setting of the warning is itself a signal of the authority and seriousness of the warning.

Finally, the rather general biblical image of the mountain as a place of encounter between God and the prophets (e.g., Elijah) stands behind certain actions of the Markan Jesus on the Mount of Olives that mark him too as a prophet. Prediction of the future is but one aspect of a prophet's role, and not the most important aspect at that, but it does seem to be included by Mark as an element of prophecy (cf. Deuteronomy 18:21–22). When the innocent Jesus is mocked (14:65), his suffering is perhaps in line with that of the prophets mocked of old (cf. Isaiah 50:5–6).[103] But when this episode of the mockers covering Jesus' face and asking him to "prophesy" about the blows is followed immediately by Peter's denial in exact fulfillment of Jesus' prophecy, one realizes that Jesus also stands in the line of prophets as a true predictor of the future. Three times the Markan Jesus is reported to be on the Mount of Olives, and each time he makes a prediction of future events.

First, at 11:1, Jesus arrives at the Mount of Olives and there "predicts" the circumstances surrounding the disciples' procurement of a colt for his entry into Jerusalem (11:2–3). Immediately afterwards the prediction is fulfilled precisely as spoken (11:4–7). The parallel prediction concerning the procurement of the upper room for the celebration of the Passover meal (14:12–15), also fulfilled immediately (14:16), is spoken at Bethany (14:3), which earlier had been associated with the Mount of Olives (11:1).[104]

Secondly, at 13:3 and following, Jesus sits on the Mount of Olives and predicts the future destruction of the temple, the coming of false prophets, the cataclysmic events of the end time, and the coming of the Son of man in glory. Within the narrative of Mark's Gospel these events are, apparently, yet to be fulfilled.

Thirdly, at 14:26, Jesus returns to the Mount of Olives and makes a fourfold prediction: (1) that his disciples will desert him, (2) that Peter will deny him, (3) that he will be raised up, and (4) that he will go to Galilee before his disciples (14:27–31). Not many verses later, the narrative reports: "And they all forsook him, and fled" (14:50). Then, almost immediately, Peter's denial is recounted just as Jesus foretold it—and in a significant narrative position. The resurrection is also recounted, concisely, just as it was concisely foretold. The process of Jesus' going before to Galilee is reported, at the close of the narrative (16:7), to have begun; its complete fulfillment remains just beyond the narrative. Because Jesus has proved to be a true prophet, a true predictor, within narrative time, his prophecies that extend beyond narrative time are given the highest credibility the Markan Gospel can offer. A prophet speaks with God and for God; with a prophet the channels of communication between heaven and earth are open, and the mountain is frequently the scene of the divine/human encounter.

Spoken by Jesus rather than about Jesus, one narrative fact or relation involving the mountains is a flash-forward at the topographical level: " 'But when you see the desolating sacrilege set up where it ought not be (let the reader understand), then let those who are in Judea flee to the mountains . . .' " (13:14). The verse poses problems of interpretation on two fronts. First, "those who are in Judea" is an extremely open-ended designation and is even expanded by the parenthetical aside that opens the text out to the reader. Second, commentators have found the command to flee to the mountains confusing. But the confusion appears to be based on the assumption that, since those who are in Judea are to flee, they are to flee *from Judea*, and furthermore, since Judea is the mountainous region in the area, the command must be read nonsensically: flee from the mountains to the mountains.[105] The Markan text, however, does not command fleeing *from* Judea but fleeing *within* Judea; only "those who are in Judea" need be concerned with fleeing, and they are to flee from where they live and work (13:15, "house"; 13:16, "field") to the uninhabited mountains.[106]

Some New Testament scholars have looked beyond the text for the meaning of this command—especially to the events of A.D. 66–70.[107] One may also look within the text, to the position of this passage within the topographical sequence and schema, in order to sense its significance. As Eduard Schweizer notes: "Above all, the overall construction of the Gospel contradicts the idea that this passage was drawn up as a document dealing with flight in the last days before the end of the world and that it was intended to appeal to men to conduct themselves properly in the last hour."[108] In the Gospel of Mark, the mountain, including the Mount of Olives from which Jesus issues this command, is a place of divine revelation, of open communication between God and human beings. May one not assume that the mountains of 13:14 share this connotation? Are not those in Judea to flee from their human-made houses and their human-made temples, now desecrated and desolate, to the God-made mountains to await a true hierophany? Discussion of the separate suborders and consideration of the integrated spatial schema must precede a *full* answer to these questions.

In summary, the mountain in Mark, as in the Hebrew Scriptures, is the place where heaven and earth meet. On the mountain, as by the sea, Jesus is divinely revealed. Like the wilderness, the mountain in Mark is an isolated area away from villages and cities; and, like the wilderness, the mountain as a topographical location is rich with significance from the Jewish Scriptures. The mountain, the wilderness, the sea—and villages, cities, the country—all are along the way that Jesus travels in the Gospel of Mark.

THROUGH TOWN AND COUNTRY

Unlike the mountain and the wilderness and the sea, villages, cities, and the country are less distinguished from one another in connotative significance and more frequently mentioned together in the topographical suborder. Designations for inhabited areas, often implying the inhabitants themselves, occur in clusters in Mark's Gospel: 5:14, "city and ... the country"; 6:36, " 'the country and villages' "; 6:55-56, "region" (*RSV* "neighborhood"), "villages, cities, ... the country." Although population density may be assumed to increase from the country to villages to the city, this fact is not stressed in Mark's narrative. Nor is the distinction between a walled city and an open village developed. Finally, the religious differentiation current in Talmudic times between a city as a place with a synagogue and a village as a place without a synagogue was not maintained in Mark (see 1:38–39)—or in the New Testament—although, as C. U. Wolf notes, "The OT duality persists in the Synoptics (Matt. 9:35; 10:11; Mark 6:56; Luke 8:1; 13:22)."[109] Thus, for Mark the duality between *city* and *village* is verbal, not theological. In addition, biblical usage of *polis* ("city"), unlike Greek usage, is paradoxically non-political.[110]

Most of the narrative facts or relations involving inhabited areas (*city, village, the country, region, marketplace*) fall into one of three basic categories concerning the spread of Jesus' influence among the people: (1) people come to Jesus from all inhabited areas; (2) the fame of Jesus spreads throughout all inhabited areas; (3) Jesus goes throughout all inhabited areas. In the first category, the topographical sequence opens with the people of a region coming not to Jesus but to John, Jesus' forerunner (1:5); and *chōra*, "region," is used metonymically for the inhabitants of the region,[111] making the narrative even more dramatic. The later movements of people to Jesus parallel this initial episode, especially at 6:55 (*region*), but also at 1:33 and 6:33 (*city*). The second category is typified by the summary statement at 1:28, "And at once his fame spread everywhere throughout all the surrounding region of Galilee." Further examples of this second category are given at 1:45 (*city*) and 5:14 (*city* and *the country*). The third category, Jesus' own movement throughout inhabited areas, is widely represented: *village* or *city*, 1:38 (*kōmopolis*); *village(s)*, 6:1 (*patris*), 6:6, 8:27; *villages, cities, the country, marketplaces*, 6:56; *region*, 5:1, 7:24, 7:31a, 7:31b, 8:10, 10:1. Relations designating the spread of Jesus' influence in one way or another are distributed throughout the first two-thirds of the Markan narrative and dramatize that Jesus was open to and received by people everywhere.

Two passages in this portion of the Gospel of Mark, however, serve as negative transformations of the narration of the open reception of Jesus and the spread of his fame. After the healing of the Gerasene demoniac, the people begged Jesus to depart from their region (*horia*, 5:17), because "they were afraid" (5:15). The awe-inspiring power of Jesus was experienced as, to borrow a phrase from Rudolf Otto, a *mysterium tremendum et fascinans;* its holy terror could both attract and repel those who witnessed it. Before healing the blind man from Bethsaida, Jesus "led him out of the village" (8:23), and after the healing Jesus said to him, " 'Do not even enter the village' " (8:26).[112] The purpose of these actions is apparently the restriction of Jesus' fame as a healer. Although it is not possible here to debate the relation of this passage to the so-called messianic secret, it is difficult, given the narrative order, not to connect the half-blindness of the man from Bethsaida (" 'I see men; but they look like trees, walking' " [8:24]) with the half-sight of Peter. Within five verses, Peter says to Jesus, " 'You are the Christ' " (8:29), and Jesus says to Peter, " 'Get behind me, Satan!' " (8:33). Obviously, Peter is in need of a second stage of insight. From this point on (8:31 is the first passion prediction), the theme of the spread of Jesus' fame, basically as a healer, recedes in the Markan Gospel, and the motif of the necessity of Jesus' suffering and death emerges more clearly.

Two passages in the first two-thirds of Mark, although embedded in accounts of Jesus' miraculous power, do not fit strictly into one of the three basic categories outlined above; nor are they negative transformations of one of these categories. Both are requests made of Jesus and "fulfilled" in startling ways. At 5:10, Legion, the unclean spirits, beg Jesus not to send them out of the region (*chōra*) of the Gerasenes but, rather, into a herd of pigs. "For the Jewish storyteller," Eduard Schweizer points out, "it is clear that the demons are well-off in Gentile territory and for this reason do not want to leave it; accordingly, the herd of pigs is a very desirable dwelling place."[113] Jesus agrees to Legion's request and the unclean spirits and the swine end up in no region at all, but in the sea. At 6:36, Jesus' disciples ask Jesus to send the multitude away, " 'to go into the country and villages round about and buy themselves something to eat.' " Jesus does not send them away, but provides in the wilderness more than enough for them to eat.

The majority of the references to inhabited areas occurring in the final third of the Gospel of Mark concern preparations made for the events of Jesus' passion. At the village (11:2) of Bethany or Bethphage, a colt is procured for Jesus' entry into Jerusalem. Branches are brought from the country (*agros*, 11:8) to line the road over which Jesus rides. Jesus remains in Jerusalem during the daytime, but leaves the city (11:19) in the evening. Preparations for the Passover meal, the Last Supper of Jesus and his disciples, are made in the city (14:13, 16). Finally, at the crucifixion, Simon of Cyrene, "who was coming in from the country" (*agros*, 15:21), carries Jesus' cross. An additional reference to *agros* in this portion of the Gospel, within a saying of the Markan Jesus, points to preparations ordered for the future. As part of his eschatological discourse, the Markan Jesus warns: " 'and let him who is in the field [or "the country," *agros*] not turn back to take his mantle' " (13:16). This latter instruction concerns the passion of the Markan community, while the former preparations concern the passion of Jesus.[114]

City, village, the country—these topographical terms, as applied in the first two-thirds of Mark's Gospel, seem almost a periphrastic way of saying "everywhere" (cf. the explicit statement of 1:45, *pantothen*). People come to Jesus from "all the cities" (6:33, my translation of *pasōn tōn poleōn*)—from everywhere. Jesus' fame spreads "in the city and in the country" (5:14)—everywhere. Jesus comes teaching and healing "in villages, cities, or country" (6:56)—everywhere. Jesus' openness and the response to Jesus are unrestricted. In the final third of Mark's Gospel, however, the topographical terms for inhabited areas are more specific in their designation. "The city" (11:19; 14:13, 16) is Jerusalem (cf. Ezekiel 7:23, LXX);[115] "the village opposite you" (11:2) is probably Bethany,[116] but possibly Bethphage.[117] One might say that the ministry of the Markan Jesus becomes more specific at this point as well; his action becomes more single-minded, his end more clear. This narrowing focus is a corollary to the growing conflict between Jesus and the Jewish religious establishment so obvious at the geopolitical level in the opposition ENVIRONS OF JERUSALEM vs. JERUSALEM PROPER.

The one remaining marker of topographical relations designates a space central to inhabited areas: *agora*, "the marketplace."[118] Together the three Markan occurrences of *agora* suggest the level at which Jesus and Jewish religious leaders come into conflict. For Jesus, the marketplace is a center of healing for all people: "And wherever he came, in villages, cities, or country, they laid the sick in the market places, and besought him that they might touch even the fringe of his garment; and as many as touched it were made well" (6:56).[119] If "the fringe of his garment" is, as Nineham contends, "a reference to the blue fringe or tassel every male Jew was required to have on the corners of his robe (see Num. 15:38f. and Deut. 22:12),"[120] then Jesus' loyalty to religious law, to sacred distinctions, is illustrated. Yet, as Jesus allows himself, in the profane marketplace, to be touched by the sick—some of whom were probably women, many of whom must have been ritually "unclean"—Jesus' overturning of the distinction between sacred and profane, the very foundation of the religious law, is dramatically portrayed.

On the other hand, for "the Pharisees, and all the Jews," so the Markan narrator explains, the marketplace is a profane space and any contact with it demands ritual purification (7:3–4). Whether the Markan Pharisees purify *themselves* after marketing[121] or purify the *things* brought from the marketplace,[122] the separation of the sacred and the profane is presupposed. For the scribes, according to a generalized saying of the Markan Jesus (12:38), the marketplace is a place in which to be recognized and honored above other persons. The reference to "long robes" (*stolai*) is to "the Jewish outer garment known as the *tallith*, of which the scribes wore a distinctively large version."[123] The garments were properly to be worn at prayer and while performing certain other scribal duties. Thus the garments served as signs of the scribes' sacral character, and the scribes depicted at 12:38 were wearing them inappropriately in public and profane places to distinguish themselves, as members of the sacred realm, from the profane. Concern for purity and honor disclose the separation of sacred and profane presupposed by the Markan scribes and Pharisees. Both passages occur in the context of discussion of the Law. In narrative time, 7:4 and 12:38 are flashbacks of typical and recurring events, while 6:56 is a summary statement of present and continuing action. All three passages, then, suggest characteristic attitudes and behavior; and the opposition between Jesus and the Jewish religious authorities thus depicted in the topographical microcosm of the marketplace is enacted in full in the Gospel of Mark.

TEXT AND READER

Throughout the discussion of the topographical sequence of Mark, relations whose subjects are ambiguous, unspecified, or hypothetical have been specially noted. Each such relation demands of the reader some involvement with the text in order to identify the character or complete the action. For example, at 1:2–3 a messenger, one whose voice will be heard " 'crying in the wilderness,' " is prophesied; and at 1:4, John the Baptist appears "in the wilderness, preaching." The connection is obvious but unstated; the reader completes the equation: John is the messenger. Similar reader involvement is elicited at 2:10. Jesus' statement that " 'the Son of man has authority on earth to forgive sins' " (2:10) is inserted into the account of the healing of the paralytic, following Jesus' words, " 'My son, your sins are forgiven' " (2:5). Thus Jesus' currently exercised authority in forgiving sins is paralleled by the stated authority of the Son of man to forgive sins on the earth, here and now. An implicit connection underlies the explicit parallelism; the reader closes the gap: Jesus is the Son of man.[124] The first element of the pair is a Markan character whose narrative actions make clear the appropriateness of the second element. Neither the earth at

2:10 nor the wilderness at 1:4 is an element of this implied equation, but the identifying topographical location of the relevant action.

The textual situation with *patris* at 6:1 and 6:4 is comparable, although at 6:4 *patris* does occur in a figure of speech, a common proverb. At 6:1 Jesus comes to *tēn patrida autou,* "his own country" or "his native village." At 6:2–3 the citizens there take offense at Jesus. At 6:4 Jesus states, "A prophet is not without honor except in his own country [*tē patridi autou*] . . . ." Thus, the reader, putting one and one together, sums up this implied equation: Jesus is a prophet. The conclusion has an air of discovery about it for the reader because the reader's perception is crucial to the identification; the identification is not presented literally but suggested by the narrative action. Whereas both references to "the wilderness" at 1:3–4 are included in the topographical suborder as spatial markers, as is "the earth" at 2:10, *patris* at 6:1 is included and *patris* at 6:4 is excluded as a non-topographical use of a topographical term. Each passage as a whole (1:2–4; 2:3–12; 6:1–4), however, has a non-topographical dimension by which the action of a specified character (John, Jesus, Jesus) is linked with the action of a generalized or ambiguous one (messenger, Son of man, prophet) on the basis of the reader's observation of narratively suggested similarities.

Such linking, via reader involvement, is also implicit in passages involving solely metaphorical usages of topographical terms: 10:29–30 (*agros*); 9:42 (*thalassa*); 11:23 (*thalassa* and *oros*). Because Jesus' saying at 10:29–30, " 'there is no one who has left [*aphēken*] . . . who will not receive . . . ,' " echoes Peter's immediately prior statement, " 'we have left [*aphēkamen*] everything . . .' " (10:28), the narrative situation appears to parallel that at 1:2–4, 2:10, and 6:1–4. Within the narrative action, Markan characters are identified implicitly; the disciples, the reader realizes, are among those who have left families, houses, lands. Yet the implied equation at 10:29–30 is not so exact as at 1:2–4, 2:3–12, or 6:1–4. Not only does the "receiving" remain in the narrative future, but also the way is left open for others to be included among those who leave lands and regain lands for Jesus' sake "and for the gospel" (10:29).

This open-endedness is clearer still at 9:42 and 11:23, where potential actions are ascribed to hypothetical subjects. At 9:38

the disciple John projects a negative example of discipleship, and at 9:42 Jesus suggests, in hyperbole, the seriousness of the failure of anyone—including, potentially, the reader—who might follow such an example. At 11:21 Peter betrays his lack of faith, and at 11:23 Jesus suggests, in hyperbole, the power available to any-one—including, potentially, the reader—who has faith. Whereas it is clear from the narrative action that Jesus is the only one to be identified with the "prophet" of 6:4, the "whoever" of 9:42 and 11:23 is flexible enough to invite the reader into the text to accept personally either the warning (9:42) or the encourage-ment (11:23). An invitation to the reader is engraved, as it were, by the Markan aside in 13:14, "(let the reader understand)." The warnings at 13:14 and 16, part of Jesus' eschatological discourse, are flash-forwards at the topographical level. The topographical directions given explicitly to "those who are in Judea" and the one "who is in the field" are implicitly offered not only to the four disciples who listen within the narrative but also to those who listen to the narrative and are thus incorporated into it. Even the reader who tries to escape the personal relevance of the open-ended "who" or "whoever" at 10:29–30, 9:42, and 11:23 is caught by the parenthetical statement at 13:14; reader, it says, this text means you!

This brief excursus is not presented as a formal exercise in "reader response" criticism,[126] which would be a considerable task in itself, but merely as a suggestive reading of an interre-lated series of topographical relations and as a reminder that, although the present study focuses on the reality of the text, the presence of the reader is always assumed. The Markan topog-raphy assists the Gospel's readers in identifying the fuller sig-nificance of John as the messenger, of Jesus as a prophet and as the Son of man, of the disciples as those who leave behind and receive anew, and possibly of themselves as those who are to have faith not hinder it, those who are to be open to the challenges of the future.

SCHEMA

To identify more fully the mythic significance of the topo-graphical suborder, one must turn from its diachronic structure, its sequence, to its synchronic structure, its schema. The narra-

Figure 7   Topographical Hierarchy

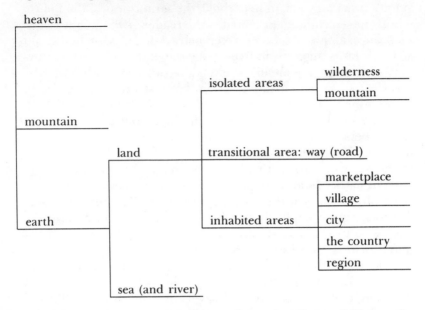

tive realities represented by the column headings of Figure 6, showing the topographical sequence, are the elements of the topographical schema. Within the schema these elements are arranged not chronologically, but abstractly, theoretically. Lying behind the mythological schema presupposed by the Markan topographical suborder is a logical hierarchy of the physical features of the earth (including heaven)—both natural and human-made—referred to in the Markan narrative. This logical hierarchy, presented as a "branching tree diagram," is given in Figure 7. Not every distinction of the logical hierarchy is manifested as an opposition within the mythological schema. The mythological schema, presented as a series of oppositions moving toward mediation, is given in Figure 8. The terms in parentheses in Figure 8 represent the nonmanifest, fundamental opposition underlying the oppositions manifest in the narrative.

HEAVEN VS. EARTH

Heaven and earth are separate realms, heaven the realm of God, earth the human realm. (For this traditional view, see Psalm

Figure 8 Topographical Schema

(promise)

heaven

land

isolated
areas

mountain   way

inhabited
areas

sea

earth

(threat)

115:16). In Mark's Gospel, the voice of God and the manifestation of God's Spirit come from heaven (1:10, 11; 9:7). At the
end time, God's power will be observed cataclysmically in heaven
(13:25a, 25b, 26, 27; 14:62). Markan characters, like all human
beings, are creatures of the earth. Limited by sickness (9:20) and
by sorrow (14:35), they fall upon the earth to which they are
bound. God's unlimited power, however, reaches from heaven to
earth (15:33). In being open to God, in turning from earth toward heaven, Jesus experiences the power of God through human actions (6:41; 7:34). The Markan opposition of heaven and
earth is rooted in the Jewish tradition; the basis of the opposition
is made plain in Hebrew Scripture, from the Pentateuch through
the Prophets.

The realm of God (heaven) is the realm of promise. God called
out a people and established a covenant with them; within God's
promises of greatness and a land, the people felt secure. But
threats to the divine promise came from the human realm
(earth); the people endangered their communal life by breaking
the covenant. The story of God's relationship with the people,
as narrated in Jewish Scripture and extended in the Gospel of
Mark, is a dynamic account of promise and threat, security and

danger. This fundamental dynamic is concretized spatially in Mark's narrative in the opposition HEAVEN vs. EARTH. On earth Jesus faces the danger of a hungry multitude, but, looking up to heaven, he provides the security of food for all (6:41). On earth Jesus faces the ultimate threat of death, but as Son of God, the promise of his presence lives on. Even the nonspatial, metaphorical usages of *ouranos* and *gē* in Mark illustrate this opposition. For example, at 10:21, the secure promise of "treasure in heaven" is opposed to the threatened danger of maintaining riches on the earth (the one obstacle to the man who would inherit eternal life; cf. Matthew 6:21).

In Lévi-Straussian language, two opposite terms with no intermediary (PROMISE/THREAT) have been replaced by two equivalent terms (HEAVEN/EARTH) that allow a third one as a mediator.[126] And what is this third term, this mediator between heaven and earth? In one sense the Markan mediator is MOUNTAIN. (See Figure 7, showing the topographical hierarchy.) The mountain is the place where earth approaches heaven and thus the scene of divine/human encounters, preeminently so for the Markan Jesus. In prayer on the mountain Jesus reaches toward God (6:46); in transfiguration on the mountain Jesus is touched by God (9:2). The words of the voice from heaven to the disciples of the transfigured Jesus on the mountain are most emphatic: " 'This is my beloved Son; listen to him' " (9:7). But all of Jesus' actions "on the mountain" point to the meeting of heaven and earth in his presence, the meeting of divine and human in him. On the mountain Jesus appoints twelve disciples, rescues a demoniac from possession, prays—and then solemnly reveals himself (on the sea), is transfigured with Moses and Elijah, teaches, and prophesies. These events exemplify the basic actions of Jesus in Mark's Gospel; and their occurrence on the mountain, the mediator between heaven and earth, confirms in the spatial order what is affirmed explicitly by the centurion: " 'Truly this man was the Son of God!' " (15:39).

Thus it is clear that in a broader sense, in the sense in which heaven and earth represent the divine and the human realms, the Markan mediation between heaven and earth is not limited to the spatial term MOUNTAIN, but is linked with the character Jesus. This is not so surprising, of course, since the topographical suborder—and, indeed, the spatial order—is but one aspect of the Markan Gospel and the character Jesus is its narrative and theological center. In Jesus, communication between heaven and earth is reestablished; God in heaven speaks to Jesus on earth (1:11; cf. 9:7); Jesus on earth speaks to God in heaven (6:41; 7:34). Furthermore, Jesus is narratively identified not only as the Son of man who has both present authority on earth (2:10) and future authority in heaven (13:26, 27; 14:62), and who thus mediates the two spheres, but also as the Son of God (1:1; 3:11; 15:39; cf. 1:11; 5:7; 9:7; 14:61).

But in an eschatological sense, so the Markan Gospel projects, the opposition between heaven and earth is not so much to be mediated as surpassed—by the power of Jesus' words: " 'Heaven and earth will pass away, but my words will not pass away' " (13:31). At that point the oppositions of the topographical suborder will be more than mediated; all spatial opposition will be invalidated by the disestablishment of its very foundation. But until that final transformation, and within the Gospel of Mark, the fundamental opposition PROMISE vs. THREAT, initially given narrative expression in the opposition HEAVEN vs. EARTH, continues to move toward mediation. The Markan spatial order affords no other instance in which movement toward the mediation of an opposition is tripled as here: (1) HEAVEN vs. EARTH is mediated by MOUNTAIN; (2) HEAVEN vs. EARTH is surpassed by Jesus' "words"; (3) HEAVEN vs. EARTH is replaced by LAND vs. SEA.

LAND VS. SEA

As PROMISE is to THREAT, as HEAVEN is to EARTH, so LAND is to SEA. The first two narrative oppositions of the topographical schema may reflect the two parallel Hebrew views of the cosmos as consisting of (1) heaven and earth (Genesis 1:1; Psalm 115: 15–16) or (2) heaven, earth, and sea (Exodus 20:11; Psalm 146:6). In the context of the topographical schema, EARTH (which includes both land and sea) signifies $g\bar{e}$ in its aspect of opposition to HEAVEN, whereas LAND signals $g\bar{e}$ in its aspect of opposition to SEA.[127] The opposition LAND vs. SEA is probably the most dramatic topographical contrast of the Gospel of Mark. As an opposition that is both natural and basic, LAND vs. SEA implicitly underlies the narrative as a whole. The Sea of Galilee is central to the spatial movements of the Markan Jesus. Jesus calls his first disciples while "passing along by the Sea of Galilee" (1:16). Jesus often encounters the crowds on the land "beside the sea" (2:13; 3:7, 9; 4:1; 5:21). Physically, the sea is a barrier between the land of Galilee and the foreign lands on its eastern shore, but Jesus easily crosses this barrier (4:35; 5:1, 21; 8:10; 8:13). At certain points in Mark, the opposition LAND vs. SEA comes to explicit expression: at 4:1, Jesus is on the sea, the crowd is on the land; at 6:47, the disciples are on the sea, Jesus is on the land.

The land, the normal and secure environment of human beings, is quite naturally opposed to the sea, a temporary place of movement for human beings and also a place that threatens (4:37–38; 6:48) and is capable of destruction (5:13; 9:42; 11:23). The land is the realm of promise. The nonspatial, metaphorical usages of $g\bar{e}$ illustrate this significance as well. For example, in the seed parables in chap. 4, the ground or earth ($g\bar{e}$) is the context of growth, the realm of promise: "The earth produces of itself . . ." (4:28). More importantly, according to the Jewish tradition underlying the Gospel of Mark, the land was created by God as the habitation for men and women over which they are "lord" (the genesis story), and a specific land was promised to the people God called out to be God's own (the exodus story).[128] But God remains Lord over the sea, and the sea remains a threatening danger to humanity. Biblical imagery, particularly in the Psalms but also in Genesis 1 and the Book of Job, frequently portrays the sea as chaos that only the Lord can order or reorder, a threat that only divine power can securely control.[129] At this point it is clear that Markan application of the term *thalassa*, "sea," rather than *limnē*, "lake," to the Lake of Galilee serves well its narrative and theological purposes. Though *limnē* is more geographically precise, the more ambiguous *thalassa* is rich in connotations from the Jewish Scriptures.[130]

The Markan Gospel presupposes this connotation of the sea as chaos, threat, danger, in opposition to the land as order, promise, security. But the Markan Gospel suggests that in the acts of Jesus the dramatic mediation of this key topographic opposition has begun. The boat might well be viewed as a mediator between the land and the sea.[131] In Jesus' experience the boat serves to extend the land, offering a dry, firm, and safe place to sit while teaching (4:1). In the experience of the disciples, the sea nearly overwhelms the boat, filling it with water and them with fear (4:37–38). The disciples cannot cross the sea even with the aid of the boat (6:48); Jesus does not even need the boat to cross the sea (6:48)—thus Jesus himself is a mediator between the land and the sea. Not only is the sea less a barrier and more a bridge between lands for Jesus, but for him the sea itself becomes as land. The disciples feel endangered by the sea (4:38). By his word Jesus calms the sea (4:39), turning aside the danger and making the disciples secure. Before Jesus' arrival the disciples are "distressed in rowing" on the threatening sea. By his coming to them Jesus treats the sea as if it were the land; he walks on the sea (6:48); for him threat becomes promise. In thus mediating the opposition LAND vs. SEA, Jesus manifests the power of God. The divine promise of security and the threat of human danger meet in Jesus and are transformed.

ISOLATED AREAS VS. INHABITED AREAS

In the process of successsive mediation fundamental to myth, the opposition LAND vs. SEA is replaced by the opposition ISOLATED AREAS vs. INHABITED AREAS. Narrative manifestation of inhabited areas is given in Mark by reference to five terms: *city*, *village, the country, region*, and *marketplace*, often occurring in clusters (6:55–56; 6:36; 5:14). In the first two-thirds of the narrative, these terms appear to function periphrastically for "everywhere"; people come to Jesus from everywhere; Jesus (or his fame) travels everywhere. In the final third of the narrative, the references to inhabited areas are concerned with preparations for Jesus' passion.

Markan narrative manifestation of ISOLATED AREAS has two foci: *wilderness* (or *wilderness place*) and *mountain*. *Erēmos*, "wilderness" or "desert," "does not necessarily stand for an arid desert, such as exists in Africa or Asia: it means an uninhabited territory, 'wild open country,' in contrast with the cultivated and inhabited sections of the land."[132] Isolation is clearly the topographic significance of *erēmos* and *erēmos topos* in Mark (e.g., 1:12–13; 1:35; 6:31–32). As a topographic location, the mountain also shares in this aspect of isolation (e.g., the mountain in the desert in Exodus; Mark 6:46; 9:2; 13:3), although it includes other aspects of significance as well. The fact that MOUNTAIN is twice represented in the topographical schema (alone as the mediator of HEAVEN and EARTH, assumed along with *wilderness* behind ISOLATED AREAS as opposed to INHABITED AREAS) illustrates two basic aspects of the Markan significance of *mountain*: revelation and retreat.[133] As a spatial location of divine revelation, MOUNTAIN mediates HEAVEN and EARTH; as a spatial location of retreat, MOUNTAIN is opposed to INHABITED AREAS. Furthermore, as Ulrich Mauser has shown, "wilderness and mountain are very often intimately correlated and the wilderness theme throughout the Bible is familiar with both elements of the mountain as they are used by Mark."[134]

In addition, Mauser, whose concern is the wilderness theme in Mark's Gospel, links the sea with the wilderness and the mountain as various isolated areas. Mark 2:13 and 3:7, Mauser argues, stress the aspect of withdrawal in relation to the sea. In Mark 4:35–41 and 6:45–52, the sea displays the characteristics of a demonic element, thus linking it with the wilderness, the dwelling place of demons.[135] Mauser's comments are well taken in light of the complex aspects of *sea*, *wilderness*, and *mountain* in the Markan narrative. But the overwhelming aspect of the sea at the mythological level in Mark is its opposition to the land, and LAND vs. SEA is "replaced" in the topographical schema by ISOLATED AREAS (*wilderness* and *mountain*) vs. INHABITED AREAS.

One might expect to associate INHABITED AREAS with security and thus with PROMISE, and ISOLATED AREAS with danger and thus with THREAT. Certainly the Jewish Scriptures tell of the wilderness as a dangerous place that threatens human existence by the absence of food and water (Exodus; Numbers) and the presence of wild animals (Isaiah 34:11).[136] Yet the accounts also affirm Yahweh's providence in the wilderness and God's future renewal of isolated areas. The Markan wilderness, like the wilderness in which the Hebrew people wandered for forty years, is a place of testing (1:13), but also a place of miraculous nourishment (6:35; 8:4). The wild beasts in the Markan wilderness, like those depicted in the renewed wilderness of Isaiah 11:6–8, are peaceful (1:13).[137] Though isolated from the people as a whole, the Markan mountain, like Mount Sinai, is a center of divine/human communication, where the promises of God are made known to God's spokesperson. Thus the Gospel of Mark follows and "fulfills" the Jewish tradition of isolated areas as, paradoxically, the realm of promise.[138] That the inhabited areas of Mark constitute the realm of threat is perhaps suggested at 1:45 ("Jesus was no longer able to enter a city," my translation), but the connection is made most clear in relation to the threat of death growing in "the city" (11:19; 14:13, 16), Jerusalem.

Nevertheless, the opposition between ISOLATED AREAS and IN-HABITED AREAS is far from absolute in Mark's Gospel; movement toward mediation is manifest. When the Markan Jesus rises "a great while before day" and goes out to a deserted place to pray (1:35), it seems to be a movement away from the clamor (THREAT) of "the whole city [which] was gathered together about the door" (1:33) to a time of calm reflection (PROMISE).[139] Yet when Simon (Peter) seeks Jesus out, Jesus responds, " 'Let us go on to the next towns [kōmopoleis], that I may preach there also; for that is why I came out' " (1:38). When the word about Jesus spreads throughout the inhabited areas, creating such a commotion (THREAT) that Jesus can no longer openly go there, Jesus withdraws to the wilderness (PROMISE). Yet when the inhabitants then seek Jesus out in the wilderness, Jesus apparently does not send them away (1.45). When Jesus withdraws with his disciples to a deserted place for rest, "For many were coming and going, and they had no leisure even to eat" (6:31), he is met by a crowd of over five thousand persons. Yet when the disciples ask Jesus to send the crowd away to buy food for themselves, Jesus feeds the entire multitude there in the desert. Jesus' withdrawal to the wilderness or to the mountain is never permanent; he always returns to the inhabited areas, to the villages and even to "the city."[140] Nor are Jesus' periodic withdrawals from the inhabited areas withdrawals from the inhabitants and their needs, for often he receives them in the wilderness. Jesus goes to the realm of PROMISE (ISOLATED AREAS), and some from the realm of THREAT (INHABITED AREAS) seek him there. But Jesus returns once more to "the city," where others seek him and condemn him to death. This final threat to human existence is carried out just outside the city.

THE WAY

Jesus' movement from the wilderness (1:12–13) to "the city" (Jerusalem) underlies Mark's story, and particular emphasis is placed upon the movement itself, upon being "on the way." WAY, or ROAD, represents the final mediation of the topographical suborder of Mark's Gospel. In a logical sense, a road is a transitional area between isolated areas and inhabited areas (see Figure 7). As outlined above in terms of the sequence, *hodos*, "way" or "road," provides a unifying framework for the topographical suborder, a framework consisting of the first and final topographic references, scattered references throughout, and a significant cluster of references (8:27 to 11:9) at the narrative turning point. Although the way has been prepared for Jesus (1:2–3), the road Jesus travels is not an easy one to follow. Its demands are strict (6:8); those who follow on the way struggle to understand not just that Jesus is the Christ (8:27–33), but what this means for Jesus (10:32–34) and for themselves, for their relations with others (9:33–37 and 10:17–22) and their relations to Jesus (10:46–52). Just as those who followed Jesus "on the road" from Galilee to Jerusalem were amazed and afraid (10:32), so too those whom he is going before on the way from Jerusalem to Galilee are amazed and afraid (16:6–8).

Hodos signals not so much another place in the Markan topography, as a way between places, a dynamic process of movement.[141] The threat of the sea, the threat of miracle-seeking crowds and inflexible religious leaders from inhabited areas, the threat of death—all have been met in Jesus by the promise of renewed communication between heaven and earth in the wilderness and especially on the mountain. The mediation of PROMISE and THREAT is a dynamic process, not a static state; it is known in the experience of being on the way. In the face of the security and danger brought together in this mediation, amazement and fear seem especially appropriate responses.

An interesting comparison may be made between the projected scene at the end of Mark—the way (road) to Galilee—and the scene at the end of the Pentateuch (or the Tetrateuch)—the wilderness, or, at least, outside the boundaries of the promised land. Some commentators read both scenes historically: Mark's

Gospel is addressed to Christians awaiting the parousia, after A.D. 70, in Galilee;[142] the priests exiled in Babylon were themselves outside the promised land when compiling the Pentateuch (or Tetrateuch). But both may also be understood more theologically: the disciples of the Markan Jesus are those who follow on the way, the way of power and also the way of suffering; the Pentateuch (or Tetrateuch) is a body of traditions preserved and presented for a (spiritually, theologically) pilgrim people, a people in the wilderness, a people on the way.[143]

The significance of the final image of the Markan Jesus as one who is in movement (on the way to Galilee, 16:7) is in marked contrast to the topographical and theological significance of the longer ending of the Gospel of Mark—16:9–20—regarded by most scholars as a later addition to the Markan text: "So then the Lord Jesus, after he had spoken to them, was taken up into *heaven*, and sat down at the right hand of God" (16:19, my emphasis). Here there is no movement and no mediation, but a return to the broadest topographical opposition, HEAVEN vs. EARTH. Jesus has withdrawn to heaven; the disciples remain on earth. Nothing is in process. The dynamic movement toward mediation witnessed through 16:8 has been undone, and a steady state of topographic opposition, of separation between heaven and earth, has been reached. But the final authentic Markan portrait of Jesus is of one who is on the way. Just so the disciples of Jesus are, according to the Gospel of Mark, those women and men, who, with fear and amazement, follow on the way.

4. Architectural Space

And he entered a house, and would not have any one know it; yet he could not be hid.

—MARK 7:24b

As outside is to inside, so topographical space is to architectural space. Markers of the topographical suborder—by the sea, on the mountain, even among the villages—locate events out-of-doors. Architectural markers locate events in relation to artificially enclosed spaces: a house, a synagogue, the temple, etc. A tomb, as a significant Markan spatial location, shares aspects with both suborders. Like a mountain, a tomb is basically an out-of-doors location. Yet, like a house, a tomb is an enclosed space, although not a dwelling—except for demoniacs (see 5:3). House, synagogue, temple—all are buildings, human constructions. A tomb, though not a building, is humanly constructed within a natural environment, "hewn out of the rock" (15:46). Because Markan characters are located spatially *inside* tombs, tombs are considered among the enclosed spaces of the architectural suborder. Commentators have called attention to various elements of the architectural suborder, generally in isolation from the system of related spaces. Jesus' teaching of the disciples "in a house" (7:17; 9:28, 33; 10:10) has been counted as evidence of the motif of the "messianic secret."[1] Other interpreters have traced the anti-temple theme in Mark.[2] The theological significance of the Markan story of the empty tomb has also been examined.[3] Yet the overall significance of these spatial locations, these architectural enclosures, may be seen more clearly when the system of their relations is observed. This interrelating of the Markan spatial locations is the present goal. By understanding the system of relations at the architectural level of the Gospel of Mark, one may be better able to understand the significance of Mark's Gospel at the theological level.

Figure 9 Architectural Relations

An action or event reported or projected in the Gospel of Mark occurs in spatial relation to:

synagōgē (synagogue) 1:21; 1:23; 1:29; 1:39; 3:1; 6:2; 12:39; 13:9
oikia (house) 1:29; 2:15; 6:10; 7:24; 9:33; 10:10; 12:40; 13:15; 14:3
      oikos (house) 2:1; 2:11; 3:20 (RSV 3:19); 5:19; 5:38; 7:17;
           7:30; 8:3; 8:26; 9:28
thura (door) 1:33; 2:2; 11:4; 15:46; 16:3
stegē (roof) 2:4
mnēmeion (tomb) 5:2; 6:29; 15:46a; 16:2; 16:3; 16:5; 16:8
      mnēma (tomb) 5:3; 5:5; 15:46b
hieron (temple) 11:11; 11:15a; 11:15b; 11:16; 11:27; 12:35; 13:1;
           13:3; 14:49
      naos (temple) 14:58; 15:29; 15:38
oikodōmai (buildings) 13:1; 13:2
dōma (housetop) 13:15
kataluma (guest room) 14:14
      anagaion (upper room) 14:15
aulē (courtyard; palace) 14:54; 14:66; 15:16
proaulion (forecourt) 14:68
praitōrion (praetorium) 15:16

RELATIONS

The sixty-five relations of the architectural suborder, in twelve categories, are cited in Figure 9. The narrative facts constituting the architectural suborder of the Markan spatial order are those relations designating events reported or projected in the Gospel of Mark in relation to *synagogue, house, door, roof, tomb, temple, buildings, housetop, room, courtyard* (or *palace*), *forecourt*, or *praetorium*. Two general observations may be made of the architectural suborder: (1) The text employs pairs of synonymous, or nearly synonymous, terms to designate each of several architectural spaces. (2) Several metaphorical applications of the architectural term *house*, one of the architectural term *door*, and one of a pronoun representing *temple* occur in the Markan text.

First, one may note the use of architectural synonyms. The English "house" translates two Greek forms: *oikia* and *oikos*. Some lexicons make a distinction between *oikia* in the strict sense as "the whole house" and *oikos* "as a set of rooms";[4] others distinguish between *oikia* as a "building" and *oikos* as a "dwelling";[5] still others distinguish between *oikia* as "the whole of a deceased person's possessions, what he leaves behind" and *oikos* as "simply his residence."[6] None of these distinctions, however, is supported by the Markan text, in which the two terms occur in comparable contexts throughout. *Oikia* is somewhat more frequent in Markan usage: twelve spatial and five metaphorical occurrences as compared with ten spatial and three metaphorical occurrences of *oikos*. For the purposes of studying the architectural suborder, *oikia* and *oikos* will be considered synonyms for "house."

The case is even clearer for *mnēmeion* and *mnēma* as synonyms meaning "tomb." *Mnēmeion*, literally "token of remembrance," especially for the dead, means possibly "monument, memorial" but generally "grave, tomb"; *mnēma*, literally "sign of remembrance," especially for the dead, means "grave, tomb."[7] But in Mark, and elsewhere (not only in the gospels but in Greek literature generally[8]), this subtle distinction is collapsed. Within the same sentence, the type of tombs among which the Gerasene demoniac lived is given as *mnēmeion* (5:2) and *mnēma* (5:3; also 5:5). Later, and again within the same sentence, the tomb in which Jesus is laid is termed *mnēmeion* (15:46a) and *mnēma* (15:46b). These three are the only Markan occurrences of *mnēma*; they are indistinguishable from the seven occurrences of *mnēmeion* as elements of the architectural suborder.

The case is somewhat less clear for *hieron* and *naos* as synonyms meaning "temple." *Hieron* may refer to the temple complex, the temple building as a whole, or specifically, the outer court, the portion of the temple open to worshippers.[9] *Naos*, on the other hand, derives from the verb *naiō*, "dwell," and refers to the temple as the dwelling place of a deity, or, specifically, that part of the temple where the god dwells, the cell or shrine of the temple, the inner sanctuary, the Holy Place of the temple.[10]

Such a distinction may be supported by the Markan text.[11] The two references to the temple as seen from the outside (13:1, 3) and the seven references to Jesus' presence in the temple, contexts that clearly disallow the meaning "Holy of Holies," employ *hieron*. On the other hand, "the curtain of the temple," which is reported split at 15:38, is likely the curtain separating the Holy of Holies;[12] and *naos* is employed. *Naos* also occurs in the statement alleged by false witnesses to have been made by Jesus: " 'I will destroy this temple [*naos*] that is made with hands...'" (14:58; cf. 15:29). Although the issue is complex, it appears that the Markan context, with its redundant and framing insistence on the falseness of the testimony (14:56, 57, 59), presents the statement as untrue to Jesus. Nevertheless, and ironically, the future action falsely linked to Jesus in a causal way, the destruction of the *naos*, is actualized in the present—by the action of God, it would appear—immediately following Jesus' death. The Holy of Holies as a separate space is destroyed by the splitting of the curtain of the *naos* (15:38).[13]

In examining the Markan *hieron/naos* references from another perspective, one notices that the Markan narrator generally employs *hieron* for "temple" (11:11, 15a, 15b, 16, 27; 12:35; 13:1, 3), while the Markan characters generally employ *naos* (false witnesses: 14:58; mockers: 15:29) or *oikos* (Jesus: 2:26; 11:17). Thus it would appear that the characters, who are portrayed as Jews, follow Jewish terminological practice, while the narrator, who is a Christian (see 1:1), follows Christian practice. The Septuagint "practically never" used *hieron* for the Jewish temple, apparently because of the pagan and cultic connotations of the term; instead the translators used simply *oikos* or *oikos hagios, oikos tou theou, oikos kuriou*—or, alternatively, *naos* or *naos hagios*.[14] The New Testament, however, does refer to the Jewish temple as *to hieron*. In so doing, are the early Christian writers challenging the religious significance of the Jewish temple?[15] The two exceptional uses of *hieron* and *naos* in Mark may suggest this conclusion. At 14:49 Jesus, in referring to his previous teaching in the temple—the *hieron*, not the *naos* or the *oikos tou theou*—speaks as one who has rejected the temple and who is at the moment he speaks being arrested by its officials. At his passion Jesus dissociates himself from Jewish devotion to the temple. At 15:38 the Markan narrator refers to the splitting of the curtain of the *naos*—not the *hieron*—perhaps to signify the end of the Jewish temple itself. At the death of Jesus the Jewish *naos* loses its function.

These two possible distinctions between *hieron* and *naos*, "temple complex"/"sanctuary proper" and Christian reference/traditional Jewish reference, need not be contradictory and may be complementary. But because the denotations and the connotations of *hieron* and *naos* in the Gospel of Mark do overlap, both terms are listed as representing *temple* in the architectural suborder. Later in this chapter, as the architectual sequence is examined in detail, the distinction between them will be noted.

Kataluma ("guest room") and *anagaion* ("upper room"), while not synonyms, are related terms defining a single space in Mark. Their close relation allows their conjunction in a presentation of the overall architectural suborder; their distinction demands comment in a discussion of the sequence in detail.

The metaphorical application of architectural terms in the Gospel of Mark must now be noted. On two occasions *oikos* ("house") appears as a metaphorical equivalent of another architectural term, *temple*. At 2:26 Jesus speaks of " 'how [David] entered the house of God, . . . and ate the bread of the Presence . . . .' " At 11:17 Jesus, quoting Isaiah, says, " 'Is it not written, "My house [God is the speaker] shall be called a house of prayer for all the nations"?' " Both statements emerge from biblical contexts (1 Samuel 21:1–6 and Isaiah 56:7). Although the phrase *oikos theou* is "a fixed term for the sanctuary in the LXX" and is "quite common" (e.g., Judges 18:31; 2 Samuel 12:20),[16] the metaphor does not appear in 1 Samuel 21:1–6, nor is the tabernacle specifically mentioned; the bread is given to David and those with him by the priest. Nevertheless, the episode of David eating the bread of the Presence from the tabernacle/temple illustrates a legitimate and traditional breakdown in the distinction between the sacred and the profane, the "holy" and the "common" (see especially 1 Samuel 21:4–5), and thus serves Jesus as a positive model in defending his disciples' disobedience of the strict letter of the sabbath law against the accusations of the Pharisees. The letter of the temple law, maintaining strict separation between sacred and profane, necessitated the activities of money-changers in the outer court of the temple, exchanging Greek and Roman (common) coins for Jewish (holy) coins for use in paying the temple tax. But, as the statement (11:17) and the actions of the Markan Jesus in the so-called "cleansing of the temple" seem to indicate, carrying out the letter of the temple law violated the spirit of the temple itself.[17] The reaction of the religious establishment to Jesus' interpretation of these biblical metaphors of the temple as the "house of God" is given at 3:6 and 11:18—they sought a way to destroy him.

On another occasion "house" is employed by the Markan Jesus not as a metaphor for a holy place, God's house, but as a metaphor for an evil realm, Satan's kingdom. By its inclusion between references to Satan in 3:23 and 3:26, the proverb of a house divided (3:25) is applied to Satan's realm.[18] The little parable of the strong man's house (3:27) is also embedded in the context of controversy regarding the source of Jesus' power (3:21–30). The import of chaps. 2 and 3, including these opposing metaphorical applications of "house" (house of God vs. house of Satan), appears to be that the opposition between sacred and profane is a false one, separating some persons and things from other persons and things, while the true opposition is between God and Satan, the divine and the demonic.

"House" (*oikia*) also occurs in a metaphorical context at 13:34–35, within the parable of the doorkeeper, and is thus linked with the metaphorical use of "door" (*thura*) at 13:29. At 13:29 Jesus says, as part of his eschatological discourse, " 'So also, when you see these things coming to pass, you know that he [the Son of man] is near, at the door [*thurais*]' " (my translation[19]). As the door marks the transition space between inside and outside, so the appearance of the Son of man " 'at the door' " signals the transition time between the present age and the eschatological age.[20] Jesus' eschatological discourse closes with the parable of the doorkeeper. Because this passage is a parable and not an allegory, a one-to-one equation of the house and the reality it represents is not to be sought; the house is the setting of a whole situation that is a narrative metaphor of the command to watch, for " 'of that day or that hour no one knows' " (13:32). Nevertheless, like the longer parables in Mark, that of the sower (4:3–20) and that of the wicked tenants (12:1–11), the parable of the doorkeeper does show marks of allegorization. The significance of the "house" at 13:34–35 in the total context of Markan architectural relations will be considered below.

Finally, "house" occurs in two sayings of Jesus that have previously been identified as metaphorical. To the common proverb given at 6:4, " 'A prophet is without honor except in his own country,' " have been added (by Mark?[21]) the phrases " 'and among his own kin, and in his own house [*oikia*].' " Despite the statement's obvious appropriateness to Jesus (marked topographically by *patris* at 6:1), the generalized statement itself does not locate any Markan event in narrative space.[22] Likewise, the paired references to "house" (*oikia*), just as the paired references to "lands" in the hyperbolic saying of the Markan Jesus at 10:29–30, must be considered primarily metaphorical despite a potentially spatial dimension.

An additional metaphor at the architectural level occurs in relation to a pronoun standing for *temple*. The context is the temple saying attributed to Jesus by the false witnesses (14:58), in which destruction of the temple made with hands is contrasted with the building of " ' "another [*allon*], not made with hands." ' " The meaning of this metaphor is not at all clear from the Gospel of Mark. Is the temple "not made with hands" the resurrected Jesus?[23] Or is the temple "not made with hands" the Christian community?[24] Both metaphors seem logically possible, and each receives narrative development elsewhere in the New Testament (John 2:19–22; 1 Corinthians 3:17; 2 Corinthians 6:16; Ephesians 2:19–22), but neither is narratively confirmed in Mark. If the metaphor of building a temple not made with hands is falsely attributed to the Markan Jesus, as 14:56, 57, and 59 seem to insist, then perhaps its truly confirmed metaphorical equivalent should not be sought in Mark's Gospel. The Markan Jesus rejects the institution of the temple, and it may be that the Markan narrator rejects the metaphor of the temple as well (as does the author of Revelation 21:22). The metaphor is presented but once in Mark—and then in a statement falsely attributed to Jesus. The connotative value of the temple is negative throughout Mark. The only positive references to the center of worship refer neither to *hieron* nor to *naos* but to *oikos*, the "house" of God. The surpassing of the temple "made with hands," a phrase employed with reference to idols in the Septuagint,[25] is mandated by the logic of Mark's narrative, but the new reality is suggested by new images.

Metaphorical applications of architectural terms are not, of course, included in the architectural suborder since they do not locate events in narrative space. But their connotative significance is not unimportant to the architectural sequence and schema. With this in mind, and with the architectural relations now established, the analysis proceeds to the diachronic sequence of their narrative manifestation in Mark's Gospel.

SEQUENCE

As the chronological arrangement of the narrative facts or relations, the sequence represents the "apparent content" of the narrative. The sequence of the architectural suborder, a complex system of sixty-five relations in twelve categories, is summarized graphically in Figure 10.

OVERVIEW

The architectural sequence of the Markan narrative opens in the synagogue (1:21) with the teaching and healing (1:23) of Jesus and the amazement and astonishment it arouses. From the synagogue (1:29) Jesus immediately goes to the house (1:29) of Simon and Andrew, where he heals as well. Such enormous crowds come to Jesus at the house in Capernaum that there is no room for them, "not even about the door" (2:2; cf. 1:33). Then Jesus travels "throughout Galilee, preaching in their synagogues and casting out demons" (1:39). Thus within the first chapter of Mark's Gospel a basic architectural pattern that continues through 6:4 is established: in synagogues and in houses Jesus preaches, or teaches, and/or heals (2:1; 3:1; 3:20 [*RSV* 3:19]; 5:38; 6:2). In addition, throughout the Gospel Jesus sends persons back to their homes, back to their daily lives, after performing a healing (2:11; 5:19; 7:29–30; 8:26). Once Jesus refuses to send people home, for they might faint with hunger on the way (8:3); he feeds them in the wilderness before dismissing them. Homes are places for health and renewed strength.

As Jesus' regular presence in the synagogue on the sabbath (1:21; 3:1; 6:2) reflects his devotion to his religious tradition,[26] his presence at home in table fellowship with "tax collectors and sinners" (2:15) reflects his challenge of that religious tradition in fundamental ways. This challenge is experienced in the synagogue itself. Thus, in this portion of the Markan narrative (1:21–6:4), synagogue and house are interwoven as architectural settings not only for teaching and healing but also for contro-

Figure 10 Architectural Sequence

An action or event reported or projected in the Gospel of Mark
occurs in spatial relation to:

synagogue	house	door	roof	tomb	temple	buildings	housetop	room	courtyard or palace	forecourt	praetorium
1:21											
1:23											
1:29	1:29	1:33									
1:39	2:1	2:2	2:4								
	2:11										
	2:15										
3:1	3:20			5:2							
				5:3							
				5:5							
	5:19										
	5:38										
6:2	6:10			6:29							
	7:17										
	7:24										
	7:30										
	8:3										
	8:26										
	9:28										
	9:33										
	10:10	11:4			11:11						
					11:15a						
					11:15b						
					11:16						
					11:27						
					12:35						
12:39	12:40				13:1	13:1					
						13:2					
					13:3						
13:9							13:15				
	13:15										
	14:3										
									14:14		
									14:15		
					14:49				14:54		
					14:58				14:66	14:68	
									15:16		15:16
					15:29						
					15:38						
				15:46a							
		15:46		15:46b							
				16:2							
		16:3		16:3							
				16:5							
				16:8							

versy. As family and scribes come together, home and synagogue merge. When Jesus is "at home" (3:20; RSV 3:19), his family thinks he is possessed and is joined there in this belief by the scribes. When Jesus is in the synagogue (6:2), those who know his family take offense at him; and Jesus realizes that, like a prophet, he is " 'not without honor, except in his own country, and among his own kin, and in his own house' " (6:4). This is a narrative turning point, and it is marked as such at the architectural level.

Between the controversy with family and scribes at home (3:20) and the controversy about family at the synagogue (6:2), a new architectural space is introduced into the narrative: the tomb. Among tombs lived the Gerasene demoniac, though his life was more death than life; his possession by a legion of unclean spirits had exiled him beyond society, beyond the realm of the living. As the tombs among which he lived (5:2, 3, 5) foreshadow the tombs of John (6:29) and Jesus (15:46a, 46b; 16:2, 3, 5, 8), so his departure from the tombs, his renewal of life through Jesus, his return to the realm of the living to preach, foreshadow Jesus' response to the tomb.[27] After this dramatic healing, Jesus sends the Gerasene home (5:19) and heads home himself.

Prior to the healing among tombs in the country of the Gerasenes, Jesus was reported only in his own home (2.1, 15,[28] 3.20) and in the home of his first disciples (1:29). But the controversy at Jesus' home (3:20) had concluded with Jesus' pronouncement that his family is " 'whoever does the will of God' " (3:35). After that point Jesus is no longer reported to be in a house that is clearly his own[29] but in houses belonging to those who listen to him (e.g., the house of Jairus, the ruler of the synagogue, 5:38). After the controversy (about family) in the synagogue (6:2), Jesus is no longer reported to be in a synagogue. Thus with the saying at 6:4, the Markan Jesus' pattern of teaching and healing in the synagogue and in his home comes to an end: "he could do no mighty work there . . . . And he marveled because of their unbelief" (6:5–6).

The beginning of a second architectural pattern is doubly marked, first by the difficult but successful mission of the disciples to houses (6:10) other than their own, and secondly by the placement of John's body in a tomb by John's disciples (6:29). These two episodes are intercalated (that is, the narration of John's death is "sandwiched" between the opening and the closing of the narration of the disciples' mission), and both episodes preview future architectural relations for Jesus. The second pattern of movement in architectural space is dominated by Jesus teaching the disciples in a house (7:17; 9:28, 33; 10:10). The house as the setting for such teaching signals not a "secret" teaching (as opposed to an "open" teaching) but rather the replacement of the synagogue as a center of teaching. A house in Mark is no place for secrets, for even when Jesus "would not have anyone know" of his presence in a house, "he could not be hid" (7:24). Houses, spatially, just as disciples, sociologically, are beginning to form the core of a new community. This second architectural pattern comes to an end at 10:17, and Jesus' metaphorical saying at 10:29–30 marks its passing and projects its return: " 'Truly, I say to you, there is no one who has left house . . ., for my sake and for the gospel, who will not receive a hundredfold now in this time, houses . . ., with persecutions, and in the age to come eternal life.' "

From this point, "houses" are left behind by the Markan Jesus and "persecution" is faced. (With one significant exception, 14:3, Jesus is no longer reported to be in a "house"; at 14:17–25, however, Jesus is presumed to be in the guest room, *kataluma*, or upper room, *anagaion*, mentioned at 14:14–15.) Outside the door (of a house) two disciples find the colt for Jesus' entry into the city of Jerusalem (11:4), the city of Jesus' passion. The architectural setting for the intensifying antagonism between Jesus and the Jewish religious establishment is, appropriately, the temple. Jesus enters the temple to look around (11:11), to cast out those who buy and sell there (11:15a, 15b, 16), and to teach (11:27; 12:35; cf. 14:49). Among other things, Jesus teaches "the great throng" (12:37) to beware of the scribes who relate themselves wrongly to architectural spaces—seeking honor in synagogues (12:39) and devouring widows' houses (12:40). Outside the temple (13:1), opposite the temple (13:3), Jesus teaches a few disciples, forewarning them of future difficulties in relation to architectural spaces—beatings in synagogues (13:9) and flight from homes (13:15). Jesus does not enter the temple again. His head is anointed with oil, like a king's, not in the seemingly wonderful buildings (13:1 vs. 13:2) of the temple but in a leper's house (14:3). Jesus is anointed for burial (14:8), not in a tomb of the dead but in a house of the living and healed. Not the temple, not the tomb, but the house is the center of Jesus' action. The role Jesus is anointed to perform is clarified within a specific room in a house: the *kataluma*, "guest room," or *anagaion*, "upper room" (14:14–15).

Jesus' role, and his relation to architectural spaces, is not easily understood, much less followed, by the Markan characters. False witnesses and mockers misinterpret Jesus' relation to the temple (14:58; 15:29). Peter follows the arrested Jesus "right into the courtyard" (*aulē*, 14:54) of the high priest's residence, but there (14:66) Peter denies Jesus, once, twice, three times, finally going out to the forecourt (*proaulion*, 14:68) to escape those who recognize him as a Galilean like Jesus. Jesus, however, does not escape the mocking of the soldiers in the palace (*aulē*, 15:16) of Pilate—or death by crucifixion.

As Jesus dies on the cross, the Markan story of the temple comes to an end with the splitting of the temple veil (15:38). Jesus' body, like John's, is laid in a tomb (15:46a, 46b), and a stone is rolled against the doorway (15:46) of the tomb. But, as the women who go to the tomb (16:2, 3) discover there (16:5), the stone has been rolled away from the doorway (16:3) and Jesus, like the Gerasene demoniac, has not remained in the realm of the dead but is returning home. So the women, too, with "trembling and astonishment," flee "from the tomb" (16:8), flee from the space beyond society's boundaries, flee from the realm of the dead, flee to . . . ?

Thus the sequence of the architectural suborder is not a static tableau of stage settings but a dynamic pattern of movement within narrative space. The buildings of the Gospel of Mark enclose more than space; they capture the varied responses made to Jesus by those around him, those he healed, taught, challenged. The Markan account of the ministry of Jesus suggests changing patterns of relation to architectural space.

FROM SYNAGOGUE TO HOUSE

The opening scene of the architectural sequence is of Jesus teaching and healing in the synagogue (1:21, 23).[30] This action in this location is typical of the Markan Jesus in the first half of the narrative, as the summary statement at 1:39 illustrates. Besides this generalized depiction of "preaching in their synagogues and casting out demons," two episodes of teaching and two of healing in the synagogue are described in more detail. The initial episodes of teaching and of healing in a synagogue are intercalated at 1:21–28. Jesus teaches (1:21); the people are astonished at his teaching (1:22); Jesus casts out an unclean spirit (1:25–26); the people are amazed, saying " 'What is this? A new teaching with authority' " (1:27, my translation[31]). Healing thus seems to be an extension of astonishing, authoritative teaching. The reported response to Jesus' second specific healing in the synagogue (3:1–6) is the beginning of a plan, among Pharisees and Herodians, to destroy Jesus. The response to the final synagogue teaching episode (6:2–6) combines astonishment and rejection. Jesus, like a prophet (6:4), is rejected among his own; never again is a synagogue the setting of the teaching or healing—or even the presence—of the Markan Jesus.[32]

Initially in the Gospel of Mark, the actions enclosed by a house parallel those enclosed by a synagogue: healing, teaching or preaching, controversy. Jesus enters a house and heals "immediately" after having left the synagogue where he has healed (1:29). "At home" (2:1) Jesus preaches and heals. So many come to Jesus that the house cannot contain them; they spill out the door (1:33; 2:2). Jesus' table fellowship with "tax collectors and sinners" in his home (2:15) disturbs the scribes, and later his family "at home" (3:20; *RSV* 3:19) joins the scribes in being disturbed at Jesus' activity. Following that controversy, Jesus is no longer reported to be in his own home,[33] but he continues to heal in the houses of those who call out to him (5:38). After healing persons, Jesus frequently sends them to their homes (2:11; 5:19), but the healer himself, like a prophet, is rejected "in his own house" (6:4).

Jesus has declared his family to be " 'whoever does the will of God' " (3:35), and he appears to have that family in mind in sending his disciples out among houses not their own (6:10). Wherever Jesus goes now, the house replaces the synagogue as the architectural setting for teaching; the questioning disciples replace the accusing scribes as listeners (7:17; 9:28, 33; 10:10); the new community has a new "gathering place."[34] But the house is not a place of withdrawal from the people, for even if Jesus "entered a house, and would not have any one know it; yet he could not be hid" (7:24). Not even the physical structure of the house could hide Jesus from those who earnestly sought him; the friends of the paralytic, "when they could not get near him because of the crowd," simply "removed the roof [stegē]" above Jesus (2:4).[35] People come to Jesus with their needs—for their own healing, for the healing of a child, for food—and he sends them all to their homes satisfied (8:26; 7:30; 8:3).

In the final section of Mark's Gosepl, neither house nor synagogue is Jesus' basic architectural location, although he speaks of the past or future spatial relations of friends and enemies to both places. Twice Jesus speaks of actions in synagogues, once as a flashback extending from past to present, once as a flashforward, projecting from present to future. Teaching in the temple, Jesus says, " 'Beware of the scribes, who like . . . to have . . . the best seats in the synagogues' " (12:38–39). (Jesus says that the scribes seek " 'the places of honor' " in private houses as well, that is, " 'at feasts.' ") As Jesus had earlier demonstrated, synagogues are to be places of authoritative teaching and healing, not of seeking honor above others. Teaching opposite the temple, Jesus says, " 'But take heed to yourselves; for . . . you will be beaten in synagogues' " (13:9).[36] Jesus' actions in synagogues provoked controversy; those who follow Jesus will also reap the fruits of that controversy in synagogues. Not only is seeking honor in synagogues enjoined (12:39), but readiness to receive beatings there is mandated (13:9).

After 10:10, the majority (five out of seven) of relations involving house as a spatial location are flashbacks or flash-forwards embedded in sayings of Jesus. (The exceptions are thura at 11:4 and oikia at 14:3.) Two sayings, involving three architectural relations, seem to portray right and wrong ways of relating to houses. Past and present scribes are wrong to " 'devour widows' houses' " (12:40, oikia).[37] Future followers must remain ready to flee their houses amid the castastophes preluding the end time (13:15, dōma and oikia). Not only is taking another's house enjoined, but readiness to give up one's own is mandated (cf. the metaphorical saying at 10:29–30). One saying, involving two architectural relations, concerns preparations for the final meal of

Jesus and the disciples in the guest room (14:14, *kataluma*) or upper room (14:15, *anagaion*).

Never after the first six chapters of Mark is Jesus reported to be in a synagogue; only once in the final six chapters of Mark is Jesus reported to be in a "house." In an ordinary setting, "at Bethany in the house of Simon the leper, as he [Jesus] sat at table" (14:3),[38] an extraordinary event took place: a woman anointed Jesus' head with oil. Such anointing is "a sign of royal dignity,"[39] more appropriately offered by the chief priest than by an unnamed woman, more appropriately set in the temple than in a house. But "Jesus Christ" (1:1), Jesus Messiah, Jesus "the anointed one," receives it in a leper's house. The implications of Jesus' messiahship are made doubly explicit: first in the house in Bethany and second in the guest room (*kataluma*, 14:14) or upper room (*anagaion*, 14:15)—of a house—in Jerusalem. Jesus accepts the anointing in the house in Bethany as anointing " 'beforehand for burying' " (14:8). Thus, as R. H. Lightfoot has observed, in Mark's Gospel "the passion narrative begins and ends with a reference to anointing," at 14:8 and 16:1.[40] In the upper room in Jerusalem (*anagaion* is stated at 14:15 and assumed at 14:17–25), Jesus offers wine as his " 'blood of the covenant' " with the promise to " 'drink it new in the kingdom of God' " (14:24–25). Both Elijah (1 Kings 17:19, 23) and Elisha (2 Kings 4:10, 11) were associated with death and "resurrection" in an "upper room" (LXX *huperōon*). Elijah carried out the resuscitation of the widow's son there, and there Elisha prophesied the birth of the wealthy woman's son, whom he later resuscitated in that space. Covenant, kingdom, messiahship involve not only a new future, a new life, but present death and burial.

OPPOSITE THE TEMPLE

But spatial location in a house is the exception in the final chapters of Mark. Chaps. 11 through 13 are dominated architecturally by the temple. As the temple is of even greater religious significance in the Jewish tradition than the synagogue, the temple provides the appropriate setting for the intensification of the conflict between Jesus and the Jewish religious establishment. And what is true of what W. F. Stinespring counts as "more than a hundred references to Herod's temple" in the New

Testament is true of the dozen or so references in Mark: "Most of these references have to do with attitudes on the part of the Jews or the early Christians toward the temple as an institution."[41] Upon entering Jerusalem, the Markan Jesus is reported to have gone into the temple and "looked round at everything" (11:11) before returning to Bethany.[42] The opposing sides are clearly established: Jesus versus the religious establishment responsible for everything going on in the temple. Jesus' second visit to the temple (11:15a) dramatizes the conflict. Maintenance of the temple ritual, based on a distinction between sacred and profane, necessitates merchants and money-changers in the outer court of the temple to exchange secular currency for the sacral currency employed in the temple and to sell to pilgrims wine, oil, salt, and animals acceptable for sacrifice. In casting out (*ekballein*, the term used in Markan accounts of exorcising demons and of the Spirit driving Jesus out into the wilderness) these functionaries of the temple (11:15b) and in refusing to "allow any one to carry anything through the temple" (11:16), Jesus calls into question the temple ritual itself and the sacred/profane distinction upon which it is based.

Nevertheless, many commentators seem to assume that at 11:16 Jesus prohibits passersby from taking a short cut through the temple. Vincent Taylor, for example, comments that "the prohibition implies a respect for the holiness of the temple and is thoroughly Jewish in spirit."[43] But Werner Kelber's view that *skeuos* (*RSV* "anything") signifies a sacred cult vessel seems more appropriate to the narrative sense.[44] Although *skeuos* has the general meaning of "thing, object, vessel, jar, dish," etc.,[45] Kelber points out that over one-third of the references to *skeuos* in the Septuagint denote sacred cult objects.[46] Yet that leaves the nearly two-thirds of the Septuagint references that do not have such a meaning; and the only other occurrence of *skeuos* in Mark, 3:27 (plural), has the general meaning of "goods." Thus it seems possible that the command concerning *skeuos* in 11:16 is more closely connected with the casting out of the buyers and sellers in 11:15 than commentators recognize. It is not just that the current merchants are dishonest and are thus to be turned out, but that no merchandising of any utensil whatsoever is to be carried out in the temple. (The biblical background supporting this reading is

suggested below.) Thus the *skeuos* of 11:16 may signify not a permanent sacred cult object used by the priests, but any object that may be sold in the outer court for use in the temple by pilgrims. Such an object would still be sacred, but this meaning would do greater justice to the immediate Markan context.[47]

Perhaps the significance of the events of 11:15–19 is to be read against the background of the expectation of the disappearance of the old temple and the construction of an entirely new temple as in Ezekiel 40–48 (or in *Ethiopian Enoch* 90:28–29), and/or the expectation of the cleansing of Jerusalem by the Messiah and the entry of "the heathen" depicted in *Psalms of Solomon* 17:32–33.[48] Jesus' actions, however, do not really function as a "cleansing," despite the traditional caption of the pericope, and no new temple is anticipated here as in Ezekiel. The final chapters of the book of Zechariah, alluded to elsewhere in Mark, present a more exact interpretive clue.[49] On the day of the Lord, reads Zechariah 14:21, "there shall no longer be a trader in the house of the Lord." There shall be no need of traders to provide sacred materials for sacrifices, for "every pot in Jerusalem and Judah shall be sacred to the Lord of hosts, so that all who sacrifice may come and take of them and boil the flesh of the sacrifice in them" (Zechariah 14:21). The distinction between sacred and profane will be invalid because "on that day" all shall be " 'Holy to the Lord' " (Zechariah 14:20). Jesus experiences the overcoming of the distinction between the sacred and the profane and so perceives no further need of traders in the temple or of the consequent carrying of any utensil (*skeuos*, 11:16) through the temple. For the Markan Jesus, "that day" is this day.[50]

In addition, the temple is a setting for the teaching of Jesus (11:27; 12:35; cf. 14:49). His teaching in the temple, like his teaching in the synagogue, inspires the astonishment of the people and the destructive plotting of religious leaders (11:18). But Jesus' teaching in the temple is portrayed more specifically than his teaching in the synagogue;[51] beyond the narrative statement that "Jesus taught," specific samples of that teaching are preserved in the temple setting. After casting out the buyers and sellers, Jesus taught that God's house is to be a house of prayer for all nations (11:17). In dialogue with the chief priests, scribes,

and elders in the temple (11:27), Jesus taught concerning the source of his authority, and to them and against them he told the parable of the wicked tenants. With the Pharisees and the Herodians, Jesus debated the paying of taxes to Caesar; with the Sadducees, the resurrection from the dead; and with one of the scribes, the great commandments. "And as Jesus taught in the temple" (12:35), he taught about the "son of David," and warned "the great throng [who] heard him gladly" (12:37) to beware the misdeeds of the scribes, and pointed out to his disciples the poor widow who gave all. Although the Markan calendar seems compressed at this point, the extent of Jesus' specific teaching set in the temple is suggested by Jesus' statement at Gethsemane: " 'Day after day I was with you in the temple teaching . . .' " (14:49).

For his final extended teaching session, however, Jesus leaves the temple (13:1), never to return.[52] The only Markan uses of the general term *oikodomē*, building, occur at this point of spatial transition. While one of Jesus' disciples is awed by the wonderful (*potapai*) buildings of the temple complex (13:1), Jesus notes that these buildings, although large (*megalas*) will someday be destroyed (13:2). The adjectives chosen to modify these two uses of *oikodomē* are interesting. *Potapos* literally means "what kind of?" but in context implies "what wonderful!" Thus the disciple's statement is really a rhetorical question, assuming an affirmative response from Jesus. Jesus' response, however, overturns this expectation. The root meaning of *megas* is "large" in size or extent, having greatness in quantity (cf. 16:4). Had greatness in quality, that is, magnificence, been intended, *megaleios* could have been more suitably employed. Largeness of size is less awesome than what the disciple perceived, and when no stone is left upon another not even largeness of size will remain. Jesus' view of the future of the temple contrasts with a common element among various eschatological hopes for the new Jerusalem: "that the future Jerusalem will be a city of ineffable glory and indescribable majesty."[53]

These opposing views anticipate Jesus' eschatological discourse to four of his disciples from the Mount of Olives, "opposite the temple" (13:3). Opposite the institution of the temple and its leaders—chief priests, scribes, and elders—is the community of

the disciples and its leaders—"Peter and James and John and Andrew" (13:3). Opposite the physical structure of the temple is its future destruction, when " 'there will not be left here one stone upon another' " (13:2)[54] and a " 'desolating sacrilege [will be] set up where it ought not to be' " (13:14; cf. Daniel 9:27). Opposite the ritual demands of the temple is the command to " 'watch' " (13:37).

Thus in chap. 13 the temple itself becomes part of Jesus' past, and its desecration and destruction part of the disciples' future and, apparently (13:14), part of the reader's present. The "sacrilege" (13:14) is not projected to destroy the temple but to make it "desolate [erēmōseōs, from erēmos, "wilderness"] by causing pious worshippers to avoid it because of the abomination, and thus depriving it of any meaning or purpose."[55] Jesus, however, abandons the temple not because its sacrality has been profaned but because he experiences a breakdown of the sacred/profane distinction. Thus the temple loses its meaning with Jesus' actions (11:15–17; 13:1–3); the loss of meaning at the time of the "desolating sacrilege" is merely confirmatory (13:14), as is the total destruction of the temple (13:2).[56]

After Jesus' final departure from the temple, the temple is brought to attention through flashbacks. Jesus reflects truly his relation to the temple: " 'Day after day I was with you in the temple [hieron] teaching . . .' " (14:49). Others report falsely Jesus' relation to the temple: " 'We heard him say, "I will destroy this temple [naos] . . ." ' " (14:58; cf. 15:29). The statements of the false witnesses and the mockers are contextually complex. Both are conversationally embedded flashbacks to flashforwards: we say that, in the past, Jesus said that, in the future, he would destroy the temple. But the Markan context, in the narrative present, presents both the accusers at the trial and the mockers at the crucifixion as false (14:56–58) or derisive (15:29) opponents of Jesus.[57]

Some interpreters, however, argue that 14:58 is regarded by the author of Mark's Gospel as false in some sense and true in some sense. According to John Donahue, "the false witnesses arise from a pre-Markan apologetic tradition, based on the use of Old Testament texts which originally had nothing to do with the temple saying of 14:58."[58] Thus Donahue holds that "the

content of the statement is true for Mk," although "the form is 'false' because it is uttered by Jesus, according to Mk at the wrong time, i.e., before his enthronement and coming."[59] Donald Juel regards the temple charge (14:58) as false at the surface level and, ironically, true at a deeper level: "the charge in 14:58 can be both 'false testimony' (Jesus never threatened to destroy the temple) and 'prophetic' (as a result of his death the old religious order symbolized by the temple comes to an end)."[60] It would seem more reasonable to accept the temple saying at 14:58 as false, according to its Markan context, and to seek not its truth but its meaning.[61]

Concerning the second occurrence of the temple saying, Donahue remarks that 15:29, within a thoroughgoing context of contempt, places on the lips of the mockers an incorrect eschatology and an incorrect understanding of Jesus' passion. "The incorrect eschatology would join the coming of Jesus as savior with the destruction of the temple which is now taking place. The incorrect understanding of the Passion would obviate the necessity of Jesus to complete the way of the cross before his vindication."[62] And Juel argues that 15:29–30, read with 14:58, is part of Mark's ironic suggestion of a deeper truth: "The version in 15:29 might indicate that the statement has been interpreted by Jesus' opponents as implying that Jesus is a magician, that he has made an impossible threat against the temple. The version of the charge in 14:58, however, might be intended to indicate the sense in which the charge is true."[63] What is clear is that the Markan Gospel makes a distinction between Jesus as an opponent of the temple and the predictor of its destruction (affirmed, for example, at 11:12–20 and 13:2) and Jesus as the destroyer of the temple (denied at 14:58 and 15:29).[64] No action of the Markan Jesus is causally related to the destruction of the *naos*, but the divine action witnessed in Jesus' death (15:37, 39) is paralleled by the divine action witnessed in the destruction of the *naos*, which no longer functions as a separate space—the Holy of Holies—once its curtain is destroyed (15:38).

There is an ironic connection between the temple saying of the false witnesses and that of the mockers. At the trial, at which the false witnesses speak, Jesus is falsely convicted of blasphemy (14:64, *blasphēmias*)—apparently on the grounds of his answer to the chief priest. At the crucifixion the passersby who echo the false witnesses actually do blaspheme (15:29, *eblasphēmoun*), with the "implicit assumption that in blaspheming Jesus they are really blaspheming God."[65] There is, in addition, an ironic connection between Jesus' statement concerning teaching in the temple and the statements of the false witnesses and the mockers concerning destroying the temple. The chief priests, scribes, and elders realized that Jesus' teaching threatened destruction of the temple system; to protect that system they destroyed Jesus. But there is "an ironic twist," as Werner Kelber points out: "If the Jewish officials sought to protect the Temple by putting Jesus to death, they merely hastened the fate of the Temple, because the very death of Jesus constitutes a prolepsis of the end of the Temple (15:37–38)."[66] When the curtain of the *naos* is destroyed (15:38), the separation of the Holy of Holies is destroyed. The separation of the sacred and the profane is thus destroyed; consequently, the foundation of the temple system is destroyed. Those who sought to connect causally Jesus' actions and the destruction of the temple (*naos*) were false witnesses, whereas the one who saw in Jesus' death, paralleled by the destruction of the veil of the temple (*naos*), the action of God, is a true witness (15:37–39).

The actual narrative event of the splitting of the temple curtain becomes also a sign-event of the destruction of the temple system and of the temple itself. Commentators on 15:38 have been divided into two groups: (1) one group that "interprets the veil as the veil which covered the entrance to the Holy of Holies, and sees the splitting of the veil as a sign that through the death of Jesus, all men and not simply Jews are given access to God," and (2) a second group that "holds that the splitting refers to the veil hung in front of the whole sanctuary, and that its splitting is a symbolic reference to the destruction of the temple."[67] But the sharp opposition of these views is not warranted by the Markan narrative. If Mark's Gospel is in part a response to the actual destruction of the temple, as a number of scholars suggest, then what is being asserted in Mark is that the present destruction of the temple buildings is not a devastating loss, since in Jesus' life and death the basis of the temple system (and Jewish exclusivism) had already been destroyed.[68]

THROUGH THE COURTYARD

Because Jesus' death is decisive in the Gospel of Mark, only after Jesus' death is it possible for a human character to witness to Jesus as the Son of God (15:39).[69] Peter tried, after Jesus' arrest, to follow Jesus; he "followed him at a distance, right into the courtyard [*aulē*] of the high priest" (14:54). But there Peter failed as a witness; in the courtyard (*aulē*, 14:66) he denied Jesus. The double references to Peter in the courtyard warming himself (14:54; 14:66–67) frame the trial of Jesus before the Sanhedrin. The intercalation of the testimony of Jesus and the denial of Peter is thus punctuated by the architectural marker *aulē*. As Schweizer remarks, "The visible parallel between Jesus and Peter makes the fundamental difference between them all the more prominent."[70] Having denied Jesus, Peter went out from the space to which he had followed Jesus; he "went out into the forecourt [*proaulion*]" (14:68, my translation). Unwilling to be identified as a follower of Jesus, Peter was unwilling to remain in the place where Jesus was. Outside, physically and otherwise, Peter denied Jesus a second and a third time. The cock crowed; Jesus was tried before Pilate, led away "inside the palace (*aulē*)" (15:16), and mocked by the soldiers.

"Palace" is an extended or synechdochical meaning of *aulē*,[71] apparently demanding clarification for Mark's readers by the juxtaposition of *praitōrion*, a Latin loanword for "praetorium," at 15:16. Markan commentators have carried on both a historical debate concerning whether the praetorium of Mark 15:16 refers to the Palace of Herod in the western part of Jerusalem or to the fortress Antonia northwest of the temple area[72] and a linguistic debate concerning whether *ho estin praitōrion* ("that is, the praetorium") is an attempt to explain "translation Greek" based on an Aramaic original.[73] But by focusing on the history and linguistics of the author's intention in using *praitōrion*, commentators have overlooked the meaning effect within the narrative itself of the use of *aulē* for both palace and courtyard. The Markan use of *aulē* for Pilate's palace as well as for the chief priest's courtyard serves not only to link Jesus' secular trial with his religious one but also to contrast Jesus' actions with Peter's. Inside the *aulē*, that is, the *praitōrion* (15:16), Jesus suffered; Peter, desiring to avoid suffering, went outside the *aulē*, into the *proaulion* (14:68), denying Jesus. Jesus' suffering led to death, and only through death could Jesus be fully affirmed both as "the Christ" (so Peter at 8:29) and as "the Son of God" (so the centurion at 15:39). This is the "beginning of the good news [*RSV* "gospel"] of Jesus Christ, the Son of God" (1:1) as proclaimed in the opening of Mark's Gospel.

As the architectural location of present action in the Markan narrative, *aulē* (14:54, 66, 68; 15:16) immediately follows *kataluma* (14:14) and *anagaion* (14:15)—*hieron* at 14:49 occurs within a flashback, as does *naos* at 14:58. That is, the intercalated account of Jesus' trial and Peter's denial follows the narration of the Last Supper. This juxtaposition of interior courtyard and interior room, not just houses in general, indicates a narrowing focus at the architectural level that is paralleled at many other levels.[74] Every effort is made to capture the reader's close attention for the final scenes of Mark, the account of Jesus' passion.

BEYOND THE TOMB

The architectural suborder of the Gospel of Mark closes at the tomb, the tomb where the crucified Jesus was laid (15:46a), the tomb whose doorway (15:46) was sealed with a stone (15:46b). Perhaps it was a tomb like those among which the Gerasene demoniac had lived (5:2, 3, 5); perhaps it was a tomb like that in which John had been laid by his disciples (6:29). But the Gerasene had, through the power of the Lord (5:19) in Jesus' word, come out from the tombs and gone home "to proclaim . . . how much Jesus had done" (5:20). And after the Markan reporting of the entombment of John, the return of Jesus' disciples from their successful mission of preaching and healing—in the manner of Jesus—is narrated. John has been killed and laid in a tomb; the work of Jesus and his disciples continues. Jesus has been killed and laid in a tomb; what shall continue?[75]

On the day after the sabbath, the women, who had followed Jesus, come to the tomb (16:2) and discover not the sealed tomb (16:3, *thura* and *mnēmeion*) and the dead Jesus of their expectations, but an open tomb (16:5) and a spokesman for a risen Jesus. The women had assumed that, after the crucifixion, the tomb was the place for ministering (cf. *diēkonoun*, "ministered," at 15:41) by the followers of Jesus. The spokesman's message challenges that spatial assumption; his spatial word from Jesus is "go" (16:7).[76] And the women do go; they go out and flee from the tomb, "for trembling and astonishment had come upon them . . ." (16:8). They had gone outside the city to the tomb, beyond the boundaries of society to the realm of the dead, to follow Jesus. But Jesus was not in that space. Jesus, who had taught concerning the resurrection (12:18–27) that God " 'is not God of the dead, but of the living' " (12:27), was no longer in the tomb. Thus the women flee from the tomb, and therefore back into society and back among the living, with the promise for themselves and for the disciples, especially Peter, that " 'there you will see him' " (16:7).[77]

OUTSIDE AND INSIDE

The women's movements in going out of the tomb parallel the apparent movement of Jesus. Even though the movements of the architectural suborder are oriented to inside spaces, architectural enclosures in Mark are sometimes more significant as places to be outside of than as places to be inside of. At critical moments Jesus and/or others are located outside the temple (13:1, 3), outside the courtyard (14:68), outside tombs (5:2, 3, 5) or the tomb (16:6, 8). In addition the outside/inside distinction is complex in regard to several architectural spaces, especially those specified toward the end of Mark's Gospel. A room is an enclosure within an enclosure (inside the inside), whereas a housetop (13:15) is the outer surface of an enclosure (outside the inside). The courtyard is an interior open space (the outside brought inside), whereas the tomb is an out-of-doors enclosure (the inside taken outside). From room to tomb—all are enclosures, yet none finally encloses Jesus or his followers. When Jesus is in the house, the door (1:33; 2:2) does not keep the crowds out; when Jesus is buried, the door of the tomb (15:46; 16:3) does not keep Jesus in. A house that seems to enclose Jesus ceases to do so when the friends of the paralytic remove the roof (2:4). The function of the roof is destroyed in order that a human being can be restored. Later the tomb seems to enclose Jesus

(15:46); but when the stone before the tomb is found rolled away (16:3), is the function of the tomb destroyed in order that humanity can be restored?

The overturning of the outside/inside distinction at the architectural level has perhaps been anticipated by the use of the terms *outside* and *inside* in key non-architectural passages in Mark. At 3:31, 32, and at 4:11, *exō* ("outside") is applied to a group of persons. At 3:31, 32, Jesus' mother and brothers are "outside"—physically, and perhaps spiritually as well—for the Markan Jesus identified his "mother" and "brothers" as "those who sat about him" and " 'whoever does the will of God' " (3:34–35). The expected criterion for being an insider, being family, is cast out, and a new criterion is brought in. Personal expectations are turned inside out. The context of 4:11 is more complex due to difficulties in determining the denotations of *to mystērion* ("mystery," translated "the secret" by *RSV*) and *en parabolais* ("in parables") as well as the connotation of the adaptation of Isaiah 6:9–10 in 4:12. Nevertheless, "those outside" appear to be in contrast with the disciples who would then, presumably, be "those inside." Being inside here, as at 3:31–35, is a matter of discipleship—but also a matter of being "given" a "mystery." Being inside is a gift, a surprise.

The teaching of the Markan Jesus is surprising to those inside the Jewish religious tradition. Paired, non-architectural uses of *exōthen* ("outside" or "without") and *esōthen* ("inside" or "within") punctuate Jesus' teaching on defilement at 7:14–23. Defilement, Jesus asserts, comes not from things outside a person, such as ritually unclean foods, but from things inside a person, evil thoughts and deeds. As the Markan parenthetical aside at 7:19 specifies, such a point of view completely overturns the Jewish system of ritual observances concerning food. Jesus' challenge turns the traditional Jewish ritual world upside down and inside out.

A parallel attack on the Jewish ritual world occurs when Jesus casts the buyers and sellers out of the temple. The counterattack by the religious leaders results in Jesus being cast out of the city (as, at the metaphorical level, the owner's son is cast out of the vineyard at 12:8). When laid in the tomb, Jesus is spatially located inside an outside inside (that is, inside an out-of-doors enclosure). But when, amazingly (16:5), the tomb is found empty, Jesus is known to be outside this inside, beyond all enclosure. This realization astonishes (16:8). Resurrection is the turning of expectations inside out.

SCHEMA

In order to appreciate more fully the significance of the surprises of the architectural suborder, one must move from its diachronic structure, its sequence, to its synchronic structure, its schema. It is by attending to the schema of the architectural suborder, the internal organization of its "bundles of relations," that one may "understand" the narrative at the architectural level. Lying behind the mythological schema presupposed by the Markan architectural suborder is a logical hierarchy of all the architectural spaces referred to in the Markan narrative. This logical hierarchy, presented as a "branching tree diagram," is given in Figure 11. The mythological schema, presented as a series of oppositions moving toward mediation, is given in Figure 12. The terms in parentheses in Figure 12 represent the nonmanifest, fundamental opposition underlying the oppositions manifest in the narrative.

HOUSE VS. SYNAGOGUE—AND TEMPLE

The initial architectural mode of the Gospel of Mark is "in the synagogue." Jesus teaches, heals, and sparks controversy in the synagogue. But the dominant architectural marker of the Gospel of Mark is *house*. Jesus is often reported to be in his home or in a house teaching or healing; those with him there are sometimes crowds, sometimes all his disciples, sometimes a few of his disciples. Also Jesus often sends people back to their own homes, frequently after a healing. A synagogue, of course, is a religious space, a sacred space; in relation to it a house, a residential space, is profane. On this basis, the two architectural terms are in opposition. Although it seems that the first-century Pharisees sought to make all of life—and perhaps especially the home— sacred, such a goal in fact accentuates the sacred/profane distinction. The Pharisaic opposition is not between the sacred synagogue (and temple) and the profane house but between those

Figure 11 Architectural Hierarchy

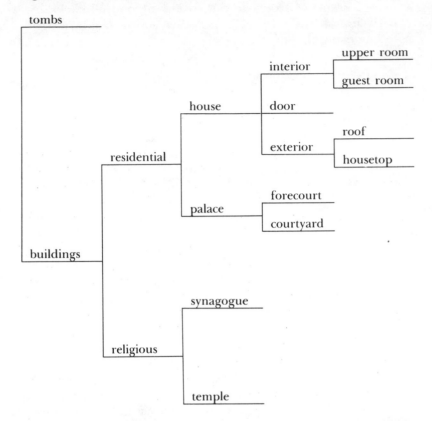

persons, places, and things made sacred by Torah observance and all other—profane—persons, places, and things. The house itself, without Torah observance, would be, for the Pharisees, profane. The Markan Jesus and the Markan narrative seem to move toward the opposite goal of disvaluing the sacred/profane distinction (see Mark 7—in its entirety). PROFANE and SACRED, the terms in parentheses in Figure 12, are "two opposite terms with no intermediary." In the mythic process of mediation they are "replaced by two equivalent terms,"[78] HOUSE and SYNA-GOGUE.

Movement toward mediation between HOUSE and SYNAGOGUE is manifest in the Markan narrative not so much by the appear-

Figure 12   Architectural Schema

(profane)

house

room

tomb

temple

courtyard

synagogue—
and temple

(sacred)

ance of a third and mediating term between the two as by the takeover of the functions of one by the other. In chap. 5, the healing (or resuscitation) of Jairus' daughter is related. Not only is this the most dramatic healing of Mark (since the girl is pronounced dead before Jesus' arrival), but it is also given special treatment by its intercalation with the healing of the hemorrhaging woman. The raising of the daughter occurs in the *house* (*oikos*) of one of the rulers of the *synagogue* (*archisynagōgos*, 5:22, 35, 36, 38). Power is not with the ruler of the synagogue, but with Jesus in the house. Immediately afterwards (6:1–6), the controversy in the synagogue crests. From then on the house is the chief architectural center for teaching, replacing the synagogue as it were. In terms of the fundamental opposition underlying the architectural schema, the sacred realm is inadequate to contain Jesus' "new teaching" (1:27), and it overflows into the profane realm.[79]

The manifestation of the sacred realm is intensified in the narrative movement from the synagogue to the temple. The synagogue is the setting for studying the Law, the temple the place for worshiping God's very presence. The potential opposition of the synagogue and the temple (see the logical hierarchy in Figure 11) is not actualized in the Markan narrative; the mythological schema represents a *selection* of distinctions from the logical hierarchy. A possible historical context of this Markan mythological position is, in the words of Wolfgang Schrage, that in "N[ew] T[estament] days the temple and the synagogue stood alongside one another, nor was there any thought of antithesis or rivalry."[80] Furthermore, after A.D. 70, the synagogue stood almost in place of the temple for Jews: "The founding of the synagogue shows that the Rabbis saw in the synagogue an equivalent of the temple, and in the *diaspora* and after the destruction of the temple it was a full substitute."[81] Such a situation quite possibly forms the background for the Markan linking of SYNAGOGUE and TEMPLE. After the destruction of the temple, the synagogue became the focal point of the Jewish community. "The fact that Judaism could withstand the disaster of 70 virtually without a break is undoubtedly to be credited in the main to the synagogue."[82] Christians, expelled from the synagogue, needed another way of dealing with the disaster of 70. Such a situation may form the background of the Markan opposition, HOUSE vs. SYNAGOGUE— AND TEMPLE.

Because both SYNAGOGUE and TEMPLE manifest the SACRED realm, it is not surprising that HOUSE, a manifestation of the PROFANE realm, is also in opposition to TEMPLE in Mark's Gospel.[83] In the final third of the narrative, the temple is the dominant architectural mode. Yet Jesus only visits the temple in Jerusalem; he stays in Bethany in the house of Simon the leper (14:3). The house is his base of opposition to the activities and leaders of the temple. The religious establishment of the temple opposes Jesus of the leper's house. In the house, rather than in the temple, Jesus becomes "the anointed one." As during Jesus' ministry the house had come to oppose the synagogue, so during Jesus' passion the more holy temple opposes the house and rejects and is rejected by the one identified with it.

Even at the metaphorical level of Mark's Gospel, *temple* is rejected, *house* affirmed. The metaphor of building a temple "not made with hands" is falsely attributed at 14:58 to the Markan Jesus, but the metaphor of the temple as the *house* of God is on his lips truly, both early and late (2:26; 11:17). Jesus' eschatological discourse opens with the prediction of the destruction of the temple and closes with the parable of the doorkeeper of the house. " 'Watch,' " the disciples, like the doorkeeper, are instructed, " 'for you do not know when the Lord [Greek *kurios*; *RSV* "master"] of the house will come. . . .'" (13:35). The meaning is transparent. As the parable begins, the master of the house is a "man," *anthrōpos* (13:34); as the parable becomes command, the master becomes Lord, *kurios*. At Mark 1:3,[84] and probably at 5:19, *kurios* is employed ambiguously to refer to Jesus as well as to God. At 13:29 the Markan Jesus speaks of the future when the Son of man will be "at the door"(*RSV* "gates"). Jesus is consistently associated with the house in Mark. "'Watch therefore— for you do not know when the Lord of the house will come. . . .'"

Both John Donahue and Donald Juel have argued that the temple "not made with hands" (14:58) signifies the Christian community.[85] The present analysis concurs in significant ways with Donahue's analysis of the "anti-Jerusalem and anti-Temple polemic which runs through the Gospel," but diverges from his conclusion that Mark "brings to a culmination" this polemic by attributing 14:58 to Jesus as a true statement in reference to the new community.[86] Indeed, the new community is opposed to the old community in Mark; and, indeed, the old community is signaled metaphorically by the "temple." But the evidence for the temple "not made with hands" as a metaphor of the new community comes not from Mark but from New Testament letters and Qumran documents.[87] It seems likely that the Markan Gospel does suggest a theological response of the Christian community to the crisis of the destruction of the temple; but, on the basis of the entire system of architectural relations as well as the immediate context of 14:58, it seems unlikely that Mark does so by "creat[ing] a Christian exegesis of Temple expectations"[88] and by imaging the Christian community as a new temple "not made with hands."

But may it not be that the house, which replaces the synagogue and stands in opposition to the doomed temple in Mark, does suggest the early Christian community?[89] With the destruction of the temple (13:2) and rejection in the synagogue (13:9), the Christian community must come together in "house churches." As Otto Michel points out, "Primitive Christianity structured its congregations in families, groups and 'houses.' The house was both a fellowship and a place of meeting."[90] Perhaps the Markan architectural symbols of *house, synagogue,* and *temple* received their power from the historical experiences of early Christians. Perhaps Mark's Gospel, in its narrative manipulation of these architectural symbols, suggested a way of responding meaningfully to those historical realities; perhaps it marked the establishment of a new ritual center after the destruction of an old one. Ever since the life and death of Jesus, so the Markan Gospel assures its readers, the sacred structures of temple and synagogue are no longer central; the new community gathers in a house to experience, witness to, and await "the Lord of the house."[91]

ROOM VS. COURTYARD

As part of the mythic process of progressive mediation, the opposition HOUSE VS. SYNAGOGUE—AND TEMPLE is replaced by an equivalent opposition, ROOM VS. COURTYARD. Since the only two narrative manifestations of a room in Mark's Gospel pertain to a room in a house, it is clear that ROOM replaces HOUSE and represents the PROFANE pole of the fundamental opposition of the architectural schema. Based on the logical hierarchy (Figure 11), however, it might appear that COURTYARD represents the PROFANE pole as well. Yet this is not the case in the Markan narrative because the courtyard referred to is "the courtyard of the high priest" (14:54), the chief official of the Jewish religious establishment. Thus COURTYARD replaces SYNAGOGUE—AND TEMPLE and represents the SACRED as the opposites move toward mediation.

Movement toward mediation between ROOM and COURTYARD, as between HOUSE and SYNAGOGUE—AND TEMPLE, is not manifest in the Markan narrative by the appearance of a third and mediating term. Rather, movement toward mediation is narratively suggested by the solemnity of the Last Supper in the upper room and the hypocrisy of the trial in the high priest's courtyard. In the guest room (14:14) or upper room (14:15), a Jewish religious ritual, the Passover meal, is enriched in meaning: the celebration of the exodus is transformed into a celebration of Jesus' death and an anticipation of the kingdom of God (14:22–25).[92] In the high priest's courtyard, a Jewish institution, a hearing, is deprived of its essential meaning: the procedures for fair and impartial evaluation are transformed into a mockery of justice.[93]

The institution of justice is desecrated in the high priest's court-yard, and the Passover meal receives a new sacral dimension in the common room.

Movement toward mediation is further implied by Jesus' acceptance of the necessity of his suffering and death in both spaces. In the room Jesus breaks the bread as his body will be broken in death and pours out the wine as his blood, his life, will be " 'poured out for many' " (14:24). Above the courtyard the Sanhedrin condemns Jesus "as deserving of death" (14:64). Jesus' acceptance of his death is not understood or shared by his disciples in either upper room or courtyard. In the room Jesus foretells his betrayal by one of his disciples. Just after Jesus and his disciples depart from the room, Jesus predicts Peter's denial. To the courtyard Peter alone follows Jesus, and just after his denial Peter departs from the courtyard.

Although significant in the process of the progressive media-tion of PROFANE and SACRED, the opposition ROOM VS. COURT-YARD is narratively manifest in but one pair of scenes in the Markan story. Greater scope is given to both its preceding op-position, HOUSE VS. SYNAGOGUE — AND TEMPLE, and its succeed-ing one, TOMB VS. TEMPLE.

TOMB VS. TEMPLE

The fundamental opposition PROFANE VS. SACRED receives its third narrative manifestation at the architectural level in the op-position TOMB VS. TEMPLE. The temple, like the (high priest's) courtyard and the synagogue, functions as a power base for the Jewish religious establishment; there also Jesus is engaged in controversy internal to Judaism. The tomb, like the (upper) room and the house, serves as home base for Jesus and his fol-lowers in opposition to the religious establishment; from there Jesus and his followers move outward. Thus TEMPLE represents the SACRED pole and TOMB the PROFANE pole of the fundamental opposition. In addition, the temple, like the (high priest's) court-yard and the synagogue, is an official architectural space built by and for the Jewish religious establishment, whereas Jesus' tomb, like the (upper) room and most, if not all, of the houses in Mark, is a space temporarily "borrowed" by Jesus. Jesus oc-cupies no space permanently.

Narrative manifestation of the opposition TOMB vs. TEMPLE is observed in the ongoing debate between Jesus and the chief priests, scribes, and elders. After challenging the religious institutions and religious leaders and criticizing their hypocritical responses, Jesus concludes that they are dead, that the temple will fall and thus serve as their tomb (cf. Mathew 23:27). In responding to the challenge of Jesus with a plot for his death, the religious leaders are acting out their conclusion that Jesus would be better dead, that Jesus' place is in the tomb. The temple was the center of the Jewish religious establishment; the Markan Jesus pointed to that center's disintegration. By consigning Jesus to the tomb, religious officials hoped to end his influence; but the tomb was found as empty as their success. Thus, whereas the religious leaders hoped that the tomb would be the end of Jesus' challenge to the sacred order, Jesus challenged that the temple of the sacred order itself would end.

TEMPLE also appears as a term in the first manifest opposition of the architectural suborder: HOUSE vs. SYNAGOGUE — AND TEMPLE. Because the temple would be thought of as "more sacred" than the synagogue, it is perhaps surprising to find TEMPLE as (also) an element of the third manifest opposition, closer to mediation of the latent opposition PROFANE vs. SACRED than is SYNAGOGUE. But in Mark's Gospel (and especially in its long conclusion) the temple that is traditionally considered sacred is considered doomed to dysfunction and nonexistence. The temple becomes less sacred as it becomes less real, as it becomes nothing. Thus it is not TOMB that leads to nothingness but TEMPLE.

Within the opposition TOMB vs. TEMPLE, it is difficult to perceive any movement toward narrative mediation in the strict sense of Lévi-Strauss's formulation in which "two opposite terms with no intermediary always tend to be replaced by two equivalent terms which allow a third one as a mediator."[94] Rather, an important breakdown of the fundamental opposition PROFANE vs. SACRED is suggested in relation to the terms of the opposition TOMB vs. TEMPLE. The profane is only considered so from the point of view of the sacred. It is the institution of the temple that reinforces the distinction between the sacred and the profane. The temple precinct is sacred as opposed to the profane marketplace; the materials for offerings and the coins used in the temple are sacred, having been sold or exchanged in the outer court of the temple expressly for that purpose; the Holy of Holies, where the priest alone confronts the presence of God, is most sacred of all and is thus separated within the temple by a curtain. So when the temple curtain is split, the temple merchants and money-changers cast out, and the total destruction of the temple itself foretold, the distinction between the sacred and profane is undermined at its foundation.[95]

The overcoming of the opposition SACRED VS. PROFANE is also suggested by the ambiguous position of the tomb in the architectural suborder. In a preliminary way, the tomb mediates between the sacred and the profane and their narrative manifestations by combining aspects of each. A tomb, of course, unlike a house or a room, is for the dead not the living. But, like a residence, a tomb is a personal or familial space.[96] Unlike a synagogue or the temple, a tomb is not holy but taboo.[97] Yet, like a religious space, a tomb is surrounded by a certain sense of awe. More significantly, the tomb marks the overcoming of the opposition SACRED VS. PROFANE by going beyond such a distinction. The distinction between sacred and profane is a societal one; and, on account of the belief in the defiling effect of contact with the dead (Leviticus 21:1; Numbers 6:6; 19:13; etc.),[98] a tomb is a space beyond society's bounds, outside the gates. According to the implications of the Markan text, the leaders of the Jewish religious establishment believed that by placing Jesus in a tomb they would be able to remove his influence beyond the bounds of society. Because the Markan Jesus does not remain in that traditionally assigned space, his death (as well as his life) serves to question the distinctions imposed by society and by tradition.[99]

Finally, Jesus himself, Jesus as the cornerstone (12:10), appears to be the mediator of the architectural suborder at a metaphorical level. Stones (*lithoi*) are mentioned on only three other occasions in Mark: (1) The Gerasene demoniac, living among tombs, bruises himself with stones until the demons are exorcized by Jesus (5:5). (2) One of Jesus' disciples exclaims that the stones of the temple are "wonderful," only to be contradicted by Jesus' words, " 'There will not be left here one stone upon another, that will not be thrown down' " (13:1, 2). (3) The women at the tomb find the stone rolled away and Jesus no longer in the tomb (15:46; 16:3, 4). While the stones of the temple will be found toppled in destruction, the stone before the tomb is found rolled away in victory. Stones and tombs and temple exhibit an intriguing affinity. Their coherence is metaphorical in the deepest sense in Mark's Gospel, for the one who foretells the destruction of the temple and who cannot be destroyed by the tomb is affirmed as " ' "The very stone which the builders rejected [and which] has become the head of the corner..." ' " (12:10).

To summarize the architectural schema, one may say that as SACRED is to PROFANE, so is SYNAGOGUE—AND TEMPLE to HOUSE, COURTYARD to ROOM, and TEMPLE to TOMB. And it must be noted that, contrary to what one might expect of "religious literature," the positively valued pole of this Markan schema, the pole manifested by the architectural spaces most closely associated with Jesus, is the PROFANE pole. But even more significant is the observation that, as the narrative progresses, both the sacred and the profane architectural spaces of Mark's Gospel are abandoned by Jesus. The room and the courtyard are but temporary settings. Jesus abandons both synagogue and temple, as, in the future, all will abandon the temple. Nor is the crucified Jesus found in the tomb. The good news cannot be kept inside.

By the close of the Gospel of Mark, no architectural space functions in its normal, expected way any longer. A house is no longer a family dwelling but has become a gathering place for the new community, replacing the rejected and rejecting synagogue. The temple is no longer a space separating sacred and profane and will become but a rubble of stones, not one on another. The tomb is no longer the prison of the dead (dark and closed) but (empty and open) it has become the threshold of renewed life. Empty tomb, ruined temple, house of gathering— Jesus' death, the destruction of the temple, the new community—all are, according to Mark's Gospel, witnesses to the breakdown of the opposition of the sacred and the profane and the breakthrough to a new reality.

5. Integrating Markan Space

And he said to them, "Do not be amazed; you seek Jesus of Nazareth, who was crucified. He has risen, he is not here; see the place where they laid him. But go, tell his disciples and Peter that he is going before you to Galilee; there you will see him, as he told you." And they went out and fled from the tomb; for trembling and astonishment had come upon them; and they said nothing to any one, for they were afraid.

— MARK 16:6–8

The complexity of the spatial order of the Gospel of Mark has demanded division into suborders for the process of detailed analysis. The unity of the Markan spatial order, however, demands integration of these suborders for a more holistic view. Because the analytical separation of the geopolitical, topographical, and architectural suborders has shattered the original integration of the text, the synthetic task might well be labeled one of reintegration. The relations of the integrated spatial order are all the relations of the three suborders combined. In the examination of the sequence of the spatial order, the focus will be on the narrative extent of relations from each of the suborders and the patterns of their diachronic relationships. Consideration will also be given to the "double ending" of the Gospel of Mark. In the analysis of the schema of the spatial order, the terms of the oppositions of the schemata of the three suborders will be combined into a new schema of oppositions moving toward mediation. This schema of the schemata will suggest a new expression of the fundamental opposition underlying the spatial order, one that may be understood as a more basic opposition underlying the nonmanifest oppositions of the three suborders. This schema of the schemata will clarify the degree to which the Gospel of Mark presents expected patterns of opposition and the degree to which it challenges such patterns.[1]

SEQUENCE

The sequence of the spatial order, a complex system of 288 relations in three suborders, is summarized graphically in Figure

13. The most obvious observation is of the dominance of relations of the topographical suborder, especially in the first half of the Gospel. Although significant groupings of geopolitical relations punctuate this topographical dominance (especially at 1:5; 3:7–8; 7:31), the way, the wilderness, the mountain(s), heaven, earth, inhabited areas, and, above all, the sea, set the main stage for Markan characters through chap. 9. At 10:1, the beginning of Jesus' journey to Jerusalem, geopolitical relations increase proportionately, as do architectural relations at 11:11, Jesus' initial entrance into the temple. Thus, while Galilee and foreign regions are the locus of narrative action, topography is of special importance; when Judea and Jerusalem become the center of narrative action, political geography and architecture increase in relative importance within the Markan spatial order. Each of the three suborders indicates breaks in the flow of the narrative action, but not precisely at the same points. A break in one suborder may be anticipated in a second suborder and recapitulated in a third. These patterns of diachronic relationships, suggested in Figure 14, elaborate and enrich the texture of the narrative.

OVERARCHING PATTERNS

The geopolitical suborder, perhaps, states the theme of the spatial order of Mark's Gospel most clearly because the many named places are perceived in three basic groups: Galilee, foreign regions, Judea. At this level, the narrative depicts a major shift at 10:1; spatially the shift is from Galilee (and foreign regions) to Judea (especially Jerusalem); theologically the shift is from a ministry of power to a ministry of suffering. Two passion predictions anticipate this break (8:31; 9:31); the third, and most complete, follows it (10:32–34). The only healing recounted after this shift is the giving of sight to blind Bartimaeus, who follows Jesus "on the way" (10:52) to Jerusalem, the city of death. The only "nature miracle" performed by Jesus after 10:1 is the cursing of the barren fig tree, an enacted metaphor of the temple's present uselessness and future destruction. R. H. Lightfoot depicts "chapter 10, with its mention of the borders of Judea, Peraea and Jericho," as "a connecting link" between the two chief sections of Mark's Gospel, the Galilean ministry, chaps. 1–9, and

Figure 13 Spatial Sequence

An action or event reported or projected in the Gospel of Mark
occurs in spatial relation to:

Political Geography	Topography	Architecture
	1:2	
	1:3	
	1:3a	
	1:3b	
	1:4	
1:5	1:5	
1:5		
1:5	1:5	
1:9		
1:9		
1:9	1:10	
	1:11	
	1:12	
	1:13	
1:14	1:16a	
1:16	1:16b	
	1:19	
	1:20	
1:21		1:21
		1:23
1:24	1:28	
1:28		1:29
		1:29
	1:33	1:33
	1:35	
	1:38	
	1:38	1:39
1:39	1:45	
	1:45	
2:1		2:1
		2:2
		2:4
	2:10	2:11
	2:13	2:15
	2:23	3:1
	3:7	
3:7		
3:7		
3:8		

Figure 13 Spatial Sequence *cont.*

Political Geography	Topography	Architecture
3:8		
3:8		
3:8		
3:8	3:9	
	3:13	3:20
3:22	4:1a	
	4:1b	
	4:1c	
	4:1d	
	4:1e	
	4:1	
	4:35	
	4:36a	
	4:36b	
	4:37a	
	4:37b	
	4:39	
	4:41	
	5:1a	
	5:1b	
	5:1	
5:1	5:2	5:2
		5:3
		5:5
	5:5	
	5:10	
	5:11	
	5:13a	
	5:13b	
	5:14	
	5:14	
	5:17	
	5:18a	
	5:18b	5:19
5:20	5:21a	
	5:21b	
	5:21c	
	5:21d	5:38
	6:1	6:2
	6:6	
	6:8	6:10
6:21		6:29
	6:31	

Figure 13 Spatial Sequence *cont.*

Political Geography	Topography	Architecture
	6:32	
	6:32	
	6:33	
	6:35	
	6:36	
	6:36	
	6:41	
	6:45a	
	6:45b	
	6:45	
	6:45c	
6:45	6:46	
	6:47a	
	6:47b	
	6:47	
	6:48a	
	6:48b	
	6:49	
	6:51	
	6:53a	
	6:53	
6:53	6:53b	
	6:54	
	6:55	
	6:56	
	6:56	
	6:56	
	6:56	
7:1	7:4	7:17
	7:24	
7:24		7:24
7:26		7:30
	7:31a	
7:31		
7:31	7:31	
7:31	7:31b	
7:31	7:34	8:3
	8:3	
	8:4	
	8:6	
	8:10a	
	8:10b	
	8:10	

Figure 13 Spatial Sequence *cont.*

Political Geography	Topography	Architecture
8:10	8:13a	
	8:13b	
	8:14	
8:22	8:23	8:26
	8:26	
	8:27	
8:27	8:27	
	9:2	
	9:7a	
	9:7b	
	9:9	
	9:20	9:28
9:30		
9:33		9:33
	9:33	
	9:34	
	10:1	
10:1		
10:1		10:10
	10:17	
	10:32a	
10:32	10:32b	
10:33		
10:46a		
10:46b	10:46	
10:47	10:52	
11:1		
11:1		
11:1	11:1	
11:1	11:2	11:4
	11:4	
	11:8	
	11:8	
	11:9	
11:11		11:11
11:11		
11:12		
11:15		11:15a
		11:15b
		11:16
	11:19	
11:27		11:27
		12:35

Figure 13 Spatial Sequence *cont.*

Political Geography	Topography	Architecture
	12:38	12:39
		12:40
		13:1
		13:1
		13:2
	13:3	
13:3		13:3
		13:9
13:14	13:14	13:15
		13:15
	13:16	
	13:25a	
	13:25b	
	13:26	
	13:27	
	13:27	
	13:31	
	13:31	
14:3		14:3
	14:13	14:14
		14:15
	14:16	
	14:26	
14:26	14:28	
14:28		
14:32	14:35	14:49
		14:54
		14:58
	14:62a	
	14:62b	14:66
14:67		14:68
14:70		15:16
		15:16
15:21	15:21	
15:22		15:29
	15:33	15:38
15:40		
15:41		
15:41		
15:43		15:46a
		15:46
		15:46b
15:47		

Figure 13   Spatial Sequence *cont.*

Political Geography	Topography	Architecture
16:1		16:2
		16:3
		16:3
		16:5
16:6	16:7	
16:7		16:8

the "last week" at Jerusalem, chaps. 11–16.[2] But, although Galilee is the dominant spatial setting of chaps. 1–10 and Judea of 10–16, the narrative in fact opens in Judea and closes with past and future looks to Galilee. Action in Judea (especially Jerusalem) as the climax to action in Galilee might represent the cultural expectation of many first-century hearers of Mark's story. Jerusalem was, after all, the culmination of many a pilgrimage. But the Markan pattern reverses this expectation: early in the narrative, Judean actions culminate in Galilee (see 1:14); late in the narrative, Judean actions again culminate in Galilee (see 14:28 and 16:7). Thus not only does the Judea-to-Galilee pattern frame the narrative at the geopolitical level, but it is intensified by repetition within the narrative.

What one hears in the topographical suborder is, perhaps, the development of the theme stated in the geopolitical suborder, for the topographical suborder is the most extensive and complex of the three. After a brief, opening emphasis on the way and the wilderness, the sea becomes the dominant topographical setting for nearly eight chapters. Way and wilderness, mountain, heaven and earth, cities, villages, and the country—all have a place in setting the scenes, but the sea dominates them all, and Jesus masters the sea. At 8:22 the last Markan journey on the sea comes to an end; at 8:27 the topographical dominance of journeys "on the way" (or "road") begins (8:27–11:9). Between these two spatial markers is recounted the only two-stage healing in the Gospels, the healing of the blind man of Bethsaida. From 8:31, the first passion prediction, forward, Jesus seeks to heal the disciples' second stage of blindness, their blindness not to the

Figure 14 Spatial Patterns

Markan Chapter	Geopolitical Suborder	Topographical Suborder	Architectural Suborder
1	Judea	way/wilderness	
2			
3			synagogue and house
4		sea (also way, wilderness, mountain)	
5			
6	Galilee (and foreign regions)		
7			
8			house
9			
10		way (also mountain, heaven/earth)	
11			
12	Judea (especially Jerusalem)		temple
13			
14			house, court-yard (flash-backs, flash-forwards to temple)
15	Galilee (flashbacks and flash-forwards)		
16			tomb

significance of power but to the significance of suffering. Thus 8:27 marks a major break at the topographical level. And yet intruding on the dominance of the way as a setting is one mountain setting, in the account of the transfiguration (9:2, 9); Jesus' mediation of heaven and earth, anticipated at his baptism and recapitulated in his eschatological discourse, peaks on this high mountain (9:2). Nevertheless, the way continues to set the pattern for this transitional mid-section of Mark's Gospel.[3] The mountain (of Olives) is featured again at chaps. 13 and 14, but the way is emphasized once more at 14:28 and, in closing, at 16:7. The geopolitical suborder suggests a major, and surprising, reversal in expectations; the topographical suborder suggests how such a reversal is possible—by following on the way. References to the way frame the Gospel and dominate its pivotal center section. Jesus is master on the sea, mediator on the mountain, and leader on the way.

The architectural suborder also presents a pivotal central focus and several key breaks. From 1:21 through 6:6, the synagogue and the house are interwoven as settings for teaching, healing, and controversy. But with the decisive break marked by the proverb at 6:4, the synagogue (and Jesus' private house) is left behind. From 6:10 through 10:16, the house is the architectural center of narrative action, absorbing, in some respects, the functions of the synagogue. At 11:11 the second major shift occurs, and attention focuses on the temple until 13:1; here the antagonism between Jesus and the religious establishment reaches its height. Several briefer architectural scenes, in a house (anointing at Bethany; Last Supper) or in a courtyard or palace (Jesus' trial and Peter's denial) or in the temple (splitting of the curtain), are followed by the final architectural setting, the tomb. But the tomb, like the architectural enclosures before it, fails to function in the expected way. Life surpasses the tomb as gathering and teaching surpass the synagogue, and prayer and praise surpass the temple.

The narrative breaks of the architectural suborder are decisive, its cadence clear: *synagogue/house/temple/tomb*. Its emphasis on a pivotal term, *house*, anticipates a similar emphasis at the topographical suborder (*way*). Thus the architectural shift from *synagogue* to *house* anticipates the topographical shift from *sea* to *way*, which is in turn echoed by the less subtle but more clear shift from Galilee to Judea. Within each suborder, the most positive element is emphatically placed in the diachronic arrangement. In the architectural suborder, dominance of the house is centered. In the topographical suborder, emphasis on the way is both central and framing. In the geopolitical suborder, culmination in Galilee is doubled. Thus the overturning of expectations, the opening up of new possibilities, the surprising presence of a new reality is a thrice-told tale in the spatial order of the Gospel of Mark. This diachronic pattern is heard as theme and variations in the integrated sequence of the geopolitical, topographical, and architectural suborders.

DOUBLE ENDING

In addition to these overarching patterns of the narrative as a whole, the Markan spatial sequence manifests a distinctive pattern in the final portion of the Gospel, chaps. 13–16. From the mountain (of Olives) Jesus foretells the passion of his later followers, the eschatological crises; the final spatial location given for these future followers is the mountains (13:14). And from the Mount of Olives Jesus goes to his own passion; the final spatial location given for Jesus is on the way to Galilee (16:7). As R. H. Lightfoot noticed some time ago, there are a number of parallels between chap. 13 and chaps. 14–15 of the Gospel of Mark.[4] As James M. Robinson has observed, chap. 13 "sets the frame of reference for understanding the passion narrative and the experience of the Church."[5] And as Norman Perrin and John Donahue have noted, chap. 13 and chaps. 14–16 form a double ending, the passion of the community (chap. 13) paralleling the passion of Jesus (chaps. 14–16).[6]

This double ending is signaled in the spatial order by the shift of setting from the temple to the Mount of Olives at chap. 13 and the shift back to the dominance of architectural enclosures at chaps. 14–16 (houses, the courtyard, the tomb). At the close of the passion of the community (chap. 13), Jesus says from the mountain, " 'And what I say to you I say to all: Watch.' " At the close of the passion of Jesus (chaps. 14–16), the young man says from the tomb, " 'He has risen, he is not here . . . . But go, tell his disciples and Peter that he is going before you to Galilee.' "

"Watch" (*grēgoreite*, from *grēgoreō*) and "risen" (*ēgerthē*, from *egeirō*) have a linguistic root in common and thus, perhaps, have some elements of meaning in common. *Grēgoreō* was a new formation in Hellenistic Greek from *egrēgora*, the perfect of *egeirō*;[7] their shared significance is "to be awake." Both the surprising experience of the empty tomb (chap. 16) and the surprising experience of the ruined temple (chap. 13), both the resurrection (chap. 16) and the parousia (chap. 13), call forth wakefulness from the followers of Jesus. Both the disciples whom Jesus is " 'going before . . . [on the way] to Galilee' " (16:7) and the later disciples who " 'flee to the mountains' " (13:14) are to be awake.[8]

SCHEMA

The mythic significance of the final spatial locations of both portions of the Markan double ending, the mountain(s) and the way, may be understood more clearly by turning from the diachronic structure of the Markan spatial order, its sequence, to its synchronic structure, its schema. A logical hierarchy of all the spatial designations included in the narrative lies behind the mythological schema presupposed by the Markan spatial order. This logical hierarchy integrates the three logical hierarchies of the three suborders. Presented as a "branching tree diagram," the spatial hierarchy is given in Figure 15. From the elements of the logical hierarchy are selected the ordered pairs of oppositions whose movement toward mediation defines the structure of the mythic narrative. This structure is outlined in the spatial schema, given in Figure 16. Denotative and connotative aspects are combined in the formation of the mythological schema. For example, the final three terms of the spatial schema (Figure 16), MOUNTAIN, TOMB, and WAY, are both connotatively rich in Mark's Gospel, based in part on their associations in the Jewish Scriptures, and denotatively strong as potential mediators, based on their positions in the logical hierarchy (Figure 15). In terms of the logical hierarchy, *mountain* is between *heaven* and *earth*, and *tomb* is between *outside* and *inside*; in addition, *way* (on the earth) may be thought of as between *mountain* (above the earth) and *tomb* (in the earth). In terms of the mythological schema, MOUNTAIN is a mediator of the first manifest opposi-

Figure 15 Spatial Hierarchy

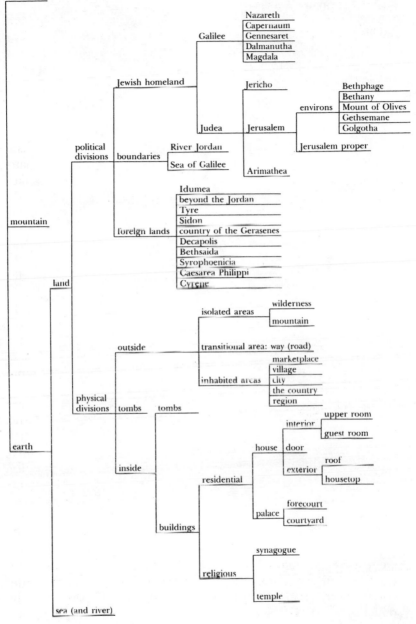

Figure 16   Spatial Schema

(order)

　heaven

　　land

　　　Jewish homeland

　　　　Galilee

　　　　　isolated areas

　　　　　　house

　　　　　　　environs of Jerusalem

　　　　　　　Mount of Olives

　　　　　　　tomb

　　　　　　　　way

　　　　　　　mountain

　　　　　　Temple

　　　　　　Jerusalem proper

　　　　　synagogue

　　　　　inhabited areas

　　　　Judea

　　　foreign lands

　　sea

　earth

(chaos)

tion, HEAVEN VS. EARTH (see Figure 8, showing the topographical schema), and WAY is the mediator of the final opposition of the spatial order, TOMB VS. MOUNTAIN (see Figure 16, showing the spatial schema). TOMB VS. MOUNTAIN represents another aspect of the integrated spacial schema: its oppositions may be formed

Figure 17   Fundamental Spatial Oppositions

SPATIAL	geopolitical	topographical	architectural
ORDER	familiar	promise	profane
vs.	vs.	vs.	vs.
CHAOS	strange	threat	sacred

of elements from different suborders. The two such oppositions of the spatial schema are its final two.

The initial two oppositions and the final mediator of the integrated spatial schema are topographical. Furthermore, the topographical schema (Figure 8), in isolation, presents two mediators, whereas neither the geopolitical schema (Figure 4) nor the architectural schema (Figure 12) presents a final mediator. Thus the geopolitical and architectural schemata are, as it were, fitted into the frame of the topographical schema, although changes are made in all the schemata in this process of integration. Perhaps the topographical frame stems from topography's more "cosmic" scale in relation to political geography or architecture; *heaven* and *earth*, or *heaven* and *earth* and *sea*, indicate "the whole universe" in the biblical tradition (see Figure 15).

The terms in parentheses in Figure 16 represent the non-manifest, fundamental opposition underlying the spatial order as a whole and may be related to the three fundamental oppositions underlying the three respective suborders as suggested in Figure 17. FAMILIAR vs. STRANGE (geopolitical suborder) and PROMISE vs. THREAT (topographical suborder) are expressed more "cosmically" as ORDER vs. CHAOS. What is threatening about the strange and strange about the threatening is their tendency toward chaos, their destruction of the security of order offered by the familiar and the promising. To link the strange and the threatening with chaos and the familiar and the promising with order is natural enough. The Markan presupposition that strange foreign lands and the threatening sea betoken chaos—as opposed to the order implied by the familiar Jewish homeland and the promise of the land itself—presents basic oppositions of the cultural code available to Mark (e.g., the Septuagint and first-century geopolitical realities in Palestine).

But when the opposition PROFANE vs. SACRED (architectural suborder) is placed within this framework in Mark (Figure 17), the expected values of the opposed terms are reversed. Mark's Gospel links SACRED with CHAOS and PROFANE with ORDER, challenging the assumption of established religion that the sacred functions to keep chaos at bay and maintain order in the world, both the human community and the cosmic universe.[9] Thus the spatial order of the Gospel of Mark both presents and challenges the expected oppositions, while moving toward their mediation at the mythic level.[10]

PRESENTING THE EXPECTED PATTERN OF OPPOSITION

For the most part, the spatial schema combines and orders the progressive oppositions of the schemata of the three suborders previously presented; in these cases summaries of the nature of each opposition will be abbreviated, stressing mainly how the opposition ORDER vs. CHAOS is manifest. This is the case with the first three narrative oppositions of the spatial schema, those pairs that present the expected pattern of opposition.

The Markan opposition HEAVEN vs. EARTH is rooted in the Jewish tradition. As creator, God ordered both heaven and earth into being from primeval chaos (Genesis 1). Thus, in the beginning, GOD, as ORDER, was in opposition to HEAVEN AND EARTH, as CHAOS. But, since heaven is traditionally considered God's dwelling place, the spatial location of the "orderer," heaven is linked with the pole of ORDER, and earth, the dwelling place of human beings who bring chaos upon God's creation (e.g., Genesis 3; 6:1–7), is linked with the opposing pole of CHAOS. As Hermann Sasse explains, "It is because the earth is the setting of a fallen creation, the theatre of sin, that it stands in a different relation to God from heaven."[11] As analysis of the topographical suborder suggested, the opposition HEAVEN vs. EARTH is mediated in Mark's Gospel spatially by MOUNTAIN and personally by Jesus. Yet, in an eschatological sense, the Markan narrative projects not the mediation of HEAVEN and EARTH, the basic poles of all spatial opposition, but their passing away, their being surpassed by the power of Jesus' words (13:31). Thus, in the end, JESUS' WORDS, as ORDER, will be in opposition to HEAVEN AND EARTH, as CHAOS. Until the end time, however, and within the

Markan spatial order, the fundamental opposition ORDER vs. CHAOS, initially given narrative expression as HEAVEN vs. EARTH, continues to move toward mediation.

The manifestation of the fundamental opposition ORDER vs. CHAOS is especially clear in the narrative opposition LAND vs. SEA. The Jewish Scriptures portray the sea as chaos that only the Lord can order. Mark accepts this connotation of the sea as chaos in opposition to the land as order. Yet mediation is manifest in the Gospel as Jesus functions in a "Lordly" role: crossing the sea as if it were a bridge and not a barrier, walking on the sea as if it were a road and not water, calming the sea by his word as if he were God, ordering the chaos.[12]

As ORDER is to CHAOS and LAND is to SEA, so is JEWISH HOME-LAND to FOREIGN LANDS. JEWISH HOMELAND (the place of residence of the central characters of the story) is related to FOREIGN LAND (a temporary place of travel for the central characters) as LAND (the familiar environment of human beings) is related to SEA (a temporary place of travel for human beings). FAMILIAR is to STRANGE as ORDER is to CHAOS. The lives of swine-keeping Gerasenes and the Syrophoenician women appear chaotic from the point of view of the Jewish life ordered by laws regulating not only worship and work but also daily food. Here again movement toward mediation is manifest in the actions of Jesus. Jesus miraculously feeds both Jews and Gentiles; he heals persons from foreign lands as well as those from Galilee and Judea; he journeys both within his home country and beyond it.

Thus the actions of Jesus (on the mountain, on the sea, in all regions) move the narrative toward mediation in regard to each of the first three narrative oppositions of the spatial schema. Furthermore, because both JEWISH HOMELAND and FOREIGN LANDS are LAND (as opposed to SEA), and both LAND and SEA are elements of EARTH (as opposed to HEAVEN), this section of the spatial schema clearly illustrates the movement toward mediation by successive opposition that Lévi-Strauss considers archetypical of myth. While assuming the cultural values that link HEAVEN, LAND, and JEWISH HOMELAND with ORDER— and EARTH, SEA, and FOREIGN LANDS with CHAOS—the Gospel of Mark systematically weakens the fundamental opposition ORDER vs. CHAOS.

CHALLENGING THE EXPECTED PATTERN OF OPPOSITION

Mediation of ORDER and CHAOS continues throughout the Markan spatial schema, but as GALILEE vs. JUDEA replaces JEWISH HOMELAND vs. FOREIGN LANDS, the Markan schema challenges the normative values of the terms of its narrative oppositions while mediating the fundamental opposition. Redaction criticism has long noted that the distinction between Galilee and Judea (or Jerusalem) is important in Mark; the present structural exegesis illustrates further that the contextual values of the terms of this distinction are pivotal for the Gospel. The Markan narrative, which manifests the traditional Jewish associations of SEA and FOREIGN LANDS with CHAOS and of LAND and JEWISH HOMELAND with ORDER, reverses the expected associations of GALILEE and JUDEA. Would not Judea, the region of Jerusalem—religious center of the Jewish people, home of the temple that ordered their worship and of the Tables of the Law that ordered their very lives—be expected to be the center of order?[13] And would not Galilee, in contradistinction to the home of the religious establishment—Galilee surrounded by foreign lands and their influence—be anticipated as a manifestation of chaos?

But in the Markan Gospel, Galilee, Jesus' homeland within the Jewish homeland, is the center of order. Wherever he journeys— to the Jordan to be baptized, to Tyre and Sidon to heal, to Jerusalem to be crucified—the Markan Jesus always returns to Galilee. Galilee forms a framework for the narrative action, ordering movements in space. In controversy with the leaders and representatives of the supposed religious order centralized in Judea, Jesus calls the established religious order into question.[14] A new and authentic order is both demanded and proclaimed by Jesus of Nazareth in Galilee; to Jesus the old order is as chaos. Chaos breaks loose when Jesus arrives in Jerusalem in Judea. The chaos of the trial, in which the Markan chief priests and elders appear to ignore their own required order, leads to the chaos of the crucifixion, complete with darkness when there should be light and the rending of the temple curtain, which makes chaos of the rigid demarcation of the sacred and profane within the religious structure. Thus JUDEA is linked with the

CHAOS pole of the fundamental opposition, and GALILEE with ORDER.

At the level of the opposition GALILEE vs. JUDEA, movement toward the mediation of ORDER and CHAOS is implied in the Markan exchange of connotations between the two regions. When Galilee (supposedly chaotic) connotes a new order, and Judea (supposedly orderly) represents chaos, the fundamental opposition is weakened. A similar movement toward mediation by the exchange of connotations or functions continues throughout the five succeeding oppositions.

The succeeding oppositions illustrate as well Mark's challenge of normative expectations with regard to the associations of OR-DER and CHAOS. Presumably, isolated areas might be associated with the dangers of hunger and thirst and attacks by wild animals and thus with chaos, and inhabited areas associated with the safety of home and family and thus with order. But the wild beasts of the wilderness, which should be dangerous (e.g., Isaiah 34:11), are peaceful in the Markan wilderness (1:13; cf. Isaiah 11:6–8). The Markan wilderness is a place of testing (1:13), but also a place of miraculous nourishment (6:35–44.; 8:4), as was the wilderness in which the Jewish people wandered for forty years. Thus the Markan Gospel reflects the twofold, paradoxical wilderness tradition of the Hebrew Scriptures, but accents the pole of ORDER over against CHAOS.[15]

The paradoxical tradition of the wilderness marks a movement toward mediation—the chaos of the wilderness promises a new or renewed order—and this movement toward mediation is carried further in Mark's gospel. Jesus' withdrawal to the wilderness to pray (1:35) seems to be a movement away from the clamor (CHAOS) of "the whole city [which] was gathered together about the door" (1:32) to a time and place of calm reflection (ORDER). Yet Jesus continues "on to the next towns" (1:38); ORDER overtakes CHAOS. Again, when the word about Jesus spreads throughout the inhabited areas, creating such a commotion (CHAOS) that Jesus can no longer openly go there, Jesus withdraws to the wilderness (ORDER). Yet, in what seems a movement toward mediation, the inhabitants come to Jesus in the wilderness (1:45; cf. 6:31–34); CHAOS comes to ORDER.

In the spatial opposition HOUSE vs. SYNAGOGUE, the expected connotations are more distinct and Mark's reversal of them more clear. A synagogue is an enclosed religious or sacred space, a house a common or profane one. Following the reasoning given above concerning Judea, the synagogue would traditionally be considered a center of order, a focal point of the regulated life of the community.[16] Markan synagogues, however, are centers of controversy, manifestations of chaos. Jesus is free to preach or teach in synagogues, but he is not a synagogue leader, and his house and the houses of his friends must serve as his base of operations, his center of order. Jesus teaches and heals in houses as he does in synagogues, but his teaching in a house is usually directed to his disciples, the core members of the new order of life he demands and proclaims. The raising of Jairus' daughter may suggest movement toward mediation within the HOUSE vs. SYNAGOGUE opposition, for the scene of this most dramatic "healing" is the house (ORDER) of the ruler of the synagogue (CHAOS). As Jesus approaches the house he sees "a tumult, and the people weeping and wailing loudly" (5:38), that is, chaos; but Jesus raises the girl, giving to her new life and reordering the lives of her parents.

The surprising Markan pattern, PROFANE is to SACRED as ORDER is to CHAOS, reappears in the spatial opposition ENVIRONS OF JERUSALEM vs. JERUSALEM PROPER. As we have seen, Jerusalem, which should be *the* center of order, is instead a center of chaos, of false accusation, of death.[17] Jesus makes his way to Jerusalem, but he makes his stay in Bethany, in the *house* of Simon the leper (14:3)—an overlap of geopolitical and architectural oppositions. Jesus enters Jerusalem in the morning and returns to Bethany in the evening; Jesus meets privately with his disciples on the Mount of Olives, including Gethsemane; and even his death takes place outside Jerusalem, at Golgotha. Jerusalem is the power base of the opposition of Jesus. Jesus' power has another base, both spatially and theologically. Jesus' round trips from Bethany to Jerusalem serve as the spatial frame for the cursing of the fig tree, generally recognized as a metaphor for the chaotic fall of Jerusalem and/or the destruction of the temple. The traditional view projects chaos as a result of the fall of Jerusalem while continuing to link order with Jerusalem it-

self.[18] The Markan Gospel, however, suggests that the chaos of
the fall of Jerusalem is archetypical of Jerusalem itself. The Markan Jesus, as the representative of the new order he proclaims,
stands over against Jerusalem, over against the temple, over
against the religious establishment. Movement toward mediation
is suggested by the Markan exchange of functions or connotations between the supposedly ordered Jerusalem and its supposedly chaotic environs; as the new order of Bethany and the
Mount of Olives, of Gethsemane and Golgotha, is set forth, the
old order of Jerusalem dissolves into chaos.

This pattern is intensified in the schematic opposition MOUNT
OF OLIVES VS. TEMPLE.[19] This opposition of a topographical/geo-
political space and an architectural one is more explicitly stated
in the Gospel of Mark than any other spatial opposition. The
two locations mark the boundaries of a significant entrance and
exit of the Markan Jesus: from the Mount of Olives (11:1) Jesus
makes his initial entry into Jerusalem and into the temple
(11:11); to the Mount of Olives (13:3) outside Jerusalem, Jesus
makes his final exit from the temple (13:1). It is as if the movements of the Markan Jesus shadow the movements of "the Lord"
in the vision of Ezekiel: "And the glory of the Lord went up
from the midst of the city [i.e., the temple], and stood upon the
mountain which is on the east side of the city [i.e., the Mount
of Olives]" (Ezekiel 11:23). But, whereas "the Lord's" departure
from the temple is followed, in Ezekiel's vision, by oracles of both
doom and hope, by a vision of a new temple, and by "the Lord's"
return to the temple (Ezekiel 43:4), Jesus' departure from the
temple is followed, in Mark's Gospel, by Jesus' prophecy of the
temple's destruction and by his eschatological discourse.[20]

Jesus sits "on the Mount of Olives opposite the temple" (13:3)
as he delivers his eschatological discourse in response to his disciples' questions concerning the time and the sign of the coming
destruction of the temple and of Jerusalem.[21] As Jerusalem is
the seat of the religious authority of the chief priests, scribes,
and elders (old order, Markan CHAOS), so the Mount of Olives
is the seat of authoritative teaching of Jesus (new order, Markan
ORDER). As a mountain, the Mount of Olives shares in the general biblical connotation of a mountain as a place of divine revelation. But the Mount of Olives also bears a unique significance.

According to Zechariah 14:4, the Mount of Olives is the destined place of the initiation of the end of the age, the apocolyptic judgment, the day of the Lord. At the Mount of Olives the new order is to break in, turning the old order of the temple to chaos. At the Mount of Olives, after the Last Supper, Jesus tells his disciples, " 'I will go before you to Galilee' " (14:28), and warns Peter of his coming denial. Thus, in his teaching from the Mount of Olives, Jesus anticipates both the eschatological end and its destruction and his personal end, his death, bringing into conjunction these two instances of the conflict of CHAOS and ORDER being overcome in a new order.

In addition to being opposed on the basis of the fundamental opposition ORDER vs. CHAOS, the Mount of Olives and the temple as spatial locations are opposed in a physical way. The relevant phrase in 13:3 is, according to Robert Bratcher and Eugene Nida, "translatable" as "the Mount of Olives 'on the opposite side of the ravine from the temple.' "[22] Thus the Mount of Olives and the temple mount are two opposed high points. The Mount of Olives is a completely natural, that is, God-made, mountain, whereas the temple, although on a natural rise, is, in a sense, a constructed or human-made mountain. Furthermore, the Mount of Olives is higher than the temple mount.[23] According to Hebrew prophecy, however, this situation is to be reversed at the end time, either by the lowering of the Mount of Olives or by the raising of the temple mount. Zechariah 14:4 suggests that the Mount of Olives will be "split in two . . . so that one half of the Mount shall withdraw northward, and the other half southward," thus lowering the mount that overtops the temple mount.[24] An oracle given in both Isaiah 2:2 and Micah 4:1 projects that "the mountain of the house of the Lord shall be established as the highest of the mountains, and shall be raised (up) above the hills . . . ." In proclaiming the future destruction of the temple from a position on the Mount of Olives, the Markan Jesus reverses these prophetic expectations as these prophetic expectations reverse physical reality.

The final opposition of the spatial schema, TOMB vs. MOUNTAIN, also has a significant physical dimension. Whereas a mountain is a high point above the general surface of the earth, a tomb is a low point below (or within) the surface of the earth.

A tomb is "hewn out of the rock" (15:46) of which a mountain may be formed. TOMB (architectural) vs. MOUNTAIN (topographical) is the second opposition (following MOUNT OF OLIVES vs. TEMPLE) formed by terms from different suborders. From the opposition of GALILEE and JUDEA through the opposition of TOMB and MOUNTAIN, the traditional associations of ORDER and CHAOS have been challenged by the Markan narrative, while movement toward mediation has been made by the exchange of connotations. Here at the close of the process of mediation, the connotations of TOMB and MOUNTAIN as representative of ORDER and CHAOS are remarkably intertwined.

In the biblical tradition a mountain is the traditional setting for a solemn divine act. The Markan Jesus' appointment of the twelve on a mountain (3:13), as well as their number, connects the establishment of the New Israel with the foundation of the old Israel at Mount Sinai (Exodus 19). A mountain is the setting for God's communication with his prophets, such as Elijah on Mount Horeb (1 Kings 19). At the Mount of Olives Jesus prophesies events that will soon come to pass: the "falling away" of the disciples, Peter's denial, his own death and resurrection, the coming of the Son of man. But most importantly, the mountain, between heaven and earth, is the traditional setting for divine revelation and for authoritative teaching: the revelation at the burning bush, the Ten Commandments, the words from the cloud at the transfiguration, Jesus' eschatological discourse. On a mountain—and among tombs—the Markan Jesus exorcises the Gerasene demoniac and is recognized as the "Son of the Most High God." And on a mountain Jesus prays alone before revealing himself to his disciples (on the sea) in the words of God to Moses from the burning bush: "I am." Thus a mountain is a center of divine order, although divine revelation may be overwhelming (chaotic) for its human witnesses; neither Moses before the burning bush nor Peter before the transfigured Jesus (9:6) knows how to respond; those who " 'flee to the mountains' " (13:14) anticipate a new order amid the chaos of the end time. But the order represented by the mountain(s) in Mark is a new order, an order that prevails after the old order has dissolved into chaos. The new order of the mountain replaces the old order (CHAOS) of the temple, of Jerusalem, of the synagogue. Thus

MOUNTAIN replaces the CHAOS pole of the fundamental spatial opposition rather than representing it; mediation is almost complete.

TOMB, on the other hand, in terms of the traditional associations available to Mark, appears to represent CHAOS. As the entrance to Sheol, the tomb is the beginning of nothingness, a void; perhaps it is a chaotic void like the primeval void before God's creation of the world. But even greater chaos is manifested at the tomb of the Markan Jesus. The stone has been rolled back; the corpse is no longer there. The women at the empty tomb are afraid—filled with awe—at Jesus' words reported by the young man, just as the men on the sea were afraid—filled with awe—at Jesus' words (4:41). But out of the chaos of the waves and out of the chaos of the grave, a new order comes. As is suggested in the saying of the young man at the tomb (" 'he is going before you to Galilee; there you will see him,' " 16:7), resurrection is a metaphor of a new order. Thus the tomb—the empty tomb—destroys the CHAOS pole of the fundamental spatial opposition and manifests ORDER; the process of mediation is nearing its end.

The Gospel of Mark has, as it were, a double ending, the passion of Jesus (chaps. 14–16) and the passion of the community (chap. 13). In the one ending, women flee from the tomb (16:8), and in the other " 'those who are in Judea [are warned to] flee to the mountains' " (13:14). In the Markan context the mountains suggest revelation, new order, in the midst of chaos, just as the shattering of the chaos of the tomb offers revelation, the new order of resurrection. The experience of the dramatic mediation of CHAOS and ORDER pointed to in the resurrection story (chap. 16) is proleptic of a similar experience pointed to in the parousia prophecy (chap. 13). The response to the chaos of Jesus' death (chap. 16) points the way for the response to the chaos of the temple's destruction (chap. 13). ORDER vs. CHAOS is, at last, mediated by a new order, and the new order is less a set of boundaries and more a direction.

The locations of the Markan Jesus' last two messages to his followers are the mountain (of Olives) and the tomb, and the common element of these messages (14:28; 16:7) points to the way, to going before. If one were to associate chaos with random movement and order with stasis, then purposeful movement would suggest their mediation and being "on the way" would represent it. The final mediator of the spatial order of the Gospel of Mark, the WAY (or road), signals not so much another place, as a way between places, a dynamic process of movement. Jesus moves from the Mount of Olives to the temple, from the environs of Jerusalem to Jerusalem proper, from Galilee to Judea on a road. Between inhabited areas a road may pass through isolated areas. Within a city or a village a road may connect house and synagogue. Jesus journeys to foreign lands by road and by sea, but the sea becomes for him as a road, for he walks on it. But, most of all, Jesus is on the move. He does not remain in one locale but travels widely. He has no place to call his own, and even his tomb is borrowed. Jesus' movements are neither static (ORDER) nor random (CHAOS) but purposeful (mediation).

The specific Markan references to the way (hodos and proagein) sharpen this image of the mediation of CHAOS and ORDER. The spatial order of the Gospel of Mark, which closes with an implication of the way, opens with an explicit biblical quotation of the term: " 'Prepare the way of the Lord' " (1:3). But the way Jesus travels is not an easy one to follow. Its demands are strict: no bread, no bag, no money (6:8). Peter confesses Jesus as "the Christ" on the way to Caesarea Philippi, but the disciples discuss who among them is greatest on the way to Capernaum. Jesus takes the difficult way up to Jerusalem, and from Jericho Bartimaeus follows him on the way. At the tomb the women who have followed Jesus to the end are told to " 'tell his disciples and Peter that he is going before you to Galilee' " (16:7), that is, he is on the way.

It is interesting to note, as Wilhelm Michaelis has, that "in the LXX [as against Philo] the metaphor of the way is not controlled by a goal which man should seek and to which he may attain. The metaphor presupposes that the command of God stands at the beginning of the way."[25] If Mark's Gospel, which often exhibits familiarity with Septuagint usage, parallels it at this point, the followers of Jesus are oriented not to Galilee, the end point of the way, but to the beginning point, Jesus. In this is the mediation, the transformation: Jesus "who was crucified" is going to Galilee before them, going where they must go—home—to begin life anew, to reorder the chaos. As those who followed Jesus "on the road" to Jerusalem were amazed and afraid (10:32), so too those who will follow him on the road from Jerusalem to Galilee are amazed and afraid.

A full discussion of the significance of "fear" in the Markan Gospel is beyond the scope of the present study, but one must at least raise the question of whether James M. Robinson's opposition of faith and fear is oversimplified for the Markan Gospel.[26] Certainly, as Robinson insists, fear or awe is not the Markan "ideal of piety," but it does seem to be part of the reality of Christian faith and experience in the Markan understanding. John Donahue's interpretation seems true to the text:

> Mark's own theology of fear and wonder comes out especially in the resurrection account (16:5, 8) and in the jarring ending to the Gospel, "for they were afraid." This motif which throughout the Gospel establishes rapport with the reader and which dictates how the reader should respond to Jesus, now becomes a symbolic reaction to the whole Gospel. Mark's reader is left, not with the assurance of resurrection vision, but simply with numinous fear in the presence of divine promise. These reactions of wonder and surprise accompany the revelation of God in Jesus, and they signify the power of this revelation to unsettle and change human existence.[27]

Amazement and fear are not signs of withdrawal but signs of engagement in the Gospel of Mark, signs of being "on the way."

"On the way," suggested at 16:7 by *proagei*, is, finally, the key mediator of the various Markan manifestations of the fundamental opposition ORDER vs. CHAOS. Redaction critics and New Testament historians have commented on the situation of the Markan community in terms that suggest its very real experience of the conflict of chaos and order. A Lévi-Straussian analysis of Mark suggests that such a conflict is fundamental in scope and mythic in presentation. The opposition is mediated, according to Mark's Gospel, by following the way of Jesus, who, as the Pharisees and Herodians ironically note (12:14), truly teaches the way of God. The way will not be easy or without fear, but "he is going before." *Hodos* is more an action than a place. The mediation made possible by Jesus' actions must be confirmed by the actions of Jesus' followers. For Mark's Gospel, the final movement toward mediation means not an end to movement, but a new meaning for movement.[28]

Perhaps the analytical procedure of, initially, eliminating met-aphorical uses of spatial terms from the spatial sequence and, finally, considering what is in effect the metaphorical dimension of the spatial schema seems self-contradictory. But the contra-diction is only a seeming one; the procedure is paradoxical. The final concern is not with individual words or phrases that may function metaphorically here or there, but with the nonmanifest significance of an entire *system* of spatial relations. If the spatial designation *way* has an overall metaphorical dimension, it is be-cause of its relative position among other spatial designations.

The tension manifest schematically by WAY is expressed se-quentially by the final, complex (topographical/geopolitical) re-lation: going before to Galilee. Being on the way is not static but dynamic. Galilee represents not a mediator but a turning point in the reversal of expectations. Life in Galilee, though filled with experiences of a new power, was not without its problems for Jesus and his followers. As W. D. Davies has concluded:

Not for [Matthew] nor for Mark was Galilee *terra Christiana*; it was no Messianic holy land in either Gospel. Failure as well as success marked the Galilean ministry from the start. That failure knew no geographic boundaries. There is no Galilean idyll for Jesus in Mark or Matthew. For them both, Galilee found much to object to in Jesus, as he found much to condemn in it. Lohmeyer and Lightfoot too easily overlooked the fact that even when the Galileans "understood" Jesus they misun-derstood him; for this reason, at the very height of his popularity there, Jesus found that he had to escape from Galilee.[29]

Thus, to be on the way to Galilee is not to escape the challenges of life but to risk involvement in the paradox of power and suf-fering. It is no wonder those who stand at the beginning of this way, whether the Markan women at the empty tomb or the Mar-kan readers, are amazed and afraid. Mediation of ORDER and CHAOS is not made easy by Jesus who was crucified and is on the way to Galilee—just possible.

The Markan Jesus has an affinity for the space between —the way (between isolated areas and inhabited areas), the mountain (between heaven and earth), the Sea of Galilee (between the Jew-ish homeland and foreign lands), the tomb (between outside and inside). The door is also a space between—between interior and exterior (see the spatial hierarchy, in Figure 15). One is thus led to compare the spatial image of Jesus "on the way" (that is, "going before") at 16:7 and the spatial metaphor of the Son of man "at the door" (*RSV* "gates") at 13:29.[30] The two images are given in the double ending of Mark. The Markan passion of Jesus (chaps. 14–16) closes spatially on the way to Galilee (16:7); the Markan passion of the community (chap. 13) closes metaphorically on the watch at the door (13:37). Watching is to seeing as being on the way is to arriving; the watching and the way are climactic in Mark's Gospel. The tension of the Markan ending reflects the tension of the Good News according to Mark: conflict between the chaos and order of life is overcome not in arriving, but in being on the way.

Notes to the Preface

1. A number of books and articles on Mark that have, in at least one aspect, a direct bearing on Markan narrative space are referred to in the notes. References are made throughout to three "standard" English-language commentaries: D. E. Nineham, *The Gospel of St. Mark* (Pelican New Testament Commentaries; Baltimore: Penguin, 1963); Vincent Taylor, *The Gospel According to St. Mark* (London: Macmillan, 1955; New York: St. Martin's, 1955); Eduard Schweizer, *The Good News According to Mark* (Atlanta: John Knox, 1970).
2. Within the field of religion, the foundational work on the concept of space has been done by Mircea Eliade, whose book *The Sacred and the Profane: The Nature of Religion* (New York: Harcourt, Brace, 1959) offers the best starting point. Chapters 4–8 of Jonathan Z. Smith's *Map Is Not Territory: Studies in the History of Religions* (Leiden: Brill, 1978) are an important second step, as they concern "the adequacy of the description of sacred space as developed within the general History of Religions represented, preeminently, by the writings of Mircea Eliade" (pp. xi–xii). Concerning "space" (or "setting") within literary texts, see Gaston Bachelard, *The Poetics of Space* (New York: Orion, 1964); Seymour Chatman, *Story and Discourse: Narrative Structure in Fiction and Film* (Ithaca: Cornell University, 1978) 138–45; and Wesley Kort, *Narrative Elements and Religious Meanings* (Philadelphia: Fortress, 1975) 20–39.
3. For my description and evaluation of the various goals and foci of structuralism, see " 'No Need to Have Any One Write'?: A Structural Exegesis of 1 Thessalonians," *Semeia* 26 (1983) 57–83, esp. 72–78; see also my "Structuralism, Hermeneutics, and Contextual Meaning," *JAAR* 51 (1983) 207–30, and the literature cited there. Three additional points of entry into the world of structuralism are Daniel Patte's *What is Structural Exegesis?* (Guides to Biblical Scholarship, New Testament Series; Philadelphia: Fortress, 1976), various issues of *Semeia* (esp. 1, 2, 3, 6, 9, 10, 15, 16, 18, 26, 29), and several monographs in the Pittsburgh Theological Monographs series of Pickwick Press.
4. The works of Lohmeyer, Lightfoot, Marxsen, and Kelber in relation to Galilee and Jerusalem in Mark, the works of Mauser and Heil in relation to the wilderness and the sea in Mark, and the works of Donahue and Juel in relation to the temple and the house in Mark (among others) are cited in Chapters 2, 3, and 4.
5. Two important structural exegeses of Mark are Dan O. Via, Jr., *Kerygma and Comedy in the New Testament: A Structuralist Approach to Hermeneutic* (Philadelphia: Fortress, 1975) and Daniel Patte and Aline Patte, *Structural Exegesis: From Theory to Practice* (Philadelphia: Fortress, 1978). Structural exegeses of aspects or portions of Mark are included in Xavier Léon-Dufour et al., *Les Miracles de Jésus selon le Nouveau Testament* (Paris: Editions du Seuil, 1977) 213–26 (regarding miracles in Mark), and The Entrevernes Group, *Signs and Parables: Semiotics and Gospel Texts* (Pittsburgh: Pickwick, 1978) 65–115 (regarding Mark 6:30–53).
6. Louis Marin, in the first of two studies making up *The Semiotics of the Passion*

Narrative: Topics and Figures (Pittsburgh: Pickwick, 1980) presents a structural analysis of the narrative space of the passion narrative—in its four canonical "variants"—by a close examination of the toponyms, the proper place names, of the texts. Marin's work presupposes familiarity with the theoretical models of Algirdas J. Greimas. Also dependent upon Greimas is Edward John McMahon's study, "The Death and Resurrection of Jesus in Luke 23:26–24:53: A Greimasian Analysis" (Ph.D diss., Vanderbilt University, 1984). McMahon argues that "Luke's system of convictions here is organized by a spatial pattern which divides persons, places, and things into a /human/ and an /outside of society/ realm, each subdivided into several spheres" (quotation from abstract).

7. Because it deals with all four canonical gospels, Marin's *Semiotics of the Passion Narrative* necessarily discusses narrative space in the passion narrative of Mark. Marin's conclusions, however, are frequently based on his own "harmony" of the gospels and are thus of limited use in the present context. Marin does offer occasional comments on one of the four "variants," but rarely on Mark. The only structural exegesis of narrative space in the Markan Gospel as a whole that is known to me is Bas van Iersel, "Locality, Structure, and Meaning in Mark," *Linguistica Biblica* 53 (1983) 45–54. For a comment on this brief study see note 1 to Chapter 5.

8. See the discussion by Patte and Patte of "hermeneutic" (not exegesis) as a "prolongation of the semantic universe of the text" and their insistence that "*a hermeneutic can be viewed as legitimate only when it respects the integrity of the text's semantic universe*" (*Structural Exegesis*, 94–112; quotation from 100).

9. Willi Marxsen, *Mark the Evangelist: Studies on the Redaction History of the Gospel* (Nashville and New York: Abingdon, 1969) 208–209. I would, however, heartily disagree with what Marxsen makes of this "conclusive inconclusiveness": "The orientation to Galilee and the imminent Parousia awaited there provide the motive for the Gospel's formation" (p. 209). See Chapters 2 and 5.

Notes to Chapter 1

1. Unless otherwise stated, all biblical quotations presented in English are from the Revised Standard Version (*RSV*) of the Bible, copyright 1952, 1946, 1971, by the Division of Christian Education of the National Council of the Churches of Christ in the United States of America. All textual analysis is based on the Greek text of the Gospel of Mark, relying on *The Greek New Testament* (ed. Kurt Aland et al.; 3rd ed.; United Bible Societies, 1975).

2. E.g., Gustaf Dalman, *Sacred Sites and Ways: Studies in the Topography of the Gospels* (London: Society for Promoting Christian Knowledge, 1935; New York: Macmillan, 1935).

3. E.g., relevant articles in the *Theological Dictionary of the New Testament* (10 vols.; Grand Rapids: Eerdmans, 1946–76); and *The Interpreter's Dictionary of the Bible* (5 vols.; Nashville: Abingdon, vols. 1–4, 1962; supp., 1976).

4. E.g., D. E. Nineham, *The Gospel of St. Mark* (Pelican New Testament Commentaries; Baltimore: Penguin, 1963) 180–81, 186, 263; and Eduard Schweizer, *The Good News According to Mark* (Atlanta: John Knox, 1970) 113, 142, 154.

5. E.g., Willi Marxsen, *Mark the Evangelist: Studies on the Redaction History of the Gospel* (Nashville and New York: Abingdon, 1969) 30–53; and Ulrich Mauser, *Christ in the Wilderness: The Wilderness Theme in the Second Gospel and its Basis in the Biblical Tradition* (Naperville, IL: Alec R. Allenson, 1963).

6. Here the influence of Lohmeyer may be traced through Lightfoot and Marxsen to Kelber. See the following: Ernst Lohmeyer, *Galiläa und Jerusalem* (Forschungen zur Religion und Literatur des Alten und Neuen Testaments 34; Göttingen: Vandenhoeck und Ruprecht, 1936). Robert Henry Lightfoot, *Locality and Doctrine in the Gospels* (New York and London: Harper, [1938]). Marxsen, *Evangelist*, 54–116. Werner H. Kelber, *The Kingdom in Mark: A New Place and a New Time* (Philadelphia: Fortress, 1974). For a critique of Lohmeyer, Lightfoot, Marxsen, and Kelber from a literary rather than historical point of view, see my "Galilee and Jerusalem: History and Literature in Marcan Interpretation," *CBQ* 44 (1982) 242–55.

7. In addition to Lohmeyer, Lightfoot, Marxsen, and Kelber on Galilee and Jerusalem, see Günter Stemberger ("Galilee—Land of Salvation?," appendix IV in *The Gospel and the Land: Early Christianity and Jewish Territorial Doctrine*, by W. D. Davies [Berkeley: University of California, 1974]) on the "Galilee hypothesis"; Mauser on the wilderness; Davies (*The Gospel and the Land*, 221–43) on Mark as a whole; Jean Calloud ("Toward a Structural Analysis of the Gospel of Mark," *Semeia* 16 [1979] 131–65) on Mark 2; and Louis Marin (*The Semiotics of the Passion Narrative: Topics and Figures* [Pittsburgh: Pickwick, 1980]) on the proper place names in the passion narratives of the gospels.

8. In a context broader than Markan studies, Edward McMahon argues for "Making Room for Space in Structuralist Exegesis" (paper presented at the annual meeting of the Society of Biblical Literature, Chicago, December 1984). As McMahon notes:

Because "space" has not been thematized as a subject for independent treatment by either literary critics or structuralist critics, it is necessary to see how space has been treated in relation to some other subject if we wish to do an archaeology of the dimension of the text. Therefore we shall see in turn how space has been treated in relationship to the codes of the narrative (Barthes) and the characters present in the text (Marin); in relationship to the problem of point of view (Uspensky, Petersen); as occurring at both the levels of narrating and narrated (Chatman, Prince, Phillips); and in organic relationship to the temporal network of the text (Bakhtin). (P. 2)

McMahon's survey concludes with a presentation of "the model proposed by Claude Lévi-Strauss which takes directly into consideration the place of space in narrative" (p. 2) and with a reference to my article "Galilee and Jerusalem." The other works McMahon refers to include: Roland Barthes, *S/Z* (New York: Hill and Wang, 1974); Marin, *Semiotics of the Passion Narrative;* Boris Uspensky, *A Poetics of Composition* (Berkeley: University of California, 1983); Norman R. Petersen, " 'Point of View' in Mark's Narrative," *Semeia* 12 (1978) 97–122; Seymour Chatman, *Story and Discourse: Narrative Structure in Fiction and Film* (Ithaca: Cornell University, 1978); Gerald Prince, *Narratology: The Form and Functioning of Narrative* (Berlin: Mouton, 1982); Gary Phillips, " 'This is a Hard Saying. Who Can Be Listener to It?': Creating a Reader in John 6," *Semeia* 26 (1983) 23–56; Mikhail Bakhtin, *The Dialogic Imagination* (Austin: University of Texas, 1981) 84–258.

9. For an excellent introduction to Mark as a literary work, as a narrative, see David Rhoads and Donald Michie, *Mark as Story: An Introduction to the Narrative of a Gospel* (Philadelphia: Fortress, 1982). This work was published after my spatial analysis was completed, but there is considerable agreement between my analysis and the conclusions reached by Rhoads and Michie—as far, that is, as their ten-page overview of the "The Settings" (63–72) goes.

10. Lévi-Strauss's most extensive application of his method of myth analysis appears in the four volumes of *Mythologiques,* translated as *Introduction to a Science of Mythology* (4 vols.; vol. 1: *The Raw and the Cooked;* vol. 2: *From Honey to Ashes;* vol. 3: *The Origin of Table Manners;* vol. 4: *The Naked Man;* New York: Harper & Row, 1969–81). However, Lévi-Strauss's most explicit explanations of his methodology occur in "The Structural Study of Myth" (*Journal of American Folklore* 68 [1955] 428–44) and "The Story of Asdiwal" (trans. Nicholas Mann, in *The Structural Study of Myth and Totemism* [ed. Edmund Leach; Association of Social Anthropologists Monographs 5; London: Tavistock, 1967] 1–47).

11. Daniel Patte, "Structural Network in Narrative: The Good Samaritan," *Soundings* 58 (1975) 221–42; quotation from 231.

12. Edmund Leach, "Genesis as Myth," in *Genesis as Myth and Other Essays* (London: Jonathan Cape, 1969) 7–23; and idem, "Lévi-Strauss in the Garden of Eden: An Examination of Some Recent Developments in the Analysis of Myth," in *Claude Lévi-Strauss: The Anthropologist as Hero* (ed. E. Nelson Hayes and Tanya Hayes; Cambridge: M.I.T., 1970) 47–60.

13. Robert M. Polzin, *Biblical Structuralism: Method and Subjectivity in the Study of Ancient Texts* (Semeia Supplements; Philadelphia: Fortress, 1977; Missoula: Scholars, 1977) 54–125.

14. D. Patte, "Structural Network"; idem, "Structural Analysis of the Parable of the Prodigal Son: Toward a Method," in *Semiology and Parables* (ed. Daniel Patte; Pittsburgh Theological Monograph Series 9; Pittsburgh: Pickwick,

1976) 71–149; see 119–42. Bernard B. Scott, "The Prodigal Son: A Structuralist Interpretation," *Semeia* 9 (1977) 45–73.

15. Marin, *Semiotics of the Passion Narrative*, 101–103, 173–74.

16. Daniel Patte, *What Is Structural Exegesis?* (Guides to Biblical Scholarship, New Testament Series; Philadelphia: Fortress, 1976) 59–76. Elizabeth Struthers Malbon, " 'No Need to Have Any One Write'?: A Structural Exegesis of 1 Thessalonians," *Semeia* 26 (1983) 57–83.

17. Norman Perrin, *The New Testament: An Introduction* (New York: Harcourt Brace Jovanovich, 1974) 26–34. Cf. G. B. Caird, *The Language and Imagery of the Bible* (Philadelphia: Westminster, 1980) 219–42. Caird describes myth (and eschatology) as "metaphor systems for the theological interpretation of historical events" (p. 219) and explains how Paul, in his letters, "is using mythical language . . . to interpret the historic event of the cross. . . . [and] also using history to reinterpret the myth" (p. 242).

18. On the limits of the application of "the methods and procedures of structural analysis (which have been scientifically proven on myths) to the biblical text and especially to the New Testament text," see Louis Marin, "A Conclusion," in *The New Testament and Structuralism* (ed. Alfred M Johnson, Jr.; Pittsburgh: Pickwick, 1976) 241–45; quotation from 241. Paul Ricoeur takes specific exception to the applicability of Lévi-Strauss's methodology—founded on analysis of myths—to biblical materials—since Judaism and Christianity emphasize history; see, e.g., two of Ricoeur's essays in *The Conflict of Interpretations: Essays in Hermeneutics* (ed. Don Ihde; Evanston: Northwestern University, 1974), "Structure and Hermeneutics" (27–61) and "Structure, Word, Event" (79–96). See also my essay "The Text and Time: Lévi-Strauss and New Testament Studies," in *Anthropology and the Study of Religion* (ed. Robert L. Moore and Frank E. Reynolds; Chicago: Center for the Scientific Study of Religion, 1984) 177–91, esp. 185–86, in which I discuss the dialogue between Ricoeur and Lévi-Strauss published as "A Confrontation" in *New Left Review* 62 (1970) 57–74 (an English translation of "Réponses a quelques questions," *Esprit* 31 [1963] 628–53).

The complex problem of defining "myth" is beyond the scope of the present study. For a summary discussion of the problem in relation to biblical materials—and bibliographical references—see Caird, *Language and Imagery*, 219–42; and Brevard S. Childs, *Myth and Reality in the Old Testament* (London: SCM, 1962) 13–21. Childs's basic "phenomenological definition" of myth—that myth is an expression of human understanding of reality (p. 17)—is assumed here. But the general attitude toward myth assumed in the present study is more atune with that sounding throughout a number of the essays in *Myth, Symbol, and Reality*, edited by Alan M. Olson (Notre Dame and London: University of Notre Dame, 1980); see the essays by H. Mason, B. J. F. Lonergan, J. Waardenburg, and H. H. Oliver. On the problem of the definition (and valuation) of myth and mythology, see also Marcel Detiene, "Rethinking Mythology," in *Between Belief and Transgression: Structuralist Essays in Religion, History, and Myth* (ed. Michel Izard and Pierre Smith; Chicago and London: University of Chicago, 1982) 43–52.

19. Lévi-Strauss, "Asdiwal," 17.

20. Lévi-Strauss, "Structural Study," 432.

21. In terms of my typology of structuralist goals, presented in "Structuralism, Hermeneutics, and Contextual Meaning" (*JAAR* 51 [1983] 207–30), analysis is not a terminal goal. Lévi-Strauss moves through analysis to theory and to ideology, whereas I move through analysis to structural exegesis.

22. Lévi-Strauss, "Structural Study," 431.
23. Ibid., 443.
24. Lévi-Strauss makes no effort to reconcile these two sets of terms; however, both discussions move in the same direction, and I have tried to make clear when possible the equivalence between the two sets of terms and processes of analysis. In addition, some problems of terminology exist within each article. Within the terminology of "The Story of Asdiwal" (facts/orders), "levels" and "orders" are used synonymously. Within the terminology of "The Structural Study of Myth" (relations/bundles), some confusion is possible concerning the meaning of "constituent units." First, Lévi-Strauss asserts that "each gross constituent unit will consist in a relation" (p. 431). Then he notes that "the true constituent units of a myth are not isolated relations but *bundles of such relations*" (p. 431). Finally, Lévi-Strauss writes of "all the notes [of an orchestra score] which are written vertically making up one gross constituent unit, i.e., one bundle of relations" (p. 432). In any case, when analyzing the structure and meaning of the myth, the bundles of relations are the important elements. I have found the terms *relations* (rather than *facts*) and *orders* (rather than *bundles*) more usable in my own discussion.
25. Lévi-Strauss, "Asdiwal," 1.
26. Ibid., 21.
27. Lévi-Strauss, "Structural Study," 442–43.
28. Lévi-Strauss, "Asdiwal," 1.
29. Lévi-Strauss, "Structural Study," 440.
30. That is, each element (A, B, C, D) is expressed in the formula as a function (e.g., "the function x," or "f_x") of a term—e.g., (a). Thus A : B :: C : D becomes $f_x(a) : f_y(b) :: f_x(b) : f_{a-1}(y)$. For a discussion of Lévi-Strauss's formula, see my "Mythic Structure and Meaning in Mark: Elements of a Lévi-Straussian Analysis," *Semeia* 16 (1979) 97–132. Note that there is an error in note 21 of this article; in the diagram of the square on page 126, the positions of $f_x(b)$ and $f_{a-1}(y)$ should be reversed and the comments below changed accordingly. See also Malbon, "1 Thessalonians," 68–72. For a discussion of Lévi-Strauss's formula in relation to Greimas's semiotic square, see my "The Spiral and the Square: Lévi-Strauss's Mythic Formula and Greimas's Constitutional Model," *Linguistica Biblica* 55 (1984) 47–56.
31. Dan O. Via, Jr., *Kerygma and Comedy in the New Testament: A Structuralist Approach to Hermeneutic* (Philadelphia: Fortress, 1975) 113.
32. Polzin, *Biblical Structuralism*, 5.
33. "Narrative space" is not to be confused with "spatial form" in narrative. A more traditional (and not entirely equivalent) term for "narrative space" is "setting." One might conceive of "spatial form" as the spatiality (in imagination and language) of synchronic or paradigmatic structure. See especially W. J. T. Mitchell, "Spatial Form in Literature: Toward a General Theory," in *The Language of Images* (ed. W. J. T. Mitchell; Chicago and London: University of Chicago, 1980) 271–99; see also Jeffrey R. Smitten and Ann Daghistany, eds., *Spatial Form in Narrative* (Ithaca and London: Cornell University, 1981). Thus, in Mitchell's terms, the present work is concerned with the interrelated "spatial form" (synchronic or paradigmatic) and "temporal form" (diachronic or syntagmatic) of "narrative space" (or "setting").
34. Concerning the fundamental relationship of space and meaning in the passion narrative, Marin writes: "Taken seriously, this relationship would permit us to come to a kind of minimal definition of the narrative in its most obvious manifestation" (*Semiotics of the Passion Narrative*, 18). In a broader context,

see Jonathan Z. Smith, "The Influence of Symbols Upon Social Change: A Place on Which to Stand," in *Map Is Not Territory: Studies in the History of Religions* (Leiden: Brill, 1978) 143: "It is through an understanding and symbolization of place that a society or individual creates itself."

35. "What Is a Gospel? Geography, Time and Narrative Structure," *Perspectives in Religious Studies* 10 (1983) 255–68; quotation from 259. Hedrick's further observations are marred, however, by an overly rigid separation of Mark as "author" and Mark as "theologian" (see, e.g., p. 267).

36. See my "The Text and Time," 177–91. With my argument for the equal importance of the synchronic and the diachronic and their interdependence, compare the argument of Mitchell for the equal importance and interdependence of "spatial form" (or spatiality) and temporality ("Spatial Form in Literature").

37. There is an important difference between the charts Lévi-Strauss presents in analyzing the Oedipus myth and the Zuni emergence myth ("Structural Study," 433 and 437) and my sequence charts. Lévi-Strauss intends to illustrate the basic structure of a complete myth, as the collection of all its variants, in one relatively simple chart; and the four columns of the chart have the relationship (reading from left to right) 1 : 2 :: 3 : 4, paralleling the mythic formula. In so charting the myth, Lévi-Strauss does not consider various orders of the Oedipus myth or the Zuni myth; but in analyzing the myth of Asdiwal, Lévi-Strauss focuses on orders, sequences, and schemata. My method of analysis draws from both procedures. And since each of my sequence charts presents the analysis not of a whole text but of one suborder (or one integrated order) alone, the columns represent not the elements of the formula but the elements of the schema. Thus my sequence charts give more detail but a less complete overall picture than Lévi-Strauss's mythic charts. In both types of chart, however, the columns point to the paradigmatic reading.

38. Here "logic" and "mytho*logic*" refer not to an Aristotelian logic but to a Lévi-Straussian "logic" of "the concrete" (see Claude Lévi-Strauss, *The Savage Mind* [Chicago: University of Chicago, 1966] esp. 1–74). After working out the distinction between the logical hierarchy and the mythological schema, I realized that Lévi-Strauss may have had a glimpse of the problem that led me to this distinction. The original version of "La Geste d'Asdiwal" (*Ecole pratique des hautes études, Section des sciences religieuses* [Extra. Annuaire 1958–1959; Paris, 1958] 3–43; reprinted in *Les Temps modernes* 179 [mars 1962] 1080–1123, see 1099) and its first appearance in English ("The Story of Asdiwal," in *The Structural Study of Myth and Totemism* [1967] 1–47, see 19) present this diagram as a schematic integration:

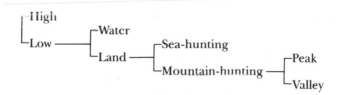

The second, and anthologized, version of the article, both in French (*Anthropologie Structurale Deux* [Paris: Plon, 1973] 175–233, see 196) and in English (*Structural Anthropology*, vol. 2 [New York: Basic Books, 1976] 146–97, see 163), provides a new schematic diagram in its place:

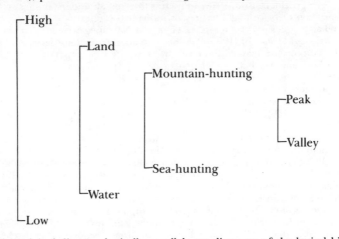

The original diagram basically parallels my diagrams of the logical hierarchies, while the second diagram parallels my diagrams of the mythological schemata. No comment is made by Lévi-Strauss concerning this revision.

39. Dan O. Via, Jr., "A Response to Crossan, Funk, and Petersen," *Semeia* 1 (1974) 223.
40. As David Rhoads has observed: "Of course, knowledge of the history and culture of the first century is a crucial aid to understanding Mark's story-world, but that is a different matter from using elements of a text to reconstruct historical events" ("Narrative Criticism and the Gospel of Mark," *JAAR* 50 [1982] 411–34; quotation from 413).
41. William Wrede, *The Messianic Secret* (Naperville, IL: Alec R. Allenson, 1972) 280–81.
42. Editorial, *Interpretation* 28 (1974) 131–32; quotation from 132. This issue of *Interpretation* is on structuralism.

Notes to Chapter 2

1. E.g., D. E. Nineham, *The Gospel of St. Mark* (Pelican New Testament Commentaries; Baltimore: Penguin, 1963); on confused geographical distinctions see 180, 186, 236, etc.; on important geographical distinctions see Nineham's labels of the larger divisions of Mark's Gospel. Also Werner H. Kelber, *The Kingdom in Mark: A New Place and a New Time* (Philadelphia: Fortress, 1974); on geographical confusion see, e.g., 58 and 60; on geographical significance see Kelber's overall approach to the pattern of the Markan Jesus' journeys and the Markan significance of the distinction between Galilee and Jerusalem.

2. Louis Marin focuses on the toponyms, the proper place names, of the passion narrative (in its four canonical "variants") in the first of two structuralist essays in *The Semiotics of the Passion Narrative: Topics and Figures* (Pittsburgh: Pickwick, 1980). Because Marin's study is both broader (all four gospels) and more narrow (primarily the passion narrative) than the present study, and because his conclusions are frequently based on his own synopsis of the gospels, his work is of limited use in the present context of analyzing all geopolitical references in their Markan context.

3. *Kananaios*, identifying Simon at 3:18, is a political—but not a geopolitical—reference. The term means "an adherent of the party later known as the Zealots" (cf. Luke 6:15), not a "Canaanite" (*Chananaios*) or an "inhabitant of Cana" (*Kanaios*). See Vincent Taylor, *The Gospel According to St. Mark* (London: Macmillan, 1955; New York: St. Martin's, 1955) 234; Henry Barclay Swete, *Commentary on Mark* (London: Macmillan, 1913; reprinted, Grand Rapids: Kregel, 1977) 61–62.

4. Robert G. Bratcher and Eugene A. Nida, *A Translator's Handbook on the Gospel of Mark* (Helps for Translators, vol. 2; Leiden: Brill, for the United Bible Societies, 1961) 50, 237, 471, 483–84, 495, 500.

5. Assuming that the term *Nazarēnos* derives from the name of the town Nazareth. See William F. Arndt, F. Wilbur Gingrich, and Frederick W. Danker, trans. and eds., *A Greek-English Lexicon of the New Testament and Other Early Christian Literature* (2nd ed.; Chicago: University of Chicago, 1979) 532; Taylor, *St. Mark*, 177–78; Eduard Schweizer, *The Good News According to Mark* (Atlanta: John Knox, 1970) 52; Nineham, *St. Mark*, 79; O. Cullmann, "Nazarene," in *The Interpreter's Dictionary of the Bible* (*IDB*) (5 vols.; Nashville: Abingdon, vols. 1–4, 1962; supp., 1976) 3 (1962) 523; H. H. Schaeder, "Nazarēnos, Nazōraios," in *Theological Dictionary of the New Testament* (*TDNT*) (10 vols.; Grand Rapids: Eerdmans, 1964–76) 4 (1967) 874–79.

6. Gustaf Dalman, *Sacred Sites and Ways: Studies in the Topography of the Gospels* (London: Society for Promoting Christian Knowledge, 1935; New York: Macmillan, 1935) 225–26.

7. The narrative might be more "reasonable" if the Syrophoenician woman were away from her native place as well, since Jesus would seem to be willing to give "crumbs" (if not "bread") to the "dogs" by traveling to Gentile ter-

ritory. See Paul J. Achtemeier, "Toward the Isolation of Pre-Markan Miracle Catenae," *JBL* 89 (1970) 287.

8. The phrase *holēn tēn perichōron tēs Galilaias* could possibly be interpreted as the region *around* Galilee (cf. Matthew 4:24). Most commentators, however, understand the phrase as *throughout* Galilee, considering the genitive epexegetic: "the whole region around, that is, Galilee" (Arndt and Gingrich, *Lexicon*, 653). See Taylor, *St. Mark*, 177; Robert Henry Lightfoot, *Locality and Doctrine in the Gospels* (New York and London: Harper, [1938]) 117; Bratcher and Nida, *Handbook*, 54–55.

9. Cf. Schweizer, *Good News*, 79.

10. For the textual argument for excluding "and Sidon" at 7:24, see Bruce A. Metzger, *A Textual Commentary on the Greek New Testament* (United Bible Societies, 1971) 95.

11. This is the only New Testament occurrence of the place name Dalmanutha. Although no such location is known for certain to New Testament scholars, it is generally assumed to represent an area along the west shore of the Sea of Galilee. There is some manuscript evidence for Magadan or Magdala at Mark 8:10, and these two place names also appear as variants in the parallel passage in Matthew 15:39. (See Arndt and Gingrich, *Lexicon*, 170; Taylor, *St. Mark*, 360–61; Nineham, *St. Mark*, 209; Bratcher and Nida, *Handbook*, 249; D. C. Pellett, "Dalmanutha," *IDB* 1 [1962] 757). Augustine identified the places mentioned by Mark and Matthew (Taylor, *St. Mark*, 361). For a different opinion of the location of Dalmanutha, see Kelber, *Kingdom*, 61.

12. So also K. W. Clark, "Galilee," *IDB* 2 (1962) 347; Bratcher and Nida, *Handbook*, 307. *Contra* Willi Marxsen (*Mark the Evangelist: Studies on the Redaction History of the Gospel* [Nashville and New York: Abingdon, 1969] 74–75), who opts for the textual variant omitting the *kai* ("and"), the Western text: *eis ta horia tēs Ioudaias peran tou Iordanou* ("to the region of Judea beyond the Jordan"; cf. Matthew 19:1). Taylor (*St. Mark*, 416–17) and Nineham (*St. Mark*, 263–64) discuss the difficulties and textual variants of this verse. Schweizer (*Good News*, 202) suggests a theological interpretation.

13. On the use of *potamos* ("river") together with *Iordanēs*, including uses in the LXX and in Josephus as well as in the New Testament, see K. H. Rengstorf, "*potamos*," *TDNT* 6 (1968) 601. On the contrast between traditional Jewish washings and baptisms in bath-houses and John's baptism in the River Jordan see Rengstorf, 602, 613–15.

14. Lightfoot notes that the two uses of "all" at 1:5 "are probably not to be regarded as picturesque exaggeration, but emphasize that which was only to be expected at the appearance of the herald of the end" (*Locality*, 114). Cf. Schweizer, *Good News*, 33; Nineham, *St. Mark*, 57.

15. On the parallels between John at the Jordan and Elijah and Elisha at the Jordan (2 Kings 2, 5, 6) see S. Cohen, "Jordan," *IDB* 2 (1962) 978. Cf. Taylor, *St. Mark*, 155.

16. See Norman Perrin, "The Use of *(Para)didonai* in Connection with the Passion of Jesus in the New Testament," in *A Modern Pilgrimage in New Testament Christology* (Philadelphia: Fortress, 1974) 94–103. Cf. Marxsen, *Evangelist*, 39ff.

17. As Marxsen (*Evangelist*, 149) has noted, 1:1 is "to be construed as the final statement of the evangelist's backward directed composition."

18. So Marxsen (*Evangelist*, 57), who regards 1:9 as redactional, at least in part, and the *Nazarēnos* passages as traditional.

19. On 16:6 cf. Lightfoot, *Locality*, 58.
20. Kelber, *Kingdom*, 45–46; following Achtemeier, "Toward the Isolation of Pre-Markan Miracle Catenae," 265–91. See also Achtemeier, "The Origin and Function of the Pre-Markan Miracle Catenae," *JBL* 91 (1972) 198–221.
21. A more detailed version of my argument appears in "The Jesus of Mark and the Sea of Galilee," *JBL* 103 (1984) 363–77.
22. Bratcher and Nida, *Handbook*, 211.
23. So also Bratcher and Nida, *Handbook*, 249.
24. Whereas Marxsen (*Evangelist*, 68–69) would agree with this outline, Kelber (*Kingdom*, 45–65) traces a somewhat different pattern. For a presentation of and argument against Kelber's outline, see my "The Jesus of Mark and the Sea of Galilee." The present reading also disagrees with Robert M. Fowler's assertion that the author of Mark "has almost no concern for the consistency of his geographical references" (*Loaves and Fishes: The Function of the Feeding Stories in the Gospel of Mark* [Society of Biblical Literature Dissertation Series 54; Chico, CA: Scholars, 1981] 66).
25. Cf. Kelber, *Kingdom*, esp. 62–63.
26. Ironically, my reading of a detoured journey, which Kelber's reading would oppose, might seem to support Kelber's view of discipleship failure in Mark, a view that I oppose. Kelber's interpretation deserves a fuller response than can be given here, but, in general, I read the data Kelber collects for "discipleship failure" as evidence of Markan pastoral concern for the difficulty of true discipleship, which affirms both the power and the suffering of Jesus. In addition to my "The Jesus of Mark and the Sea of Galilee," see Johannes Schreiber, *Theologie des Vertrauens: Eine redaktionsgeschichtliche Untersuchung des Markusevangeliums* (Hamburg: Furche-Verlag, 1967), esp. 203–210; and Robert C. Tannehill, "The Disciples in Mark: The Function of a Narrative Role," *JR* 57 (1977) 386–405, esp. 398–400.
27. Marxsen (*Evangelist*, 64) reads 3:7–8 in support of his view that Mark's Gospel is a (historical) call to await the (temporal) parousia in (geographical) Galilee. For Nineham (*St. Mark*, 112–13) the multitude of 3:7–8 represents "all Israel," which gathers to Jesus and from which "he creates the new community which was expected in the last time." (Cf. Lightfoot, *Locality*, 119; E. Lohse, "Siōn—Hierosoluma," *TDNT* 7 [1971] 330) Schweizer (*Good News*, 79) suggests that "the locations named form an outline of the Gospel of Mark . . . ." (See also Taylor, *St. Mark*, 226–27.)
28. Taylor, *St. Mark*, 437; Bratcher and Nida, *Handbook*, 329.
29. Cf. Taylor, *St. Mark*, 437–38; Nineham, *St. Mark*, 278.
30. Nineham, *St. Mark*, 294; Schweizer, *Good News*, 227.
31. "Bethphage" may mean literally "house of figs" or "house of unripe figs" (Arndt and Gingrich, *Lexicon*, 140; K. W. Clark, "Bethphage," *IDB* 1 [1962] 396), and "Bethany," "house of dates" (Taylor, *St. Mark*, 453).
32. E.g., Schweizer, *Good News*, 230–36; Nineham, *St. Mark*, 299; C. H. Bird, "Some *gar* Clauses in St. Mark's Gospel," *JTS* n.s. 4 (1953) 177–79. *Contra* Taylor, *St. Mark*, 458–60.
33. Herbert G. May and Bruce M. Metzger, eds., *The Oxford Annotated Bible: Revised Standard Version* (2nd ed.; New York: Oxford University, 1973) 1175, note on Matthew 5:1.
34. Taylor, *St. Mark*, 453; Schweizer, *Good News*, 227.
35. J. B. Curtis, "Corruption, Mount of," *IDB* Supp. (1976) 186. Curtis points out that a mural from the synagogue at Dura-Europas combines Ezekiel's

vision of the valley of the dry bones with the cleft-in-the-mountain motif. See also Curtis, "An Investigation of the Mount of Olives in the Judeo-Christian Tradition," *HUCA* 28 (1957) 137–80.

36. Others have translated this name, *har ham mashhîth*, as "Mount of Corruption," suggesting that it "may well be a derisive corruption of *har hammishhâ*, 'Mount of Ointment,' an extrabiblical synonym for 'Mount of Olives,' " (G. A. Barrois, "Corruption, Mount of," *IDB* 1 [1962] 701).

37. Curtis, "Corruption, Mount of," *IDB* Supp. (1976) 186–87.

38. Arndt and Gingrich, *Lexicon*, 153; Taylor, *St. Mark*, 551; Nineham, *St. Mark*, 391; Schweizer, *Good News*, 311.

39. Arndt and Gingrich, *Lexicon*, 153; Taylor, *St. Mark*, 551; K. W. Clark, "Gethsemane," *IDB* 2 (1962) 387.

40. Bratcher and Nida, *Handbook*, 484; Arndt and Gingrich, *Lexicon*, 164.

41. Schweizer, *Good News*, 345.

42. See K. W. Clark, "Golgotha," *IDB* 2 (1962) 439.

43. Following Bratcher and Nida (*Handbook*, 471): "the *kai* 'also' should not be omitted (as done by RSV)."

44. On *akoloutheō* as a signal of discipleship see Metzger, *Textual Commentary*, 78; Taylor, *St. Mark*, 169; Bratcher and Nida, *Handbook*, 41. On *diakoneō*, root of the title of the early church office of "deacon," as a sign of service see Bratcher and Nida, *Handbook*, 34.

45. For a further discussion see my "Fallible Followers: Women and Men in the Gospel of Mark," *Semeia* 28 (1983) 29–48, esp. 40–46.

46. So also Taylor, *St. Mark*, 608. Cf. 14:27–28, *RSV*.

47. Cf. Schweizer, *Good News*, 273; and see Chapter 3.

48. E.g., Marxsen, *Evangelist*, 115, n. 175; Kelber, *Kingdom*, 146; Bird, "*gar* Clauses," 334, 337, 338, 340, 341, 348.

49. Lightfoot, *Locality*, 55, 70, but *contra* 63.

50. Ibid., 112–13.

51. Some ancient manuscripts read "the scribes and the Pharisees" rather than "the scribes of the Pharisees" at 2:16. Metzger argues, however, that the "more unusual expression *hoi grammateis tōn Pharisaiōn* is to be preferred, since the tendency of scribes would have been to insert *kai* after *hoi grammateis* under the influence of the common expression 'the scribes and the Pharisees' " (*Textual Commentary*, 78).

52. Because the immediately preceding geopolitical reference (10:1) includes two place names, Judea and beyond the Jordan, without clearly delimiting the itinerary, the spatial location of the encounter between Jesus and the Pharisees at 10:2 is uncertain. Judea seems more likely, however, because Judea, not the area beyond the Jordan, would have been the home territory of the Pharisees, and because the next geopolitical reference (10:32) is the road up to Jerusalem.

53. David Green, in translating Schweizer (*Good News*, 154), illustrates the "impossibility of the route of travel" by an analogy closer to home: "going from New York to Washington by way of Boston down the Mohawk Valley." Marxsen (*Evangelist*, 70) sees in the verse the "inconsistencies [that] naturally occur whenever an author elects to combine his own with traditional ideas." Taylor (*St. Mark*, 352–53) outlines the scholarly debate on 7:31.

54. Cf. Schweizer, *Good News*, 154, commenting on 7:31.

55. Caesarea Philippi was famed for an ancient, "pagan" shrine in a cave, dedicated by the Greeks "to Pan and the Nymphs" (D. C. Pellett, "Caesarea Philippi," *IDB* 1 [1962] 480). Thus the road to Caesarea Philippi, a place

that had long stirred religious sensibilities, provides an especially appropriate setting for the religious question of Jesus and Peter's confessional response. For a different explanation of the appropriateness of Caesarea Philippi as a location at this point in the Markan narrative, see Schweizer, *Good News*, 171.

56. Cf. William Wrede, *The Messianic Secret* (Naperville, IL: Alec R. Allenson, 1972) 142, n. 35.
57. So also Kelber, *Kingdom*, 62–63.
58. K. W. Clark, "Galilee, Sea of," *IDB* 2 (1962) 348.
59. See G. H. Boobyer, "Galilee and Galileans in St. Mark's Gospel," *Bulletin of the John Rylands Library* 35 (1952) 334–48; C. F. Evans, " 'I Will Go Before You Into Galilee,' " *JTS* n.s. 5 (1954) 3–18.
60. Claude Lévi-Strauss, "The Structural Study of Myth," *Journal of American Folklore* 68 (1955) 440.
61. Ibid.
62. Cf. Lightfoot, *Locality*, 124–25.
63. Ibid., 114.
64. Cf. Marxsen, who, also citing Lightfoot, comments on 1:5: "in all remaining parts of Mark's Gospel the characterization of Judea and Galilee is reversed" (*Evangelist*, 94).
65. Marin (*Semiotics of the Passion Narrative*, 23–35) presents the following "toponymic articulations" for the Markan passion narrative:

   (Mount of Olives vs. Jerusalem Temple // Temple vs. Bethany)
   (Bethany vs. Jerusalem-Temple)
   (outside of the city vs. Jerusalem-Temple)
   (Temple vs. Mount of Olives)
   (Bethany vs. the city vs. Mount of Olives)

66. E. Lohse, "*Siōn—Hierosoluma*," *TDNT* 7 (1971) 324.
67. Ibid.
68. See G. Fohrer, "*Sion—Hierosoluma*," *TDNT* 7 (1971) 311–12.
69. Ibid., 312–17.
70. For a discussion of the Markan Gospel as both myth and parable, see my "Mark: Myth and Parable," *BTB* 16 (1986) 8–17. See also note 10 to Chapter 5.
71. It is, perhaps, this tension that is sensed by scholars who, following Ernst Lohmeyer (*Galiläa und Jerusalem* [Forschungen zur Religion und Literatur des Alten und Neuen Testaments 34; Göttingen: Vandenhoeck und Ruprecht, 1936]), consider the opposition of Galilee and Jerusalem in isolation from the total Markan spatial context; see, e.g., Lightfoot, *Locality*, 156; Marxsen, *Evangelist*, 91–92, 97; Kelber, *Kingdom*, 23, 85. Although the Markan tension is clear, the equation of it—to a greater (Marxsen and Kelber) or lesser (Lightfoot) degree—with the expectation of a literal, imminent parousia in late first-century Galilee is not; see my "Galilee and Jerusalem: History and Literature in Marcan Interpretation," *CBQ* 44 (1982) 242–55.

Notes to Chapter 3

1. If one flew low enough, of course, one would also see specific buildings, such as houses, synagogues, the temple; but these spatial locations are more usefully investigated as part of an architectural suborder.
2. E.g., Eduard Schweizer, *The Good News According to Mark* (Atlanta: John Knox, 1970) 181; D. E. Nineham, *The Gospel of St. Mark* (Pelican New Testament Commentaries; Baltimore: Penguin, 1963) 237; Günter Stemberger, "Galilee—Land of Salvation?," appendix IV in *The Gospel and the Land*, by W. D. Davies (Berkeley: University of California, 1974) 419; Werner H. Kelber, *The Kingdom in Mark: A New Place and a New Time* (Philadelphia: Fortress, 1974) 72–82.
3. E.g., Schweizer, *Good News*, 109, 141; Nineham, *St. Mark*, 146–47, 180–81; Stemberger, "Galilee," 418.
4. Willi Marxsen (*Mark the Evangelist: Studies on the Redaction History of the Gospel* [Nashville and New York: Abingdon, 1969] 30–53) has considered the meaning of the initial wilderness references in Mark 1, and Ulrich Mauser (*Christ in the Wilderness: The Wilderness Theme in the Second Gospel and its Basis in the Biblical Tradition* [Naperville, IL: Alec R. Allenson, 1963]) has broadened this consideration to include all the Markan references to wilderness, as well as, in a subsidiary way, references to mountain and sea.
5. William F. Arndt, F. Wilbur Gingrich, and Frederick W. Danker, trans. and eds., *A Greek-English Lexicon of the New Testament and Other Early Christian Literature* (2nd ed.; Chicago: University of Chicago, 1979) 309; G. Kittel, "*erēmos, erēmia,*" *Theological Dictionary of the New Testament (TDNT)* (10 vols.; Grand Rapids: Eerdmans, 1964–76) 2 (1964) 657.
6. Arndt and Gingrich, *Lexicon*, 636.
7. For which see Schweizer, *Good News*, 123.
8. E.g., Schweizer, *Good News*, 123; Nineham, *St. Mark*, 165; Vincent Taylor, *The Gospel According to St. Mark* (London: Macmillan, 1955; New York: St. Martin's, 1955) 299; H. H. Schaeder, "*Nazarēnos, Nazōraios,*" *TDNT* 4 (1967) 874; K. W. Clark, "Galilee," *Interpreter's Dictionary of the Bible (IDB)* (5 vols.; Nashville: Abingdon, vols. 1–4, 1962; supp., 1976) 2 (1962) 347.
9. At 13:26 and 14:62 the language is patterned after Daniel 7:13, more closely at 14:62.
10. Robert D. Bratcher and Eugene A. Nida, *A Translator's Handbook on the Gospel of Mark* (Helps for Translators, vol. 2; Leiden: Brill, for the United Bible Societies, 1961) 211, 505.
11. See Chapter 2 for an interpretation of this detoured journey as it is marked at the geopolitical level.
12. Of those seventeen occurrences, twelve are singular and five are plural. Of nine spatial uses, three are plural. The idea of more than one heaven is Jewish, but "it is not always possible to decide with certainty just where this idea is really alive and where it simply survives in a formula" (Arndt and Gingrich, *Lexicon*, 594).

13. Arndt and Gingrich, *Lexicon*, 593–95; see also H. Traub, *"ouranos," TDNT* 5 (1967) 514.
14. See C. von Rad, *"ouranos," TDNT* 5 (1967) 504–507.
15. Arndt and Gingrich, *Lexicon*, 595; Taylor, *St. Mark*, 470; Nineham, *St. Mark*, 307.
16. Arndt and Gingrich, *Lexicon*, 595; Bratcher and Nida, *Handbook*, 360.
17. Taylor, *St. Mark*, 429. Cf. Matthew 6:19–21.
18. Arndt and Gingrich, *Lexicon*, 594.
19. Arndt and Gingrich (*Lexicon*, 594) list 6:41 and 7:34 among the nonfigurative uses of *heaven*.
20. Arndt and Gingrich, *Lexicon*, 593; cf. Bratcher and Nida, *Handbook*, 420.
21. The idiom is, apparently, Hebraic (Nineham, *St. Mark*, 360).
22. Arndt and Gingrich, *Lexicon*, 157.
23. Cf. Arndt and Gingrich, *Lexicon*, 350; Mauser, *Wilderness Theme*, 108.
24. See Schweizer, *Good News*, 198.
25. See Nineham, *St. Mark*, 305. Cf. Matthew 17:20; 21:21; 1 Corinthians 13:2.
26. Arndt and Gingrich, *Lexicon*, 553–55; W. Michaelis, *"hodos," TDNT* 5 (1967) 42–43.
27. Cf. Arndt and Gingrich, *Lexicon*, 554; Michaelis, *"hodos," TDNT* 5 (1967) 43.
28. Arndt and Gingrich, *Lexicon*, 554; Michaelis, *"hodos," TDNT* 5 (1967) 87; Bratcher and Nida, *Handbook*, 322; Taylor, *St. Mark*, 479.
29. Michaelis (*"hodos," TDNT* 5 [1967] 69) cites this passage as an example of the difficulty of drawing a line between literal and metaphorical uses of *hodos* in the New Testament.
30. Within the broader scope of all biblical literature, M. H. Pope ("Way," *IDB* 4 [1962] 817–18) defines *way* as a "common biblical metaphor for courses of nature, modes of human and divine conduct, attitude, habit, custom, undertaking, plan, purpose, fate, and the like" and lists numerous Old and New Testament examples. (Cf. Michaelis, *"hodos," TDNT* 5 [1967] 49–56, 69–91.) The metaphorical or figurative use of *hodos* is early in the Greek tradition as well; Michaelis (*"hodos," TDNT* 5 [1967] 43) cites examples from Pindar, Heraclitus, Thucydides, Democritus, and Plato. Cross-cultural examples of the metaphorical application of *way* within religious traditions are numerous—from the Eightfold Noble Path of Buddhism to the Chinese Tao.
31. Arndt and Gingrich, *Lexicon*, 13–14; see also Bratcher and Nida, *Handbook*, 164.
32. Arndt and Gingrich, *Lexicon*, 14; O. Michel, *"oikos—oikia," TDNT* 5 (1967) 131.
33. Henry Barclay Swete, *Commentary on Mark* (London: Macmillan, 1913; reprinted, Grand Rapids: Kregel, 1977) 232. Cf. Taylor, *St. Mark*, 435.
34. Taylor, *St. Mark*, 301.
35. See Arndt and Gingrich, *Lexicon*, 461; H. Strathmann, *"polis," TDNT* 6 (1968) 530.
36. *Contra* Michaelis, *"hodos," TDNT* 5 (1967) 66–67.
37. Bratcher and Nida, *Handbook*, 8–9; Taylor, *St. Mark*, 153; Schweizer, *Good News*, 31; Nineham, *St. Mark*, 60; see also Matthew Black, *An Aramaic Approach to the Gospels and Acts* (3rd ed.; Oxford: Clarendon, 1967) 99.
38. Bratcher and Nida, *Handbook*, 6–7, 9.
39. The phrase *hodon poiein* does not mean "make a road" but "go along a path." Thus Jesus and the disciples are not trampling the grain down as

they go across the field (as Schweizer, *Good News*, 72, assumes), but walking along a regular path through the field. This idiom is used comparably in the Septuagint text of Judges 17:8. In classical Greek the expression would be *hodon poieisthai*—"journey," "go along" (Taylor, *St. Mark*, 215; Bratcher and Nida, *Handbook*, 96–97).

40. On the Elisha parallel, see Lewis S. Hay, "Mark's Use of the Messianic Secret," *JAAR* 35 (1967) 24.

41. See Taylor, *St. Mark*, 304.

42. Cf. Schweizer, *Good News*, 217; Taylor, *St. Mark*, 437; Nineham, *St. Mark*, 278.

43. E.g., Taylor (*St. Mark*, 449), observing connections among 8:3, 10:52, and 11:1–11.

44. E.g., Kelber, *Kingdom*, chapter IV; see especially 67–69.

45. Kelber, *Kingdom*, 69. Kelber's view of "the way" in Mark seems circumscribed by his prior convictions concerning parousia expectation, discipleship failure, and polemic against a false eschatology (on this latter point see p. 142, n. 36).

46. Michaelis, *"hodos,"* *TDNT* 5 (1967) 52.

47. *Proagein* may be understood in two senses: (1) "to go before," "to precede," or (2) "to lead," "to go at your head." Both Taylor (*St. Mark*, 549, 608) and Nineham (*St. Mark*, 445–46) discuss the arguments given for each sense and conclude that at 14:28 and 16:7 the first is intended. Cf. also Robert Henry Lightfoot, *Locality and Doctrine in the Gospels* (New York and London: Harper, [1938]) 52, n. 2. The second sense is preferred by C. F. Evans (" 'I Will Go Before You Into Galilee,' " *JTS* n.s. 5 [1954] 3–18); and, although Evans's article is filled with interesting observations, his conclusion concerning *proagō* in Mark appears overly influenced by his reading of the other gospels and by his conviction that Galilee is (simply) a symbol for the Gentile mission. Intertwined with the argument over the sense of *proagō* is that of whether the reference to "seeing" Jesus in Galilee is to a resurrection appearance or to the parousia or to some other reality.

48. Cf. Lightfoot, *Locality*, 60; Marxsen, *Evangelist*, 75; Taylor, *St. Mark*, 608.

49. Cf. Bratcher and Nida, *Handbook*, 293.

50. It would be intriguing, but beyond the scope of the present study, to investigate the development of the significance of "the way" (*hodos*)—from the plentiful and interrelated "way" passages of Mark, to the Lukan story of Jesus' resurrection appearance "on the way" (24:32, 35) to Emmaus, to the designation of early Christiantiy as "the Way" in Acts (9:2; 19:9, 23; 24:22), to the emphatic statement of the Johannine Jesus: "I am the way" (14:6). According to Kelber (*Kingdom*, 71, n. 6): "Functionally, the *hodos* motif in Mark already approaches the personalized, Johannine sense (John 14:6)." Wayne G. Rollins finds a connection between the designation of the Christian movement as "the Way" and the Markan sense of "the way" (*The Gospels: Portraits of Christ* [Philadelphia: Westminster, 1963] 42–43).

51. Mauser (*Wilderness Theme*) isolates three emphases: (1) danger and divine help (Pentateuch); (2) rebellion, curse (Psalms); (3) renewal (Prophets). I read Mauser's evidence as a case for the double, paradoxical aspect of the Hebrew tradition of the wilderness—negative and positive, danger and help, curse and renewal.

52. Mauser, *Wilderness Theme*, 21.

53. Ibid., 51.

54. Shemaryahu Talmon ("The 'Desert Motif' in the Bible and in Qumran

Literature," in *Biblical Motifs: Origins and Transformations* [ed. Alexander Altmann; Cambridge: Harvard University, 1966] 31–63) depicts two "major classes of connotations" of the wilderness (Hebrew *midbar*): (1) spatial connotations drawn from geophysical reality, in which wilderness imagery "crystallizes abject fear, destruction, and desolation, which the Israelite perceived in desert reality (Isaiah 14:17; Zephaniah 2:13)" (p. 45), and (2) temporal connotations drawn from Israel's history, in which two themes, "Divine grace" and "Israel's sin and punishment," may be included, although the latter "is of much greater impact on the 'desert motif' in Biblical literature" (p. 48; see also Talmon, "Wilderness," *IDB* Supp. [1976] 946–49). According to Talmon, only an other-worldly view suggests positive connotations for the wilderness, and descriptions of "the nomadic ideal" in Hebrew literature reflect rather "Christian literature with a monastic orientation when 'retreat from the world' is raised from the status of a temporary disengagement to that of a theological ideal" (" 'Desert Motif,' " 63). On this latter point, see also Talmon, "The Biblical Concept of Jerusalem," *JES* 8 (1971) 300–16.

55. The prologue, 1:1–13, and more particularly the temptation of Jesus, 1:12–13, is of special importance in Mauser's overall view of Mark (see 77–102, but also passim). Despite agreement on many details, I am not here—on the prologue or throughout Mark—following Mauser's basic interpretation, which stresses the wilderness as the scene of Jesus' victory over Satanic forces.

56. Mauser, *Wilderness Theme*, 80–81; Taylor, *St. Mark*, 153; Bratcher and Nida, *Handbook*, 8; Kittel, "*erēmos, erēmia,*" *TDNT* 2 (1964) 659.

57. Cf. Mauser, *Wilderness Theme*, 80–83; Marxsen, *Evangelist*, 37, 46.

58. Bratcher and Nida, *Handbook*, 11, 5.

59. Schweizer, *Good News*, 31.

60. Mauser (*Wilderness Theme*, 98, n. 1) associates the action of the Spirit in 1:12 with the Old Testament motif of the "power of the Spirit to lift up the prophet and remove him to some distant place" (e.g., 2 Kings 2:16; 1 Kings 18:12; Ezekiel 8:3).

61. See Nineham, *St. Mark*, 64; Mauser, *Wilderness Theme*, 99; Kittel, "*erēmos, erēmia,*" *TDNT* 2 (1964) 657, n. 1.

62. Mauser (*Wilderness Theme*, 101, n. 2) finds "the angel motif" an important one in many stories of the exodus (e.g., Exodus 14:19; 23:23; 32:34; 33:2).

63. Nineham, *St. Mark*, 64; following Taylor, *St. Mark*, 164.

64. Quoted by Nineham, *St. Mark*, 64; cf. Schweizer, *Good News*, 42–43; Mauser, *Wilderness Theme*, 100–101.

65. Cf. Mauser, *Wilderness Theme*, 98–99. *Contra* Kittel, "*erēmos, erēmia,*" *TDNT* 2 (1964) 658.

66. Arndt and Gingrich, *Lexicon*, 309.

67. A "typically Markan" phrase, according to Mauser, *Wilderness Theme*, 104–105.

68. Some commentators ignore this reference to *erēmos topos* (e.g., Schweizer, *Good News;* Nineham, *St. Mark*); others insist that here it cannot mean wilderness but only "a lonely spot" because there was no wilderness or desert near Capernaum (e.g., Taylor, *St. Mark*, 183; Bratcher and Nida, *Handbook*, 60). Similar responses are made to *erēmos topos* at 1:45. These responses ignore the fact that the term is functioning theologically within a network of topographical markers, not simply literally in a geographic sense. Mauser (*Wilderness Theme*, 103–105) fully recognizes this fact.

69. See Nineham, *St. Mark,* 83–84.
70. See Arndt and Gingrich, *Lexicon,* 410; Bratcher and Nida, *Handbook,* 61–62.
71. K. W. Clark, "Galilee, Sea of," *IDB* 2 (1962) 348. While Matthew follows Mark in using "Sea of Galilee" (e.g., Matthew 4:18), Luke employs "lake (*limnē*) of Gennesaret (*Gennesaret*)" (e.g., Luke 5:1), and John explains that the Sea of Galilee is the Sea of Tiberias (John 6:1).
72. Black, *Aramaic Approach,* 133; cf. Arndt and Gingrich, *Lexicon,* 350. The Septuagint refers to the same body of water as the *Sea* of Chinnereth: Numbers 34:11, *thalassēs Chenera;* Joshua 12:3, *thalassēs Chenereth;* Joshua 13:27, *thalassēs Chenereth.*
73. For a fuller examination of the significance of the sea in the Markan Gospel, see my "The Jesus of Mark and the Sea of Galilee," *JBL* 103 (1984) 363–77.
74. This is the central theme of John Paul Heil's exegesis of the Markan "sea-walking" pericope as a "'sea-rescue' epiphany" (*Jesus Walking On the Sea: Meaning and Gospel Functions of Matt 14:22–23, Mark 6:45–52 and John 6:15b–21 [Analecta biblica* 87; Rome: Biblical Institute, 1981]).
75. For a detailed analysis of the language of the boat trips, see Robert M. Fowler, *Loaves and Fishes: The Function of the Feeding Stories in the Gospel of Mark* (Society of Biblical Literature Dissertation Series 54; Chico, CA: Scholars, for Society of Biblical Literature, 1981) 63–68, 235.
76. See Nineham, *St. Mark,* 148.
77. See Schweizer, *Good News,* 142.
78. See Taylor, *St. Mark,* 328; Schweizer, *Good News,* 142. With Mark 6:47 *(en mesō tēs thalassēs),* depicting the disciples on the Sea of Galilee, compare Exodus 14:16, 22, LXX *(eis meson tēs thalassēs),* depicting Moses and the Israelites on the Red (Reed) sea.
79. Nineham, *St. Mark,* 178–79, 209; Taylor, *St. Mark,* 359–60, 324; Schweizer, *Good News,* 157; Mauser, *Wilderness Theme,* 138.
80. Taylor, *St. Mark,* 553; Bratcher and Nida, *Handbook,* 447.
81. See Arndt and Gingrich, *Lexicon,* 85.
82. Arndt and Gingrich, *Lexicon,* 727–28; Taylor, *St. Mark,* 317.
83. Cf. James M. Robinson, *The Problem of History in Mark* (Studies in Biblical Theology 21; London: SCM, 1957) 39.
84. See H. Sasse, "*gē,*" *TDNT* 1 (1964) 679.
85. See Taylor, *St. Mark,* 501–18; Nineham, *St. Mark,* 357.
86. The phrase "from the ends [singular in the Greek] of the earth to the ends [singular in the Greek] of heaven" is unusual. More common phrases are "from the [one] end of the earth to the [other] end of the earth" (LXX: Deuteronomy 13:7; Jeremiah 12:12) and "from the [one] end of heaven to the [other] end of heaven" (LXX: Deuteronomy 4:32; 30:4; Psalm 18:7 [*RSV* 19:6]; cf. Matthew 24:31). The scriptural cosmography underlying all three phrases is that of the heaven as a half circle overarching the flat earth. Mark appears to have combined the two more usual phrases. See Taylor, *St. Mark,* 518–19; Schweizer, *Good News,* 275–76; Bratcher and Nida, *Handbook,* 416–17; Sasse, "*gē,*" *TDNT* 1 (1964) 679; H. Traub, "*ouranos,*" *TDNT* 5 (1967) 516–17.
87. See Sasse, "*gē,*" *TDNT* 1 (1964) 679.
88. For further references see Traub, "*ouranos,*" *TDNT* 5 (1967) 514–20; and Sasse, "*gē,*" *TDNT* 1 (1964) 678–79.
89. On Jesus (in Mark 2) being "at the point of conjunction" on a "trajectory

of values [that] is established" on the "cosmic axis (heaven-earth)," see Jean Calloud, "Toward a Structural Analysis of the Gospel of Mark," *Semeia* 16 (1979) 149.

90. Such a view is perhaps anticipated in certain portions of the Hebrew Scriptures: Lamentations 3:44; Job 22:13–14; Ecclesiastes 5:2 (cited by von Rad, "*ouranos*," *TDNT* 5 [1967] 507).

91. Nineham, *St. Mark*, 58.

92. See Taylor, *St. Mark*, 160.

93. Neither the Matthean nor the Lukan parallel to the baptism employs the Markan verb *schizō*, "split," in reference to the heavens. Thus, even though Matthew and Luke parallel Mark's use of *schizō* in reference to the temple curtain at the time of Jesus' crucifixion (Mark 15:38; Matthew 27:51; Luke 23:45), only in Mark is this incident connected linguistically with the opening of the way between heaven and earth depicted at Jesus' baptism (Mark 1:10). Neither Mark's use of *schizō* in reference to the heavens nor to the temple curtain parallels any of the eleven uses of *schizō* in the LXX, including three uses in the Apocrypha. Isaiah 64:1 (LXX 63:19) and Ezekiel 1:1 employ *anoigō*, "open," in reference to the heavens and is linguistically paralleled by Matthew 3:16 and Luke 3:21 but not Mark 1:10. If the Markan use of *schizō* has a LXX precursor, it is most likely to be found in Zechariah 14:4, "the Mount of Olives shall be split (*schisthēstai*) in two," a passage with which the Markan Gospel may be assumed on other grounds to be familiar. The splitting of the Mount of Olives, of the heavens, of the temple curtain—all refer to the radical beginning of a new era. It is possible, however, that Mark 1:10 is influenced by Isaiah 63:19 in the Hebrew text, where *qrs* ("rend," "tear") is used, as opposed to *pth* ("open") at Ezekiel 1:1 (Traub, "*ouranos*," *TDNT* 5 [1967] 529, n. 261).

94. See Traub, "*ouranos*," *TDNT* 5 (1967) 529–30.

95. See Taylor, *St. Mark*, 391; Nineham, *St. Mark*, 235–36; J. C. de Moor, "Cloud," *IDB* Supp. (1976) 168–69; A. Oepke, "*nephelē*," *TDNT* 4 (1967) 903–10.

96. Oepke, "*nephelē*," *TDNT* 4 (1967) 908.

97. See Mauser, *Wilderness Theme*, 114.

98. See Robinson, *Problem of History*, 45, n. 1.

99. William Wrede, *The Messianic Secret*, (Naperville, IL: Alec R. Allenson, 1972) 136.

100. So also Nineham, *St. Mark*, 115.

101. Cf. Schweizer, *Good News*, 142.

102. Mauser, *Wilderness Theme*, 111, 116.

103. See John R. Donahue, S.J., *Are You the Christ? The Trial Narrative in the Gospel of Mark* (Society of Biblical Literature Dissertation Series 10; Missoula: Society of Biblical Literature, 1973) 98–99.

104. Cf. Schweizer, *Good News*, 297; and Nineham, *St. Mark*, 295. *Contra* Taylor, *St. Mark*, 537–38.

105. E.g., Marxsen, *Evangelist*, 182–84; Kelber, *Kingdom*, 121. Both Marxsen and Kelber make "sense" of the imperative statement at 13:14 by reading it as a command to go to Galilee.

106. Cf. Schweizer, *Good News*, 273.

107. Marxsen, *Evangelist*, 171–72, 192, n. 151; Kelber, *Kingdom*, 120–21; Mauser, *Wilderness Theme*, 110.

108. Schweizer, *Good News*, 273.

109. C. U. Wolf, "Village," *IDB* 4 (1962) 784.

110. Strathmann, *"polis," TDNT* 6 (1968) 523–30. Howard Clark Kee's perception of "a clear antipathy towards the city in Mark" *(Community of the New Age: Studies in Mark's Gospel* [Philadelphia: Westminster, 1977] 103) is based on a generalizing analysis that lumps hills and mountain, the sea, the desert, the "green grass," villages, and fields in one positively valued category and stresses the several references to "the city" of Jerusalem as the opposing negative category. This "clear preference for villages and open spaces in contrast to cities (1:38, 45; 5:14; 6:6b, 11, 31; 8:4, 27; 11:2, 11; 13:3)," Kee suggests, should probably be seen against the aim of the Ptolemies, Seleucids, and Romans to urbanize Palestine (90–91).

111. Arndt and Gingrich, *Lexicon,* 889.

112. But see Taylor, *St. Mark,* 372, on the textual difficulties of 8:26.

113. Schweizer, *Good News,* 114.

114. The two "passions" in Mark will be discussed more fully in Chapter 5.

115. See Strathmann, *"polis," TDNT* 6 (1968) 524.

116. Gustaf Dalman, *Sacred Sites and Ways: Studies in the Topography of the Gospels* (London: Society for Promoting Christian Knowledge, 1935; New York: Macmillan, 1935) 255.

117. See Taylor, *St. Mark,* 452; Bratcher and Nida, *Handbook,* 342.

118. See B. H. Throckmorton, Jr., "Market place," *IDB* 3 (1962) 278.

119. Thus the marketplace is the center of healing in inhabited areas, whereas the sea is the center of healing (3:7–10) in open areas. Both 6:56 and 3:7–8 are parts of summary statements in the Markan narrative, and both exhibit a cluster of spatial markers. The similarities, differences, and functions of 3:7–12 and 6:53–56 are discussed by Kee, *Community,* 60–61.

120. Nineham, *St. Mark,* 186. So also Bratcher and Nida, *Handbook,* 218.

121. *RSV*; Arndt and Gingrich, *Lexicon,* 12.

122. Black, *Aramaic Approach,* 54. On the debate see Bratcher and Nida, *Handbook,* 222; Taylor, *St. Mark,* 336; Nineham, *St. Mark,* 193–94.

123. Nineham, *St. Mark,* 333.

124. See Norman Perrin, *A Modern Pilgrimage in New Testament Christology* (Philadelphia: Fortress, 1974) 23–40.

125. For an application of reader response criticism to the Gospel of Mark, see Fowler, *Loaves and Fishes,* 149–79; and idem, "Who Is 'The Reader' of Mark's Gospel?" *Society of Biblical Literature Seminar Papers 1983* (Chico, CA: Scholars, 1983) 31–53.

126. I have not found it possible to illustrate clearly throughout the topographical schema the details of the process of progressive mediation by which "one of the polar terms and the mediator becomes replaced by a new triad and so on" (Claude Lévi-Strauss, "The Structural Study of Myth," *Journal of American Folklore* 68 [1955] 440). For the illustration of this process within the geopolitical schema, see Chapter 2.

127. So also Arndt and Gingrich, *Lexicon,* 157. See Calloud, "Toward a Structural Analysis," 150.

128. For citations of biblical uses of *gē* in reference to "the land of promise," see Sasse, *"gē," TDNT* 1 (1964) 677–78.

129. See especially Psalm 107:23–29 and Job 38:1–11. For additional citations see B. W. Anderson, "Water," *IDB* 4 (1962) 808–10, and L. Goppelt, *"hudōr," TDNT* 8 (1972) 319, 323. On the biblical background of the "sea-walking motif" as a manifestation of divine power, see Heil, *Jesus Walking On the Sea,* 37–56.

130. Cf. Johannes Schreiber, *Theologie des Vertrauens: Eine redaktionsgeschichtliche Untersuchung des Markusevangeliums* (Hamburg: Furche-Verlag, 1967) 209.
131. Ernest Best suggests that, because the two sea miracles are "the only miracles from which the disciples [representing the Christian community] benefit," the use of the boat in the Markan sea miracles "leads easily to the development within the later church of the ship as a symbol for the Christian community" (*Following Jesus: Discipleship in the Gospel of Mark* [Journal for the Study of the New Testament Supplement Series 4; Sheffield, England: JSOT, 1981] 232–33).
132. Bratcher and Nida, *Handbook*, 8.
133. Cf. Mauser, *Wilderness Theme*, 109.
134. Ibid., 109–110; see 109–119.
135. Ibid., 124–28.
136. See also Jonathan Z. Smith, "The Influence of Symbols on Social Change: A Place on Which to Stand," in *Map Is Not Territory: Studies in the History of Religions* (Leiden: Brill, 1978) 134–36.
137. It is interesting to note that both Matthew and Luke delete the reference to the peaceful wild beasts (security, promise) and add an emphasis on hunger (danger, threat) in the story of Jesus' testing in the wilderness.
138. If, however, Talmon (" 'Desert Motif,' " esp. 37) and Pedersen (see Mauser, *Wilderness Theme*, 36–37) are correct in reading the Hebrew tradition of the wilderness not as paradoxical but as dominantly negative, then the Markan Gospel is completely in tension with traditional expectations at this point.
139. Cf. Kittel, "*erēmos, erēmia,*" *TDNT* 2 (1964) 658; Lightfoot, *Locality*, 117.
140. Robert Funk interprets this Markan evidence historically, commenting that 1:14–15 indicates Jesus' "rejection of messianic groups dwelling in the wilderness and his movements into the villages and towns" ("The Wilderness," *JBL* 78 [1959] 205–214; quotation from 213).
141. *Hodos* has maintained a double meaning as a place or as an action from the time of Homer (Michaelis, "*hodos,*" *TDNT* 5 [1967] 42–43).
142. Marxsen, *Evangelist;* Kelber, *Kingdom.*
143. Cf. Ralph W. Klein, *Israel in Exile: A Theological Interpretation* (Philadelphia: Fortress, 1979) 148 (see also pp. 125–48): "P [the Priestly writer in the Pentateuch] ends his narrative with old Israel on the verge of the land and full of hope, and that is *where* and *how* he wanted his audience to understand themselves as well." On liminality and the wilderness motif in the Hebrew Scriptures, see Robert L. Cohn, *The Shape of Sacred Space: Four Biblical Studies* (Missoula: Scholars, 1980). Cf. Jonathan Z. Smith's observation of a culture whose "cosmological conviction" is shattered: "liminality becomes the supreme goal rather than a moment in a rite of passage" ("Birth Upside Down or Right Side Up?," in *Map Is Not Territory,* 170). See also Smith's preface to *Map Is Not Territory* (esp. xii–xv), and his chapters 4–7 in general, on the prevalence of "utopian" ("no-place")—rather than "locative"—views of the world in Mediterranean religions during the Greco-Roman period.

Notes to Chapter 4

1. William Wrede, *The Messianic Secret* (Naperville, IL: Alec R. Allenson, 1972) 54–55, 66, 134–36, 141–42; G. H. Boobyer, "The Secrecy Motif in St. Mark's Gospel," *NTS* 6 (1960) 230; Lewis S. Hay, "Mark's Use of the Messianic Secret," *JAAR* 35 (1967) 21. For a different view see Theodore J. Weeden, *Mark—Traditions in Conflict* (Philadelphia: Fortress, 1971) 157–58.
2. John R. Donahue, S.J., *Are You the Christ? The Trial Narrative in the Gospel of Mark* (Society of Biblical Literature Dissertation Series 10; Missoula: Society of Biblical Literature, 1973) 113–35; idem, "Temple, Trial, and Royal Christology (Mark 14:53–65)," in *The Passion in Mark: Studies on Mark 14–16* (ed. Werner H. Kelber; Philadelphia: Fortress, 1976) 68–69. Donald Juel, *Messiah and Temple: The Trial of Jesus in the Gospel of Mark* (SBLDS 31; Missoula: Scholars, for SBL, 1977) 127–39. Cf. Ernst Lohmeyer, *Lord of the Temple: A Study of the Relation Between Cult and Gospel* (Edinburgh and London: Oliver and Boyd, 1961), chapter 2.
3. John Dominic Crossan, "Empty Tomb and Absent Lord (Mark 16:1–8)," in *The Passion in Mark: Studies on Mark 14–16* (ed. Werner H. Kelber; Philadelphia: Fortress, 1976) 135–52; idem, "A Form for Absence: The Markan Creation of Gospel," *Semeia* 12 (1978) 41–55.
4. Alexander Souter, *A Pocket Lexicon to the Greek New Testament* (Oxford: Clarendon, 1916) 172, 173.
5. William F. Arndt, F. Wilbur Gingrich, and Frederick W. Danker, trans. and eds., *A Greek-English Lexicon of the New Testament and Other Early Christian Literature* (2nd ed.; Chicago and London: University of Chicago, 1979) 557, 560–61.
6. O. Michel, "*oikos—oikia,*" *Theological Dictionary of the New Testament (TDNT)* (10 vols.; Grand Rapids: Eerdmans, 1964–76) 5 (1967) 131.
7. Arndt and Gingrich, *Lexicon*, 524.
8. O. Michel, "*mimnēskomai—mnēma, mnēmeion,*" *TDNT* 4 (1967) 681, 679.
9. Arndt and Gingrich, *Lexicon*, 372; G. Schrenk, "*hieros—hieron,*" *TDNT* 3 (1965) 232–33.
10. O. Michel, "*naos,*" *TDNT* 4 (1967) 880–81; Arndt and Gingrich, *Lexicon*, 533; *The Analytical Greek Lexicon* (Grand Rapids: Zondervan, 1970) 275.
11. Robert G. Bratcher and Eugene A. Nida, *A Translator's Handbook on the Gospel of Mark* (Helps for Translators, vol. 2; Leiden: Brill, for the United Bible Societies, 1961) 349, 463; Vincent Taylor, *The Gospel According to St. Mark* (London: Macmillan, 1955; New York: St. Martin's, 1955) 457, 566; Juel, *Messiah and Temple*, 127–28. See also W. F. Stinespring, "Temple, Jerusalem," *The Interpreter's Dictionary of the Bible (IDB)* (5 vols.; Nashville: Abingdon, vols. 1–4, 1962; supp., 1976) 4 (1962) 551. *Contra* Schrenk, "*hieros—hieron,*" *TDNT* 3 (1965) 235.
12. So also Robert Henry Lightfoot, *The Gospel Message of St. Mark* (Oxford: Clarendon, 1950) 56; Taylor, *St. Mark*, 596; Bratcher and Nida, *Handbook*, 493; Arndt and Gingrich, *Lexicon*, 533. *Contra* Juel, *Messiah and Temple*, 140–

42; and Donahue, *Trial Narrative*, 201–203. See also Michel, *"naos," TDNT* 4 (1967) 885, n. 21.

13. According to Donahue, the distinction between *hieron* and *naos* "connotes a difference between tradition and redaction since Mark uses *hieron* in those places which show his strongest redaction" (*Trial Narrative*, 105). Theodore Weeden also assumes that the use of *naos* reflects a Markan source ("The Cross as Power in Weakness [Mark 15:20b–41]," in *The Passion in Mark: Studies on Mark 14–16* [ed. Werner H. Kelber; Philadelphia: Fortress, 1976] 121–34). According to Weeden, 14:58, 15:29, and 15:38 derive from a source belonging to Mark's opponents and reflecting "*a divine man Christology conjoined with a realized eschatology which depicts Jesus as the destroyer of the old Temple and builder of the new*" (128), a Christology and eschatology Mark opposes. It is not my purpose here to support or dispute the argument concerning tradition and redaction; even if a distinction is made between tradition (*naos*) and redaction (*hieron*), this does not preclude a distinction in the meaning effect of these terms in the present Markan text.

14. Schrenk, *"hieros—hieron," TDNT* 3 (1965) 233. However, *hieron* is used for both pagan temples and the Jewish temple in the Apocrypha, Josephus, and Philo.

15. So Schrenk, *"hieros—hieron," TDNT* 3 (1965) 235. Cf. Lohmeyer, *Lord of the Temple*, 60.

16. Michel, *"oikos," TDNT* 5 (1967) 120.

17. *Contra* Lohmeyer, who interprets 11:17 "historically": "Plainly to be seen here is the view of the Galilean layman who works and lives far from the cultic centre of the Jewish faith, and venerates the temple merely as the chief synagogue; for 'house of prayer' is a fixed expression for the synagogue of the Jewish congregations" (quoted by Michel, *"oikos," TDNT* 5 [1967] 121). Yet both synagogue and temple are rejected, not venerated, by the Markan Jesus.

18. See Bratcher and Nida, *Handbook*, 120; D. E. Nineham, *The Gospel of St. Mark* (Pelican New Testament Commentaries; Baltimore: Penguin, 1963) 124

19. Cf. Arndt and Gingrich, *Lexicon*, 365.

20. According to J. Jeremias, the use of a spatial image to denote time is Hellenistic (*"thura," TDNT* 3 [1965] 173–74), and the non-Semitic origin of the expression in Mark 13:29 is confirmed by the formal—and classical—use of the plural for one door (cf. Matthew 24:33; James 5:9) (p. 174, n. 8).

21. So Nineham, *St. Mark*, 167.

22. Michel (*"oikos—oikia," TDNT* 5 [1967] 131) considers this a figurative use of *oikia*, meaning "family" or "household."

23. See Nineham, *St. Mark*, 406; Michel, *"oikos—oikodomē," TDNT* 5 (1967) 146–47. Consider the reference to "in three days"—but see Werner H. Kelber, "Conclusion: From Passion Narrative to Gospel," in *The Passion in Mark: Studies on Mark 14–16* (ed. Werner H. Kelber; Philadelphia: Fortress, 1976) 171–72; Juel, *Messiah and Temple*, 144—and compare John 2:19 22 (see Schrenk, *"hieros—hieron," TDNT* 3 [1965] 244–45; Michel, *"naos," TDNT* 4 [1967] 883–84).

24. Eduard Schweizer, *The Good News According to Mark* (Atlanta: John Knox, 1970) 329; Michel, *"oikos—oikodomeō," TDNT* 5 (1967) 139, and *"naos," TDNT* 4 (1967) 883; Lohmeyer, *Lord of the Temple*, 76, 105, and passim; Elisabeth Schüssler Fiorenza, "Cultic Language in Qumran and in the New Testament," *CBQ* 38 (1976) 169; Ernest Best, *Following Jesus: Discipleship in the Gospel of Mark* (Journal for the Study of the New Testament Supplement

Series 4; Sheffield, England: JSOT, 1981) 213–25; Donahue, *Trial Narrative*, 108–13; Donahue, "Temple, Trial," 69–71; Juel, *Messiah and Temple*, part II. For a critique of the arguments of Donahue and Juel see below.

25. Taylor, *St. Mark*, 566.
26. See Schweizer, *Good News*, 51; Nineham, *St. Mark*, 110.
27. Cf. James M. Robinson, *The Problem of History in Mark* (Studies in Biblical Theology 21; London: SCM, 1957) 40.
28. The Gospel of Mark is not known as a model of clear pronoun reference, and the *autou* at 2:15 is a case in point. While some commentators simply point out the ambiguity, most take "his house" to refer to Levi's house. I find, however, that arguments from the immediate Markan context and from Matthean and especially Lukan alteration, as well as from the overall position of the "house" as an architectural space in Mark's Gospel, suggest the opposite conclusion: *tē oikia autou* at Mark 2:15 refers to Jesus' house. For my argument in full, see "*Tē Oikia Autou:* Mark 2:15 in Context," *NTS* 31 (1985) 282–92.
29. It is possible that at 9:33 the reference to Capernaum qualifies the house as Jesus' home. According to Taylor, the house at 9:33 is "presumably that of Peter as in i. 29" (*St. Mark*, 404). Bratcher and Nida agree, adding that Peter's house, "it would seem, had become Jesus' 'home' in Galilee" (*Handbook*, 293). However, the idiom used in 2:1, where Jesus' home in Capernaum is first mentioned, *en oikō* ("at home"), is not used at 9:33—*en tē oikia* ("in the house"). Nor does a possessive adjective modify "the house" as at 2:15; nor does a reference to Jesus' family, *hoi par' autou*, signal the house as his personal home as at 3:20–21. In fact the bare phrase employed at 9:33, *en tē oikia*, appears uniquely generalized, as each of its three other Markan occurrences is modified by a genitive noun or pronoun (2:15; 6:4; 14:3).
30. See W. Schrage, "*synagōgē*," *TDNT* 7 (1971) 830.
31. Following *The Greek New Testament* (3rd ed.; ed. Kurt Aland et al.; United Bible Societies, 1975). *Contra* the *Revised Standard Version*.
32. Thus, in Mark's Gospel, Jesus attends only Galilean synagogues. The same is true in Matthew, but Luke 4:44 replaces "throughout all Galilee" of Mark 1:39 with "of Judea."
33. But see note 29 above.
34. *Synagōgē*, deriving from *synagō*, "gather" or "collect," originally meant "the act of gathering," and then was applied to "the place or the building in which the gathering takes place" (Taylor, *St. Mark*, 172; Bratcher and Nida, *Handbook*, 44; I. Sonne, "Synagogue," *IDB* 4 [1962] 477–78). The initial Markan use of *synagō* occurs in conjunction with "house," 2:1–2. Cf. *episynagō*, "gather together," in conjunction with door (of the house) at 1:33. But see also *episynagō*—which shares the same root as *synagōgē* and which has acquired an "eschatological note" from its use in the LXX (Schrage, "*synagōgē*," *TDNT* 7 [1971] 843)—in conjunction with the universe (heaven and earth) at 13:27.
35. See Jean Calloud, "Toward a Structural Analysis of the Gospel of Mark," *Semeia* 16 (1979) 150–51.
36. See Schrage, "*synagōgē*," *TDNT* 7 (1971) 831, 834.
37. Despite a possible synechdochical extension—houses as "a summary way of saying 'their belongings,' 'their fortunes' " (Bratcher and Nida, *Handbook*, 392; cf. Michel, "*oikos—oikia*," *TDNT* 5 [1967] 131)—the term has clear spatial dimensions; the scribes really do take possession of the widows' houses, spatially relocating the widows. While suggesting that "and household goods" is implied along with "houses," Arndt and Gingrich (*Lexicon*, 557) list 12:40

among the literal uses of "house." "Devour," of course, is applied metaphorically.

38. The setting is ordinary—but extraordinarily specified: not just "in the house" but at table in the house of Simon the leper in Bethany near Jerusalem. People, places, and times all become increasingly specific in the Jerusalem section of the Gospel. Instead of the Gerasene demoniac and the Syrophoenician woman, we meet Simon of Cyrene, Joseph of Arimathea, and Mary Magdalene. Not only geopolitical regions (e.g., Galilee, Judea) and towns (e.g., Capernaum, Jericho) are labeled in the spatial setting, but also many specific locations in the environs of one city, Jerusalem (Bethany, Bethphage, Mount of Olives, Gethsemane, Golgotha), and even one specific house, the house of Simon the leper in Bethany. Time is chronicled not by "in those days" (1:9) or "on the sabbath" (1:21), but by "two days before the Passover" (14:1), "the third hour" (15:25), and "very early on the first day of the week" (16:2). This increasing specificity narrows the focus of the narrative, "zooming in," as it were, on the passion story.

Louis Marin argues differently. In his structural analysis of the toponyms (proper place names) of the passion narrative in its four canonical "variants," Marin observes "a progressive obliteration of the toponyms in the central sequences: Jerusalem, and then the Temple disappear. Whenever they exist, they are translated, e.g., Golgotha" (p. 34). In place of the "obliterated" toponyms are "substituted" the homes of the actors (Annas, Caiaphas, Pilate, Herod, elders); thus the toponyms are "translated into common nouns in order to be able to enter more directly into one or several signifier systems" (p. 34). After the Last Supper, trial, death, and resurrection, the toponyms are "resurrected"—"invested with a new signifier system" (*The Semiotics of the Passion Narrative: Topics and Figures* [Pittsburgh: Pickwick, 1980] 39). While Marin's thesis may have some merit in relation to his meta-text (the four gospels combined), it has very little to commend it in relation to Mark.

39. Taylor, *St. Mark*, 529.

40. Robert Henry Lightfoot, *Locality and Doctrine in the Gospels* (New York and London: Harper, [1938]) 56.

41. W. F. Stinespring, "Temple, Jerusalem," *IDB* 4 (1962) 551.

42. Taylor (*St. Mark*, 458) and Nineham (*St. Mark*, 294) quite rightly reject the view that here Jesus is presented as a pilgrim "seeing the sights."

43. Taylor, *St. Mark*, 463, citing *Berakoth* 9:5. Cf. Henry Barclay Swete, *Commentary on Mark* (London: Macmillan, 1913; reprinted, Grand Rapids: Kregel, 1077) 256; Nineham, *St. Mark*, 304. Schweizer agrees but finds 11:16 "strange, while in it Jesus appears to be more than a reformer," while in 11:15 "Jesus' symbolic action is not part of a reform" (*Good News*, 233). I find the shortcut hypothesis of 11:16 nearly as easy to dismiss as the tourist hypothesis of 11:11.

44. Werner H. Kelber, *The Kingdom in Mark: A New Place and a New Time* (Philadelphia: Fortress, 1974) 100–101.

45. Arndt and Gingrich, *Lexicon*, 754.

46. Kelber, *Kingdom*, 101, n. 43.

47. While questioning Kelber's lexical assumption to this minor extent, I agree with his redaction critical conclusion that the "omission of 11:16 by Matthew and Luke is a *testimonium e silentio* to an anti-temple slant in Mark" (*Kingdom*, 101, n. 44).

48. Schweizer, *Good News*, 233. Cf. Taylor, *St. Mark*, 463–64.

49. Schweizer (*Good News*, 231), C. F. Evans (" 'I Will Go Before You Into

Galilee,'" *JTS* n.s. 5 [1954] 7), and Richard H. Hiers ("Purification of the Temple: Preparation for the Kingdom of God," *JBL* 90 [1971] 87) suggest a possible connection between Zechariah 14:21 and the Markan passage. Yet all three scholars consider the event a "cleansing" of the temple.

50. The contrary view interprets Jesus' actions as a reestablishment of the sacredness of the temple that had been profaned by the abuses of the merchants and money-changers (Taylor, *St. Mark*, 463; Schrenk, "*hieros—hieron*," *TDNT* 3 [1965] 243–44).

51. This greater specification of Jesus' teaching is part of a broader narrative pattern. See note 38 above.

52. Cf. Schweizer, *Good News*, 267.

53. E. Lohse, "*Siōn—Hierosoluma*," *TDNT* 7 (1971) 326.

54. See Schrenk, "*hieros—hieron*," *TDNT* 3 (1965) 245: "this sorrowful word opens the way for the liberation of the community from the *hieron*."

55. G. Kittel, "*erēmos, erēmia—erēmōsis*," *TDNT* 2 (1964) 660.

56. Juel (*Messiah and Temple*, 198) views the "temple cleansing" (11:15–17) as "a prophetic anticipation of the impending destruction of the temple."

57. Weeden, "Cross as Power," 125–26; Kelber, "Conclusion," 171.

58. Donahue, *Trial Narrative*, 72.

59. Donahue, "Temple, Trial," 67, n. 18.

60. Juel, *Messiah and Temple*, 206.

61. Donahue's separation of "content" and "form" is not entirely clear (see "Temple, Trial," 66–71). And none of the other ironically true statements that Juel mentions ("recognition" statements by the unclean spirits [3:11], the high priest [14:61], the centurion [15:39]), occur in contexts at all similar to the double insistence on the falseness of the witnesses (14:56, 57) and their failure to agree (14:56, 59) on the temple charge (14:58). While Juel has shown that it might have been possible to interpret a statement such as Mark 14:58 as "true" in some sense in a first-century Christian context, he has not shown convincingly that the Markan Gospel presents such an interpretation (see *Messiah and Temple*, 197–209). Juel's conclusions are also questioned—although on somewhat different grounds and with a clearly different alternative reading from the above—by George W. E. Nickelsburg ("The Genre and Function of the Markan Passion Narrative," *HTR* 73 [1980] 180, 183). More problematically, Schweizer (*Good News*, 234) admits that Mark has designated the statement "as false testimony against Jesus" but assumes the saying itself to be true, "a genuine saying of Jesus," and continues his commentary *on Mark* on the basis of its truth—an untenable situation. Taylor (*St. Mark*, 566–67, 591) places himself in a similar situation. For additional arguments in the debate concerning 14:58 in its Markan context, see Taylor, *St. Mark*, 566–67, and Nineham, *St. Mark*, 406–7.

62. Donahue, *Trial Narrative*, 196–98, quotation from 198. Cf. Weeden, "Cross as Power"; Kelber, "Conclusion."

63. Juel, *Messiah and Temple*, 124.

64. So also Weeden, "Cross as Power," 126; Kelber, "Conclusion," 171.

65. Schweizer, *Good News*, 349.

66. Kelber, "Conclusion," 171. Cf. Dan O. Via, *Kerygma and Comedy in the New Testament: A Structuralist Approach to Hermeneutic* (Philadelphia: Fortress, 1975) 129–30; Juel, *Messiah and Temple*, 142.

67. Donahue, *Trial Narrative*, 201–202. Taylor (*St. Mark*, 596) would be in the first group, along with Nineham (*St. Mark*, 430) and Schweizer (*Good News*, 355).

68. Other texts may also be read in part as attempts to help Jews or Christians cope with the destruction of the temple; often, as in Josephus and Philo and various New Testament and post-apostolic texts, but not in Mark, "temple" is applied as a metaphor of the body, or the community, or the whole of creation. See the sources cited by, but not necessarily the interpretations offered by, Schrenk ("*hieros—hieron*," *TDNT* 3 [1965] 241–47) and Michel ("*naos*," *TDNT* 4 [1967] 882–89). On the targums, see Juel, *Messiah and Temple*, 195. The Markan Gospel, however, seems to reject the temple at both the literal and the metaphorical levels.

69. Earlier in the story, unclean spirits had recognized Jesus as "Son of God" (3:11) or as "Son of the Most High God" (5:7). The superscription of the omniscient narrator (1:1) functions differently from the confession of one of the narrator's characters.

70. Schweizer, *Good News*, 328.

71. *Analytical Greek Lexicon*, 59. *Aulē* may also mean "palace" at Matthew 26:3 and Luke 11:21 (so *RSV*), although neither is a parallel passage to Mark 15:16.

72. Arndt and Gingrich, *Lexicon*, 697; Taylor, *St. Mark*, 579; F. D. Gealy, "Praetorium," *IDB* 3 (1962) 856.

73. Taylor, *St. Mark*, 585.

74. See note 38 above.

75. Cf. Heinz-Dieter Knigge, "The Meaning of Mark: The Exegesis of the Second Gospel," *Int* 22 (1968) 68.

76. Lightfoot contrasts 14:3–9 and 16:1; while the anointing at Bethany is accepted with high praise, "by the time of the second attempt it is found that the body neither needs nor can admit anointing at the hands of human love. This love must henceforth seek to satisfy itself in other ways than this" (*Locality*, 56).

77. Compare and contrast Daniel Patte and Aline Patte, *Structural Exegesis: From Theory to Practice* (Philadelphia: Fortress, 1978) 84–88. Our analyses agree that the tomb suggests a realm beyond or outside society; they disagree in evaluating the behavior of the women. Although the Pattes' analysis is too complex to summarize briefly, we may note that their interpretation assigns to the women a negative value because (in part) they represent, by their presence at the tomb, human beings outside of society. My analysis calls attention to the fact that, according to Mark, the women were turned around by their experience of the unexpected events at the tomb; "they went out and fled from the tomb" (16:8), that is, away from the realm outside society and (presumably, to be sure, in Mark's open ended Gospel—but *to* where else could they flee given the place *from* which they fled?) back into society. On this point, compare Lightfoot: " . . . the empty tomb is stressed, but, this once done, it is not further dwelt upon; the women's thoughts are turned away at once from the grave at Jerusalem at the present moment to Galilee and the future reunion with the disciples there" (*Locality*, 85).

78. Claude Lévi-Strauss, "The Structural Study of Myth," *Journal of American Folklore* 68 (1955) 440.

79. As Günther Stemberger notes specifically of 9:28, but also suggests more generally, "the house which Jesus and his disciples enter . . . is more a literary-theological idea than a real house" ("Galilee—Land of Salvation?," appendix IV in *The Gospel and the Land: Early Christianity and Jewish Territorial Doctrine*, by W. D. Davies [Berkeley: University of California, 1974] 419).

80. Schrage, "*synagōgē*," *TDNT* 7 [1971] 822.

81. Ibid., 822–23.
82. Ibid., 828.
83. Marin interprets the opposition in this way:

    In effect, the house and the supper room constitute for a hermeneutic of meaning, by a deciphering of the text, the metaphors of Jerusalem and the Temple. . . . inside of Jerusalem there is a home which is "like" Jerusalem and in this home, a supper room which is "like" the Temple is in Jerusalem, its center and its summary. But this double process is connected by a double displacement of Jesus in the space. He has entered into Jerusalem and into the Temple; and he has left them. Then again he has entered into the city, into a home, and in this home, into a supper room to celebrate the Passover; and this being done, the house is "like" Jerusalem and the room "like" the Temple (*Semiotics of the Passion Narrative*, 44–45).

84. Bratcher and Nida, *Handbook*, 8–9; Taylor, *St. Mark*, 153; Schweizer, *Good News*, 31; Nineham, *St. Mark*, 60. Cf. Matthew Black, *An Aramaic Approach to the Gospels and Acts* (3rd ed.; Oxford: Clarendon, 1967) 99.
85. Donahue, *Trial Narrative*, esp. 108–109; and idem, "Temple, Trial," esp. 69–71; Juel, *Messiah and Temple*.
86. Donahue, "Temple, Trial," 68–69. Juel (*Messiah and Temple*, 57–58) contends that the temple charge (14:58) "has a place in the trial as part of the messianic imagery." Jesus is "not only the Messiah who must suffer and die; he is also the Messiah who will build the eschatological temple 'not made with hands.' "
87. As Donahue notes ("Temple, Trial," 69). Juel also argues primarily on the basis of extra-Markan texts (Exodus 15:17; Colossians 2:11; Ephesians 2:11; Hebrews 9:11, 23–24; 1 Corinthians 3:16; 2 Corinthians 6:16; Ephesians 2:20–22) and extra-biblical texts (Qumran documents, targumic traditions, rabbinic traditions). It is interesting to note that the preferred designation for the temple in the seven Qumran texts Juel discusses (*Messiah and Temple*, 159–80) as relevant to Mark 14:58 is "house."
88. Donahue, "Temple, Trial," 68.
89. In discussing "the poetics of space," Gaston Bachelard argues that "both room and house are psychological diagrams that guide writers and poets in their analysis of intimacy" (*The Poetics of Space* [New York: Orion, 1964] 38; see 3–37). But Bachelard's focus on the house as an image of intimacy illustrates the individualism of modern Western culture; in the first-century Jewish and Greco-Roman world of Mark the intimacy of the house is communal; the house is an image of family, of community.
90. Michel, *"oikos," TDNT* 5 (1967) 130. Concerning a trend in Judaism to understand "house" as "the people of God, the true religious community," see Sverre Aalen, " 'Reign' and 'House' in the Kingdom of God in the Gospels," *NTS* 8 (1962) 215–40; quotation from 240. Cf. Lohmeyer, *Lord of the Temple*, 62–69. On the interrelated sociological and theological significance of "house," see John H. Elliott, *A Home for the Homeless: A Sociological Exegesis of 1 Peter, Its Situation and Strategy* (Philadelphia: Fortress, 1981). Elliott's discussions of "The Significance and Function of the *Oikos* in the Greco-Roman World" (170–82) and "in the Old and New Testaments" (182–200) are especially helpful.
91. Structuralist observations concerning the way in which HOUSE functions in the Markan narrative in opposition to SYNAGOGUE and TEMPLE are neither based upon nor offered as conclusive evidence for external historical con-

clusions. Structural exegesis focuses on the internal relations of the text. Yet a Gospel, as myth interpreting history and history functioning as myth (Norman Perrin, *The New Testament: An Introduction* [New York: Harcourt Brace Jovanovich, 1974] 26–34), can be abstracted from its historical context only analytically, not finally. In terms of the broader historical context of Mark, it is interesting to compare Jonathan Z. Smith's observations about *house* and *temple* in the second-century autobiography of Thessalos, the magician: "Once more a traditional pattern has been altered. The vision does not take place in a temple but rather in an *oikos*. . . . the locus of religious experience has been shifted from a permanent sacred center, the temple, to a place of temporary sacrality sanctified by a magician's power" ("The Temple and the Magician," in *Map Is Not Territory: Studies in the History of Religions* [Leiden: Brill, 1978] 181–82). Smith regards *Thessalos* as a "direct witness" to the Late Antique shift from the temple to the holy person as the chief locus of revelation (p. 189), from the archaic temple and court cultus to a human group, a religious association, as the "new enclave protecting man against external, hostile powers" (p. 187). John Donahue has, as he states in *The Theology and Setting of Discipleship in the Gospel of Mark* (Milwaukee: Marquette University, 1983), been influenced by my argument here—more by the argument *for* the communal significance of "house" for Mark than by the argument *against* the communal significance of the temple "not made with hands" for Mark (see especially p. 62, n. 46). Best looks on both the temple "not made with hands" and the "house" as Markan images of "the church" (*Following Jesus*, 213–29).

92. Marin argues that, in the passion narrative, the room is to the house as the Temple is to Jerusalem (see note 83 to this chapter). The room functions for Jesus and his disciples as the Temple functions for the Jews; thus the room becomes the Temple. "The Temple is the place where the hero eats, i.e. sacrifices and is sacrificed in a meal" (*Semiotics of the Passion Narrative*, 44). One problem with Marin's interpretation is its failure to take seriously the consistently negative connotations of the Temple at least in Mark.

93. Nineham, *St. Mark*, 398; see Taylor, *St. Mark*, 644–46. Procedural irregularities portrayed in the Markan account include passing a death sentence during the night, passing a death sentence before the second day, convening the second session on the same day as the first (the day began with sunset), holding the trial on the day of the Passover, holding the trial in the high priest's house rather than in the official chamber, and not requiring independent agreement of witnesses' testimony (Donahue, "Temple, Trial," 61; Schweizer, *Good News*, 322–24). See especially Juel, *Messiah and Temple*, 59–64.

94. Lévi-Strauss, "Structural Study," 440.

95. Lohmeyer's observation that the "traditional holiness" of the "cult" is overturned and replaced by the "eschatological holiness" of the "gospel" (see *Lord of the Temple*, 101, 103, 107) is not unrelated at this point. But the total architectural system of the Markan Gospel suggests that more is at stake than the replacement of one sacred order with another sacred order. It would appear, however, that Lohmeyer does sense the newness of the neither-sacred-nor-profane/both-sacred-and-profane order in relation to "the Meal," the Lord's Supper (see p. 104).

96. "The tradition of the family tomb would seem to be the most important factor in the data which pertain to burial and tombs in both OT and NT times" (E. Meyers, "Tomb," *IDB* Supp. [1976] 908).

97. According to "popular belief, . . . the burial ground is a sinister place, for the souls of the dead wander there" (Michel, "*mimnēskomai—mnēma, mnēmeion*," *TDNT* 4 [1967] 680).
98. See W. L. Reed, "Tomb," *IDB* 4 (1962) 664.
99. Dominic Crossan sees the story of the empty tomb, which he regards as a Markan creation, not as a challenge to the established religious (Jewish) tradition but as a challenge to a rival Christian tradition within the Markan community, a tradition that stressed "the abiding presence of Jesus to intervene and save his own at any time and any place" ("A Form for Absence," 52; see also "Empty Tomb and Absent Lord"). In my judgment, Crossan tends to overemphasize the negative, polemical aspect of the empty tomb narrative in relation to its positive, constructive aspect (but see his comment in "A Form for Absence," 53). Louis Marin sees in the story of the women at the tomb (which he studies in all three synoptic "variants") two foci, the absence of a body and the presence of a word: "absence of the real object here and now = presence of the message whose referent is always and already elsewhere" ("The Women at the Tomb: A Structural Analysis Essay of a Gospel Text," in *The New Testament and Structuralism* [ed. and trans. Alfred M. Johnson, Jr.; Pittsburgh Theological Monograph Series 11; Pittsburgh: Pickwick, 1976] 73–96; quotation from 87). Mark's words for Marin's "always and already elsewhere" are *en tē hodō*, "on the way."

Notes to Chapter 5

1. After the completion of this research, a short article dealing with the syntagmatic and paradigmatic relationships of five Markan spatial locations appeared (Bas van Iersel, "Locality, Structure, and Meaning in Mark," *Linguistica Biblica* 53 [1983] 45–54). Syntagmatically, van Iersel suggests that "there are five constitutive parts in Mark forming a concentric structure around the lexemes 'desert,' 'Galilee,' 'way,' 'Jerusalem,' and 'tomb' " (p. 54). Paradigmatically, van Iersel suggests the following oppositions—in terms of a (Greimasian) semiotic square: Galilee vs. Jerusalem (a vs. b), Galilee vs. the tomb and the desert (a vs. non-a), Jerusalem vs. the way (b vs. non-b), the way vs. the tomb and the desert (non-b vs. non-a). While these conclusions are interesting, problems result from the fact that the analysis is based on five spatial locations abstracted from the total Markan spatial framework; the absence of the lexeme "sea" seems particularly problematic.
2. Robert Henry Lightfoot, *Locality and Doctrine in the Gospels* (New York and London: Harper, [1938]) 112, cf. 132. So also Willi Marxsen, *Mark the Evangelist: Studies on the Redaction History of the Gospel* (Nashville and New York: Abingdon, 1969) 56.
3. Of the seven Markan uses of *hodos* from 8:27 through 10:52, Matthew repeats but two (20:17, paralleling Mark 10:32; 20:30 paralleling Mark 10:46) and Luke only one (18:35, paralleling Mark 10:46).
4. Robert Henry Lightfoot, *The Gospel Message of St. Mark* (Oxford: Clarendon, 1950) 48–59. Lightfoot draws out the parallels to chap. 13 only as far as chap. 15. As will be seen below, I perceive the parallels continuing through chap. 16.
5. James M. Robinson, *The Problem of History in Mark* (Studies in Biblical Theology 21; London: SCM, 1957) 50.
6. Perrin has suggested that Mark 13 and Mark 14–16 are "parallel," that "the passion and the parousia of Jesus stand in a certain tension with each other," that Mark's Gospel draws to a close with a "twin climax of the apocalyptic discourse . . . and the passion narrative" (*The New Testament: An Introduction* [New York: Harcourt Brace Jovanovich, 1974] 148, 159). This idea has been further developed by Donahue, who has depicted the double ending as "the passion of Jesus and the passion of the community" (lectures given at the Vanderbilt Divinity School, Fall 1977). The positions of Perrin and Donahue represent developments, based on more detailed literary analysis, of the more historically oriented positions of Etienne Trocmé and Rudolf Pesch. Trocmé holds that Mark 1–13 made up the earliest form of the Gospel, and that later this work was editorially combined with an independent document that we might call the "Passion according to Saint Mark" (Mark 14–16), to form the canonical Mark. Thus the New Testament Gospel of Mark may be understood as "the 'second edition, revised and supplemented by a long appendix' of an earlier Gospel" (*Formation of the Gospel According to Mark* [Philadelphia: Westminster, 1975] 215–29; quotation from 240). Pesch, on

the other hand, posits that Mark 13 was added after the Gospel was complete in order to counter a false eschatology (*Naherwartungen: Tradition und Redaktion in Mk 13* [Düsseldorf: Patmos Verlag, 1968]). My observations concerning the double ending of Mark are in line with the literary analysis of Perrin and Donahue and do not judge the issue of the historical creation of the Gospel of Mark.

Frank Kermode suggests, with good reason, that Mark 13 is intercalated between 1–12 and 14–16:

And indeed apocalypse, which is the genre Mark adapts in his thirteenth chapter, is the great literary vehicle of the moment of epochal transition, the period that is interposed between the past and the imminent end. Mark places his own "little apocalypse" in the space between his account of the ministry and his account of the Passion. It is the largest of his intercalations, in fact, an analepsis that is certainly homodiegetic, an incursion of the future, properly terrible, properly ambiguous, into a narrative which proleptically shapes and sanctifies it (*The Genesis of Secrecy: On the Interpretation of Narrative* [Cambridge, MA and London: Harvard University, 1979] 127–28).

7. William F. Arndt, F. Wilbur Gingrich, and Frederick W. Danker, trans. and eds., *A Greek-English Lexicon of the New Testament and Other Early Christian Literature* (2nd ed.; Chicago and London: University of Chicago, 1979) 167.
8. Norman R. Petersen's argument concerning chaps. 1–12 and 14–16 in the light of chap. 13 ("When is the End not the End? Literary Reflections on the Ending of Mark's Narrative," *Int* 34 [1980] 151–66) might be related in some ways to my discussion of the Markan double ending, but our overall readings of Mark differ considerably.
9. In light of this Markan pattern, Jonathan Z. Smith's questioning of Eliade's assumption that chaos is linked with the profane is of interest. Smith writes that

chaos is never profane in the sense of being neutral. . . . Rather, chaos *only* takes a significance within a religious world view. Chaos is a sacred power; but it is frequently perceived as being sacred "in the wrong way." It is that which is opposed to order, which threatens the pardigms and archetypes but which is, nevertheless, profoundly necessary for the very creativity that is characteristic of Eliade's notion of the Sacred ("The Wobbling Pivot," in *Map is Not Territory: Studies in the History of Religions* [Leiden: Brill, 1978] 88–103; quotation from 97).

10. As stated in Chapter 1, the question under investigation has been not whether the Gospel of Mark is a myth, but whether attention to a mythic dimension contributes to an understanding of the Gospel of Mark. The process of mediation by successive oppositions, illustrated in the spatial order, exemplifies the mythic dimension of Mark. But the importance to Mark's Gospel of *challenging* the expected pattern of opposition suggests another dimension as well, a dimension that might best be called parabolic. For a discussion of the Markan Gospel as both myth and parable, see my "Mark: Myth and Parable," *BTB* 16 (1986) 8–17.
11. H. Sasse, "*gē*," *Theological Dictionary of the New Testament (TDNT)* (10 vols.; Grand Rapids: Eerdmans, 1964–76) 1 (1964) 680. See also G. von Rad, "*ouranos*," *TDNT* 5 (1967) 508.
12. According to Howard Clark Kee, "Redemption is not seen by Mark as extrication from a hostile context in which man lives, but as renewal and or-

dering of that context, exemplified by these cosmic powers [especially power over the sea] he described working through Jesus" (*Community of the New Age: Studies in Mark's Gospel* [Philadelphia: Fortress, 1977] 121).

13. See Jonathan Z. Smith, "Earth and Gods," in *Map Is Not Territory*, 112–15.

14. Commentators who seek in Mark's Gospel the "history of Jesus" suggest that Jesus "manifested a freshness and independence of mind as to the meaning and application of the Law, consonant with the religious spirit of the *galil*," that is, consonant with "the modified orthodoxy of Jews in the *galil* [Galilee] of the Gentiles" (K. W. Clark, *The Interpreter's Dictionary of the Bible* [5 vols.; Nashville: Abingdon, vols. 1–4, 1962; supp., 1976] 2 [1962] 347).

15. If, however, Shemaryahu Talmon ("The 'Desert Motif' in the Bible and in Qumran Literature," in *Biblical Motifs: Origins and Transformations* [ed. Alexander Altmann; Cambridge: Harvard University, 1966]) is correct in reading the tradition of the wilderness in the Hebrew Scriptures not as paradoxical but as dominantly negative—emphasizing chaos (37, 43), then the Markan reversal of expectations at this point is even more dramatic. Ulrich Mauser (*Christ in the Wilderness: The Wilderness Theme in the Second Gospel and its Basis in the Biblical Tradition* [Naperville, IL: Alec R. Allenson, 1963]) recognizes that "the desert has an affinity to the chaotic state of the world that Yahweh overcame when he created the cosmos according to his good will" (51), but Mauser also perceives a prophetic theme of the renewal of the wilderness which, one might add, has an affinity to the ordered state of the world that Yahweh created and recreates. Central to Mauser's thesis is Jesus' conquering of the forces of evil, of Satan, in the chaotic wilderness (132 and passim). When chaos is conquered, one might add, it is ordered.

16. "The goal and centre of the synagogue and its gatherings are thus the passing on, the unfolding and applying of the *nomos* [law] and *paradosis* [tradition] with a view to practical obedience to the Law [Torah]" (W. Schrage, "*synagōgē*," *TDNT* 7 [1971] 822).

17. That the view of Jerusalem as an ordering center was still held by first generation Christians is exemplified by "the fact that prior to 70 the Palestinian Church tolerantly paid the temple tax (cf. Mt. 17:24–27) in spite of its conviction that there was no compulsion.... Even if this is simply to avoid giving offence to Judaism, it does at least point to a deliberate attachment to the common sanctuary" (G. Schrenk, "*hieros—hieron*," *TDNT* 3 [1965] 243). Presumably, it is this very attachment (or, rather, after A.D. 70, longing) that the Markan Gospel seeks to break. Although Mark's Gospel inverts the traditional image of Jerusalem as an ordering center (on which see E. Lohse, "*Siōn—Hierosoluma*," *TDNT* 7 [1971] 323–24), such an image is projected of Jerusalem in Luke-Acts and of the new Jerusalem in Hebrews and Revelation (ibid., 330–38); however, each of these Christian texts does, in its own way, suggest that "Jerusalem" has been, is being, or will be surpassed.

18. See Shemaryahu Talmon, "The Biblical Concept of Jerusalem," *JES* 8 (1971) 310.

19. This opposition is included in Louis Marin's list of "toponymic articulations" for the Markan passion narrative:

(Mount of Olives vs. Jerusalem-Temple // Temple vs. Bethany)
(Bethany vs. Jerusalem-Temple)
(outside of the city vs. Jerusalem-Temple)
(Temple vs. Mount of Olives)
(Bethany vs. the city vs. Mount of Olives)

(*The Semiotics of the Passion Narrative: Topics and Figures* [Pittsburgh: Pickwick, 1980] 23–25).

20. Werner Kelber sees in Ezekiel 11:23 a "precedent" for Mark's "anti-Zion posture." This fits Kelber's argument well: ". . . Ezekiel theologized in the aftermath of the Babylonian destruction of the temple. . . . Historically, it is the Roman destruction of Jerusalem and its sanctuary which forced the anti-Zion theology upon Mark" (*The Kingdom in Mark: A New Place and a New Time* [Philadelphia: Fortress, 1974] 106). However—and significantly—Kelber fails to note that Ezekiel 11:23 is paired with Ezekiel 43:2–4, and that together these references move just as "strictly within the bounds of the Davidic Zion tradition" (p. 106) as Kelber recognizes that Zechariah 14 does. The opposed points of view of Ezekiel and Mark are to be seen in the broader context of Jewish and Christian scriptures. As Jonathan Z. Smith notes:

It is revealing that the Hebrew Scriptures, in the two great traditions that cherish them, do not end, in their present Late Antique redactions, with the same passage. The Jewish collection ends with the promise of 2 Chronicles 36.23 of a rebuilt Temple and restored cultus. The Christian collection ends with the promise of Malachai 4.5 of the return of the *magus* Elijah—a promise fulfilled in the figure of John the Baptist who reinterprets an archaic water-ritual of purification into a magical ritual that saves ("The Temple and the Magician," in *Map Is Not Territory*, 189).

Or, as Christian tradition would emphasize: a promise fulfilled in the figure of John the Baptist who prepares the way of the Lord Jesus Christ.

21. On the appropriateness of the Mount of Olives, i.e., outside the temple, as a setting for the eschatological discourse, see also Marin, *Semiotics of the Passion Narrative*, 66–67.

22. Robert G. Bratcher and Eugene A. Nida, *A Translator's Handbook on the Gospel of Mark* (Helps for Translators, vol. 2; Leiden: Brill, for the United Bible Societies, 1961) 397.

23. See Eduard Schweizer, *The Good News According to Mark* (Atlanta: John Knox, 1970) 267.

24. Cf. W. Foerster, "*oros*," *TDNT* 5 (1967) 481, 484.

25. W. Michaelis, "*hodos*," *TDNT* 5 (1967) 56.

26. See Robinson, *Problem of History*, 68–78.

27. John R. Donahue, S.J., "Jesus as the Parable of God in the Gospel of Mark," *Int* 32 (1978) 369–86; quotation from 381. Thomas E. Boomershine agrees that the women's amazement and fear have positive connotations in Mark, but he also argues that their flight and silence have negative connotations. The function of this conflict of connotations is "to invite the audience to identify with a sympathetic character who makes a radically wrong response to the fulfillment of the passion and resurrection prophecies . . . [and] to appeal for repentance from the wrong response and for reinforcement of the right response" ("Mark 16:8 and the Apostolic Commission," *JBL* 100 [1981] 225–39, quotation from 237). See also my "Fallible Followers: Women and Men in the Gospel of Mark," *Semeia* 28 (1983), esp. 40–46.

28. In this light, the conclusion of Karl Ludwig Schmidt concerning *proagō* statements such as 16:7 appears amazingly cautious: "This is perhaps a Christological expression" ("*agōgē—proagō*," *TDNT* 1 [1964] 130). And the conclusion of Wayne G. Rollins concerning Markan *hodos* statements seems

especially apt: "... it appears that Mark's Gospel is an engraved invitation to come along on *the Way* of God, following Christ" (*The Gospels: Portraits of Christ* [Philadelphia: Westminster, 1963] 43). See Mark 8:34–35.

29. W. D. Davies, *The Gospel and the Land: Early Christianity and Jewish Territorial Doctrine* (Berkeley: University of California, 1974) 241.

30. In the Gospel of John, Jesus *becomes* both "the way" (14:6) and "the door" (10:9).

Index of Biblical References

Index of Modern Authors